The Book of
Medical
Blunders

D1146433

THIS IS A CARLTON BOOK

DEDICATION

For PAUL SAVORY, to whose unfailing kindness and generosity
we owe so much and for MOM and DAD.

Text and design © Carlton Books Limited, 1999

A CIP catalogue for this book is available from the British Library

ISBN 1 85868 703 9

Printed and bound in Great Britain

The Book of Medical Blunders

Real-life accounts of the most horrific medical disasters and those who survived their ordeal

Martin and Karen Fido

Contents

INTRODUCTION

Hardly a month goes by without some medical crisis or scandal appearing in the news. Much of the reason lies in political questions: Has Britain's National Health Service been so underfunded and over-managerialized that it no longer serves the public? Are the concepts of competition, an internal market, and visible value for money misplaced in the provision of health services? Does the Clintons' failure to find a workable way of instituting health care for all mean that Americans must inevitably enjoy the finest possible service for the world's rich, with health provisions that would disgrace a peasant economy for the poor and middling in Appalachia or parts of the inner cities?

These problems relate to much larger questions. The increasing expansion and longevity of the population, and the growing range of ever more expensive treatments makes it difficult to see how any economy can ever afford to provide the best care available for everyone. We have tried to avoid discussing supposed "mistakes" that rest on alleged misuse of or underprovision of resources. And we do not think this is the place to debate whether public spending on health should necessarily outweigh public spending on education, defence, or the preservation of the Queen's peace.

We are aware of the undertow of opinion blaming big multinational companies for a failure to direct research and development into new areas, and an undue control of the provision of medical services that become distorted in the interest of their profits. Although our treatment of some scandals might suggest that we endorse this uncritically, we do not wish to suggest that we have studied the global question sufficiently to assert that these cases represent the norm. We are equally aware of the innocent ignorance which allows simple mistakes.

We are, in fact, concerned with mistakes and mishaps as much as malevolence and malignancy. "Doctors bury their mistakes," is an old saying. With a free press thirsty for scandal at any price, they are lucky if they can do so today. While we can be as angry as a tabloid editor about shifty cover-ups and evasions, we hope that we are also willing to acknowledge that erring is human and we ourselves have made copious errors in our time. So we hope our strongest notes of righteous indignation have been reserved for deliberate dishonesty or greed.

One of us had the experience, last year, of being under the knife at one hospital at the very time when it was in the news vying for the title of "worst hospital in Britain" after a run of scandals. And it was very surprising to recover from the anaesthetic and learn that the surgeons had closed up their work without removing what they promised to remove, because they really had no idea what it was, and their pre-operative scans had failed to indicate that it would need plastic surgery to close up again after a full operation. We do not regard that as a mistake or mishap, or in any way the fault of the surgeons and histologists involved. Rare conditions may take anyone by surprise in any situation, and an immediate confession of ignorance is the best and most competent way to deal with them before referring them on to some one better qualified.

On the other hand, we were both extremely disturbed by the unfeeling and inconsiderate quality of nursing offered to an elderly relative in a hospital a year previously. But that could not be accounted a medical mistake in terms of this book. It caused the old lady no actual worsening of her condition. And it was caused either by sheer individual bad manners or by the pressures of overwork and understaffing, or, indeed, as a consultant to whom we complained suggested, an all too common misinterpretation of guidelines handed down from above. In this book it is only our business to criticise such guidelines if they lead to measurable medical failures.

We have definite opinions about the ways in which medicine is best organised – a slightly different opinion for each author! So we hope that any appearance of bias will be accepted as nothing but an appearance. Sympathy with the patient is normally overriding. But our final examination of quacks and impostors and the world of patent medicines goes some way to suggest that the patient in an open market may get the medicine he deserves.

Martin and Karen Fido
Canterbury, 1996

7

DANGEROUS DRUGS

"I had rather undertake the practice of physick with pure air, pure water and good food alone than with all the drugs in the Pharmacopeia."

THOMAS SYDENHAM

Thus spake "the English Hippocrates", Dr Thomas Sydenham, in 1676. and he was eminently sensible. The "herbs, simples, drugs and spices" of his day owed everything to old wives' tales and ludicrous medical theories. By and large these ranged from the sick-making and dangerous to the bland and useless. Hardly anything physicians gave their patients to ingest had the sort of physical and chemical reactions with bodily workings that we expect of drugs today, unless they were purgatives or emetics. Physicians were quite keen on "discharging excess of humours" by vomiting and excreting no less than by cupping and bleeding. All in all, the sick man of the seventeenth century might just as well have bought a love philtre from a gypsy as a medicinal drug from a physician, unless he was constipated.

Nor had things greatly improved 200 years later. In 1883, Oliver Wendell Holmes, the American physician and humourist, wrote:

"If the whole materia medica as used, could be sunk in the bottom of the sea, it would be all the better for mankind and all the worse for the fishes."

The physician's little black bag still rattled with a wide range of laxatives and emetics but very little else. The more honest doctors admitted that tender loving care (which they had already christened "TLC") was very often all they could prescribe by way of a curative. However, things were improving with regard to the treatment of symptoms or the alleviation of pain. Acetyl salicylic acid, the analgesic component of aspirin, had been discovered – within ten years it would be manufactured and marketed by Bayer in the familiar tablet form. It was, and still is, a remarkably useful drug, but it has also proved to have its dangers.

ASPIRIN

In 1763, the Reverend Edward Stone, vicar of Chipping Norton, prepared a number of mashes and brews and tried them experimentally on villagers, asking them to report which actually made a difference to them. The potion acquiring the most positive reaction was a brew of willow bark. Mr Stone had discovered salicylic acid, a painkiller with far better capacity for reducing fever than quinine, the imported cinchona bark extract. Unfortunately, Mr Stone's brew tasted vile and rasped on the mouth and throat.

A similar compound found in meadowsweet, spirin, was a great improvement. Refined to acetyl salicylic acid it ultimately gave us the aspirin that we know today. Principally used for relieving headaches and feverish or rheumatic muscular pains, aspirin also has the capacity to thin the blood. It is useful to patients with narrow arteries as it reduces the risk of dangerous blood-clotting. It is also useful to arthritics because it reduces inflammation of the joints. However it does create a risk of internal bleeding. For this reason, a mild "Junior Aspirin", with a sweet citric taste, was prepared for children.

How Aspirin Killed Children

After nearly a hundred years as the most widely used drug in the pharmacopoeia, aspirin was suddenly and hurriedly withdrawn from all preparations for children. Research in America suggested that it was linked to Reye's syndrome, a very rare disease occasionally suffered by infants and children after they have had viral infections like influenza, chickenpox and gastro-entiritis. Although there were never more than between three and seven cases per million children, the disease attacked the liver and brain and proved fatal in half of the cases.

Ralph Reye, an Australian doctor, reported its existence in 1963. He noted that early symptoms were vomiting, lassitude, drowsiness and confusion. Subsequently, as the brain inflamed, there could follow delirium, coma and death.

By 1982, the surgeon-general in America had been convinced that enough evidence existed to show a link between aspirin and Reye's syndrome. He ordered that the medication was not to be given to children or teenagers with 'flu or chicken-pox. Within four years the incidence of Reye's syndrome in America had been halved.

British Sang-Froid

When the American research findings were first reported in 1982, Mrs Audrey Harrington wrote to the Department of Health asking them to take note and follow the surgeon-general's ban. Her 11-year-old daughter Katie had died of Reye's syndrome the previous year. The British Committee on the Safety of Medicines, however, declined to make any recommendation until a full survey of the research material and further testing had been carried out. When the successful effect of banning aspirin in America was announced, MP Jack Ashley pressed the British government for similar action. Nothing happened until the studies were completed in June 1986. Suddenly, aspirin was prohibited from being given to children under the age of twelve, or used in any preparations intended for children. Ashley protested that the Department of Health's dilatory inactivity must have resulted in children suffering Reye's syndrome unnecessarily over the previous eighteen months. The Department's bland reply was that:

"No causal link has been firmly established.... There was no point in unduly alarming people or causing panic until a significant study was completed in the UK." Clifford Harrington, Katie's father, was furious. There had been 181 cases in the UK since his wife first wrote to the Department.

The Harringtons were active in the National Reye's Syndrome Foundation, and knew how many bereaved parents were shocked to learn that warnings against the use of aspirin in childhood fevers had been issued in America as early as 1982.

"It's almost like thalidomide all over again – complacency, secrecy, bureaucratic bungling and a lack of care for innocent children," was Mr Harrington's comment.

••

NARCOTICS

••

Used wrongly, or taken to excess, any drug can be dangerous. So can anything else, for that matter. It is possible to kill some one by making them drink too much water, and yet water is neither a drug nor a poison. Similarly, King John supposedly died of a surfeit of lampreys. Yet this small, eel-like fish is perfectly edible.

"Dangerous drugs" are those substances or preparations which alter mood or perception, and which are taken for recreation rather than medication. American law uses the term "narcotics" (sleep-inducing drugs) as a synonym.

Traditional Recreational Drugs

Most cultures discover one or more substances that give a heightened sense of well-being or relaxation, and which may be enjoyed by perfectly healthy people. Alcohol derived from fermented vegetable matter has been enjoyed almost universally. Its capacity to relax inhibition can make it a valuable lubricant for social intercourse. There are also considerable dangers ranging from self-induced inefficiency through habitual drunkenness to chemically induced vitamin deficiency, neuritis, and the withdrawal symptom, *delerium tremens*. However, America's disastrous attempt to ban alcohol entirely in a society which had become accustomed to it showed that most people consider its dangers an acceptable risk.

Nicotine temporarily narrows the arteries and so slows the flow of blood to the brain. This can allow users increased concentration or general relaxation, whichever seems most desirable at the time. Taken directly, either by eating or spraying on the skin, it is highly toxic. When taken in the very reduced dosage of smoked tobacco, it is difficult (though not impossible) to reach the stage of nicotine poisoning. Unfortunately, the nicotine-laden tobacco tars are unquestionably related to lung cancer. The habit of breathing in smoke is also bad for the respiratory system.

Marijuana offers a mild cocktail of effects: a sense of well-being; sudden increases in appetite; misguided belief in one's own (and one's company's) wit; and an almost comatose enjoyment of auditory, visual and tactile sensations. Like alcohol, however, it may result in self-induced inefficiency and a short-term inability to concentrate.

Opium was habitually smoked in Mandarin China with no worse social and personal effects than those that result from the social use of alcohol. It induces a pronounced feeling of well-being and is sometimes accompanied by extremely colourful dreams or daydreams. Coca leaf was chewed with limes for flavouring by the Indians of the Andes. It has a mild locally numbing effect, and generally masks feelings of hunger and fatigue.

Coffee and tea are mild general stimulants. Chocolate contains a chemical known to be produced by the brain in a state of sexual pleasure, although chocolate is by no means an aphrodisiac.

These recreational drugs have usually found their place in the pharmacopoeia at one time or another. Alcohol has been used as a stimulant and a tonic, and was for a long time included in sedative preparations for babies. The opium derivatives, morphine and heroin, gave us the first (and still some of the most powerful) effective general painkillers, of particular use in treating cancer sufferers and burn victims, for example. Cocaine, extracted from the coca-leaf, makes an excellent local anaesthetic.

The main danger with the majority of these drugs is the failure by the user to recognize that they can be habit-forming. This may lead to a dependency marked, at best, by an almost overpowering craving; at worst by severely unpleasant withdrawal symptoms.

As an increasingly effective range of mood-altering drugs have been added to the pharmacopoeia by twentieth century medical research, a significant black market in medication for recreational purposes has appeared on the streets.

Useful Drugs

From the unfortunately useless pharmacopoeia condemned to the fishes by Oliver Wendell Holmes, medicine has moved to ever-refined drugs that really work. It was the painkillers morphine and cocaine that were the first to appear. Then in the 1930s the sulpha-drugs proved effective against bacteria. The 1940s and 1950s saw the development of barbiturates – sedative drugs that brought tranquillity to the anxious and sleep to the insomniac. The antibiotics that followed were even more effective against bacteria. Anti-histamines brought down inflammation. Amphetamines reduced congestion and stimulated energy. Finally, whole ranges of ever-varying drugs with ever-varying effects were gradually developed. Many of them wound up on the streets. Some were obtained quite legitimately by wealthy celebrities whose doctors prescribed them.

••

CELEBRITY SPOT

ELVIS PRESLEY

In public, Elvis Presley was profoundly opposed to the recreational drug culture endorsed by his younger rivals, The Beatles. Yet he died of polypharmacopy – the over-use of a wide range of drugs with conflicting effects. The drugs Elvis is believed to have taken during the course of his last tour included:

Amytal – a barbiturate with a highly hypnotic effect

Biphetamine – a stimulant for the central nervous system, known to street drug-users as "Black Beauties"

Dexedrine – a powerful amphetamine stimulant

Dilaudin – a narcotic two-and-a-half times more powerful than heroin. Its use is intended solely for such agonizing conditions as massive serious burns or terminal cancer

Percodan – a concoction of five pain-killing drugs, the most important of which is a narcotic that acts in the same way as morphine

Quaaludes – a very strong tranquillizer intended mainly for disturbed mental patients. Known as "wall-bangers", they induce uncontrolled gait and slurred speech.

In 1995 Presley's physician, Dr George Nichopoulos, was struck off the register by the Tennessee Medical Board. Dr Nichopoulos protested that this was a witch-hunt, because he had been Elvis' doctor at the time of his death. When Elvis died in 1977 he had taken Dilaudin and Valmid in the search for sleep. His fallen body was also surrounded by four additional used syringes whose contents were never established. His drug dosages were as outrageous as his gluttonous consumption of unhealthy junk foods, which had blown him up to gross obesity.

THALIDOMIDE

The worst drug disaster of all. Thalidomide was a worldwide tragedy affecting 8,000 children in 46 countries – more than 400 of them in Great Britain. It created a legal battle that ran and ran, as drug companies all over the world tried to escape the enormous expense of the damage claims brought against them.

It was a story of tears as parents broke down under the stress and children wondered if life was ever going to be worthwhile. It was also a story of incredible human triumph as fearfully deformed children grew up to overcome their handicaps to lead fulfilling lives in workplace and home.

First Warning

In 1959, the German chemical company Chemie Grünenthal received a letter from a Dr Voss, warning that he had found patients who seemed to be suffering side effects, including peripheral neuritis (nerve damage) from the use of one of their patent sedatives. It is quite normal for doctors to report suspected deleterious side effects from new drugs, but the majority of such reports turn out to be false alarms. Grünenthal were unperturbed by the doctor's communication and continued to market the drug under a number of brand names.

This, however, was not the last complaint they were to receive over the next two years. Other doctors similarly reported symptoms occurring to patients who took the drug thalidomide. The symptoms included dizziness, constipation, cramps and numbness in the fingers.

Grünenthal's response was cold and unethically commercial. They denied having received previous reports. They concealed the number of warnings they had received, and they suppressed publication of reports about the link between thalidomide and peripheral neuritis.

In July 1961 the company made their first settlement. Dr Kersten Thiele, a Düsseldorf minister, was paid DM750 (about £150) in recognition of his claim that thalidomide had caused him nerve damage. The amount was small. Indeed, the damage was not outrageous. However, using their influence, and a lot of money, Grünenthal continued to counter negative reports with positive ones. Thalidomide sold freely over every counter in the world – this was Grünenthal's ambition. They seemed prepared to go to any lengths: they harassed doctors who opposed them, even using private detectives to dredge up damaging information against them.

McBride Blows the Whistle

In November came the first serious warning of the scourge awaiting the unborn. 34-year-old Dr William McBride was a relatively unknown Australian obstetrician and gynaecologist with a relatively large practice. He was struck by the appearance of an unusual number of babies with birth defects. He looked for a common factor. It seemed to him that the malformations had always occurred when the mothers had taken thalidomide during pregnancy. He wrote a short letter to The Lancet outlining his fears.

The letter would make him famous, and bring him the resources to open his own research centre, Foundation 41. Dr McBride had correctly identified the source of the worst pre-natal mishap in medical history.

The Tragedy of Mr Flawn

In Australia, thalidomide was marketed by the Distillers' Company, a subsidiary of the UK Distillers' Company, manufacturers of Johnny Walker whisky and Gordon's gin. Their chemical branch manufactured the drug under licence from Grünenthal and sold it under the trade name Distavan. When McBride's letter appeared, Distillers' Australia promptly wrote to the parent company in England asking for their comments.

The letter was received by John Flawn, the export manager responsible for distribution to Sydney. Mr Flawn turned pale when he read McBride's accusation – he and his pregnant wife Judith had been taking thalidomide regularly as a sleeping aid.

On January 9 1962 Mrs Flawn gave birth. Her son Alexander was one of the worst-damaged thalidomide children to be born in the United Kingdom. One of his arms was short and misshapen with a thumbless hand. The other hand had six fingers. His face was paralyzed on one side and his palate was more than cleft – it was a gaping hole. One ear was missing, the other grossly deformed.

Worse than all of this, it became apparent that his brain was damaged. He was deaf and dumb. He had poor vision in the left eye. It seemed that normal communication would never be possible for him. Mr Flawn was not an irresponsible profiteer – he honourably used the product he sold, and gave it to his wife. They paid a devastating price for it.

Alexander's Progress

Not until 1976 did Alexander start to make real progress. During that year Mr Flawn gave his son a red scribbling diary. Alexander became fascinated by the lines and dates in the book and started to recognize words and copy messages. At Roffley House special school he learned to copy out long entries. To him, writing seemed like something magical. However they still had work to do to socialize him – by the age of 16 Alexander still needed constant watching.

...Meanwhile back in Germany

Dr McBride's observations were confirmed by Dr Widikund Lenz. Further research proved that thalidomide taken in the first three months of pregnancy could be responsible for the limb deformity phocomelia, which causes children to be born with appendages like seal's flippers in place of arms or legs.

Grünenthal could hold out no longer. The drug was withdrawn. Nothing more could be done but wait and see how many disabled children were presently in the womb. However, the public prosecutor's office at Aachen took up the case immediately, seeking to see whether Chemie Grünenthal was open to criminal proceedings. The wheels of justice ground exceedingly slowly. It took four years before indictments were handed down against nine Grünenthal executives, charging them with intent to commit bodily harm and involuntary manslaughter. The trial of the first seven ran for another two years, and a further two years later all hearings were suspended. But Grünenthal would be forced to pay in the end.

What it Does

Thalidomide is a compound derived from glutamic acid: one of the life-sustaining amino-acids which make up protein; and pthalic acid – a derivative of benzene. Work on the chemistry of amino-acids did much to increase our understanding of life in the second half of the twentieth century.

Thalidomide had been developed as a sleeping pill. The previous generation of sedatives – the barbiturates – had two obvious faults. They were highly addictive. And they were very dangerous if accidentally taken in overdose quantities. Thalidomide avoided these weaknesses. It was soothing to the tummy as well as calming to the mind, and so became the choice prescription for pregnant women suffering from morning sickness. This was a catastrophe. Taken between the fifth and eighth weeks of pregnancy, thalidomide is the strongest teratogenic drug ever synthesized by man.

Thalidomide's teratogenic effects ranged from the mild – a missing or shortened finger or two, or a slightly bent arm or wrist – to the truly horrifying. Babies were born with some or all their limbs missing; sometimes with hands or feet protruding from armless and legless shoulders and hips; sometimes with fingerlike appendages replacing whole limbs, or the condition phocomelia with a flipper-like limb replacing the normal arm or leg.

Babies were born with one or both ears missing, and heard through mere openings in the head. Some had no ears and no working hearing mechanism inside the head. For some of the victims, laborious, painful and infection-risking operations to create ear-like appendages were largely cosmetic and, according to one not entirely unsympathetic surgeon, merely performed to assuage the guilt of doctors and parents.

Some babies were born without eyes. Many were born unable to raise their eyes or heads, so that they could only see things at or below their own eye-level. They born with cleft lips or palates. They were born with malformed genitals or no genitals at all. They were born with no anal openings to allow bowel movements to pass. They were born with damaged brains.

By 1962, 400 thalidomide-damaged children had been born in the United Kingdom. In Germany, where the drug had been sold widely under a variety of brand names, there were 2,600. In Japan the free-enterprise-worshipping authorities were completely irresponsible, and allowed the drug to continue unrestricted selling over the counter, even after its horrible effects were known. Thus they caused several hundred unnecessary deformed births. By 1962, Japan had 1,000 such children. Australia had 39 and New Zealand eight.

And doctors estimated that perhaps twice as many infants were born dead, thalidomide having wrought such havoc with their internal organs that they had no hope whatsoever of sustaining life.

TERATOGENIC

A nasty word for a nasty thing. It means liable to produce malformed off-spring: derived from the Greek noun Teratos – monster; and the verb-stem gen – to produce or give birth to.

WHAT THE MOTHERS SAID

"When Alex was born I was frightfully brave, I cut off all my feelings. This was a terrible mistake because I didn't come alive again for seven years."

JUDITH FLAWN

"When my baby was born I had him at home. My husband fainted and was kept under doctor's care. I couldn't look at the baby when the nurse was washing him. I was in a terrible state, but I said to myself, 'He is mine.' God gave him to me and if he had nothing, he was still my baby.

"We have an old custom in the area where I lived. People would come in, find the baby's hand, and put a shilling in it. When they couldn't find his arm or hand to do this, it upset them. When I took him out for a walk, it was like a circus with children following me saying, 'Look at that kid. He's got no arms.' Thank God I got over that."

MRS J. POLLOCK

"My son keeps asking me, 'Mummy, please don't let me have any more operations.' He has only one kidney. He had to have a colostomy. He has an abnormality of the penis and may be sterile. His hands are not normal. He has sight only to eye level.

"There is a possibility of more operations, but I keep my fingers crossed and pray that God will be good and the body will have its own capacity for healing."

MRS JULIA POPE, WHOSE SON HAD 42 OPERATIONS
BEFORE HE WAS TEN YEARS OLD

"They didn't allow me to see him. When they gave him to me, his face was split, hanging apart like a butcher's slab. The doctor was crying and said my baby wouldn't live. But he did, and... they sent him home with his face stitched up. He was my own flesh and blood and had to be cared for. I didn't cry outwardly but inside I screamed. I've never left the house from that day since."

Hospitals Appalled

Experienced obstetricians and nursing staff were often completely unprepared for the shocking effects such malformed babies would have on their mothers. One woman was not told that her swaddled child had no arms until she took him home and started to bath him. Another had to be kept sedated behind screens for several days. Unknown to the staff, she crept out on the fourth night and tried to suffocate her baby. As the infant wriggled and struggled the words "Thou shalt not kill" ran through the poor woman's head again and again. She returned home, but had to be treated for severe depression for the next three years.

Mrs Florence Evans described her own feelings on receiving her armless disfigured son from the sympathetic hospital staff:

America Escapes

With 400 cases in Britain and 2,600 in Germany, the USA with its giant population of 180 million should have suffered 10,000 children with birth deformities from the thalidomide plague. In fact, there were just 16 cases in total. American chemical companies proved to be extremely cautious compared with their European and Japanese counterparts.

Most important of all, the federal Food and Drug Administration (FDA) imposed stringent standards before allowing new medications to be marketed. The traditional land of the snake-oil salesman was not prepared to let the glorious principle of free enterprise allow the practice of poisoning for profit.

Richardson-Merrill arrive on the scene

Chemie Grünenthal had no immediate success in finding an American company to take up their new wonder sleeping pill in 1957. Smith, Kline and French refused it. Lederle refused it. It was a year later when Richardson-Merrill - descendant of the famous Vick's Vapo-Rub company - accepted the poisoned chalice and bought exclusive US rights.

Richardson-Merrill knew that early tests had shown the drug was lethal to dogs and cats if given in high doses.

It is understandable that this caused them little concern: raise the dose high enough and you can kill an animal with anything.

By the time they made that application, they had spent 19 months investigating their purchase. They sent out over two million tablets for clinical trials by more than a thousand doctors who, in turn, had given them to 20,000 patients. No results were reported that seemed seriously adverse to Richardson-Merrill. The company went ahead and manufactured 10 million tablets and acquired the materials to market 15 million.

On December 12 1960 they wrote to the FDA sending details of the tests that had been carried out, and asking permission to launch the drug on the market from March 6 1961 under the brand name Kevadon.

Dr Frances Kelsey National Heroine

On November 10 1960 the FDA responded. Richardson-Merrill's application was inadequate, the agency stated. The drug could not be licensed without further and better tests. The licensing agent responsible for this historic rejection was a 46-year-old woman, new to the FDA and handling her first case on their behalf. Dr Frances Kelsey's husband was a pharmacologist, and he wrote the memorandum on the chemical tests for her.

It was a blistering attack.

> "The section entitled 'Chemical Comparison of Thalidomide and Glutathemide' is an interesting collection of meaningless pseudo-scientific jargon, apparently intended to impress chemically unsophisticated readers...

> "The data are completely meaningless as presented.... "I cannot believe this to be honest incompetence."

FDA MEMORANDUM ON APPLICATION FROM RICHARDSON-MERRILL TO MARKET THALIDOMIDE

Nor was that the end of the Kelseys's suspicion that Richardson-Merrill's application was incomplete. Dr Kelsey spotted a letter in the British Medical Journal in which a Dr Florence commented on the suspected link between thalidomide and peripheral neuritis. She felt this must have been something of which Richardson-Merrill were aware, yet their application made no mention of it. Dr Kelsey sent the company a stiff reprimand on May 5:

> *"The burden of proof that the drug is safe – which must include adequate studies of all manifestations of toxicity which medical or clinical experience suggest – lies with the applicant. In this connection we are much concerned that apparently evidence with respect to the occurrence of peripheral neuritis in England was known to you but not forthrightly described in the application."*

Richardson-Merrill's executives were furious. They said threateningly that the letter was "somewhat libellous", and tried to go over Dr Kelsey's head to the medical director of the FDA. Dr Kelsey fought her corner staunchly. Summoned to explain her collision with a highly respected medicines manufacturer, she upped the ante and said that she now also wanted additional testing to show that thalidomide was safe for pregnant women. Dr Kelsey hadn't actually predicted that thalidomide would prove teratogenous but she asked the right question, and she asked it before Dr McBride and Dr Lenz had made their findings known.

Her bosses backed her. Before Richardson-merrill could come up with a revised application, the thalidomide story had become known. Grünenthal had withdrawn the drug. America was saved from the disaster that hit other countries.

On July 15 1962, the Washington Post wrote an article headlined "Heroine of the FDA Keeps Bad Drug off the Market". Dr Kelsey and her agency received a flood of favourable press coverage. She was finally awarded a gold medal by President Kennedy.

Compensation

Richardson-Merrill should have given Dr Kelsey another gold medal. Her intransigent insistence that they come up with further evidence in relation to the drug's safety must have saved them a fortune in damages.

The first case against them was brought by Thomas and Joanne Diamond on June 17 1969. The couple from Pennsylvania were suing on behalf of their son David. They asked for $2 million. Richardson-Merrill settled out of court.

Shirley Carrick of Los Angeles was just 16 years old and still in high school when she gave birth to a deformed daughter, Peggy. When she brought suit against Richardson-Merrill, the jury awarded Peggy $2.5 million, and Shirley $250,000. The company fought back, applying for a retrial. this was refused, but the damages were reduced to $775,000. Richardson-Merrill appealed again, and this time settled out of court for $500,000.

Had Dr Kelsey allowed their sales to go forward as projected, they might well have had to meet claims that exceeded $5 billion in total. At 1970s values, one wonders whether the company could have survived.

Family Problems

Mothers were not alone in being affected by the births of hideously deformed babies. Fathers and even siblings suffered traumatically, although some fathers made some of the mothers' suffering even worse.

This was particularly likely when the drug-related cause was unknown to the family. Some of the damaged children were three years old before their parents learned that heredity was not to blame. One poor mother of a brain-damaged boy was aggressively told, "It's your fault. It's inherited from your family." Another father said to his wife as he abandoned her, "If it weren't for you I wouldn't have the son I have." Yet another, seeing his child for the first time in hospital, said, "If you bring that monster home, I leave." Of course, she did. Unfortunately, he kept his word.

Medical experience did not necessarily protect men from shock. Although Stanley Jones was a psychiatric nurse, he still fainted on seeing his son David's deformity.

David Mason became nationally known for his determined fight to win proper compensation for his daughter Louise. Yet his first reaction on seeing her was very different. Louise appeared as a little head and torso with what looked like four flowers sprouting at the corners; a bright wine-red stain over the face, and a flattened nose. "Surely you're not going to allow a child in this state to live," Mason expostulated – and felt over-whelming guilt and remorse as the doctor quietly responded, "Mr Mason, I can't help you." Mrs Mason was sedated at the time and not allowed to see Louise.

In Liège, a Belgian couple went further. They poisoned their eight-day-old, legless daughter with the help of their family doctor. All three were charged with murder but were acquitted to rousing cheers from the 1,000 supporters who had crowded the courtroom for the week of their trial.

Not all of the stories were so sad. One little boy provided some justifica-tion for old-fashioned evasiveness when discussing sex with children. he had been told that santa Claus was going to bring him a little brother or sister for Christmas, and when he saw her with no arms, observed inno-cently, "I suppose Santa must have done that when he brought her down the chimney."

One adoptive father rose to the challenge, earning the gratitude of his son, national prominence in a book and television documentary film, and a place in the Exhibition of British Genius. Leonard Wiles supplied "giant's shoulders" to support his crippled son.

Terry Wiles – "On Giant's Shoulders"

At 60, van driver Leonard Wiles would probably have been seen by con-ventional social workers as too old to adopt a child, let alone a totally hand-icapped five-year-old of mixed race. Since Leonard's wife Hazel at first wished to have nothing to do with Terry, the little boy Leonard had come across in Chailey Heritage Craft School and Hospital in Surrey, sceptics would have been even more certain that no good could come of this.

The school authorities, however, rightly spotted the deep humanity of the elderly man, and for the next two years little Terry made home visits to

Leonard Wiles, and Hazel soon responded to his outgoing personality. When the boy was nine years old, the couple formally adopted him.

Terry was the illegitimate son of a black father and white mother. He was abandoned at a hospital in East Anglia, and ended up at Chailey Heritage to be fitted with artificial limbs and taught the simple crafts deemed appropriate for the handicapped. Terry has no legs. His body, little over two feet tall when he reached full growth, rests on a pad of pelvic muscle. In place of arms he has short flippers. One eye hung halfway down his face when he was born, and had to be removed. When he was seventeen he wrote his own description of his life for inclusion in Marjorie Wallace's book about the Wiles family.

> *"I would describe my life as a never-ending road with its bumps and smoothness. Sometimes I would be travelling on smoothly and then suddenly I would hit a bump of sadness in my life, but that bump would die away into nothing. Then I came to a hole when I thought life was not worth living. But as usual I carried on. Then I suddenly met two loving parents who ended my journey and who protected me from life's handicaps. My father is a pioneer in his way because he invents machines to help me and other physically handicapped children to lead a normal life."*

Len Wiles's Inventions

Len's first important observation was that Terry's artificial limbs were not only extremely painful, they actually impeded the boy. He could move more effectively by rolling himself around on the floor with his flippers. So Len dispensed with traditional prosthetics and designed a mobile chair that Terry could operate himself. He decided not to mimic the lifting and walking equipment of normal people, but to make full use of Terry's individual muscular skills.

Len was earning just £30 a week as a driver, and he had to use his spare time to design the gadgets that would make active life possible for his son. He poured his cash and energies into the job, and soon found himself in deep debt before Terry finally received a compensation payment of £5,000.

Len's imaginativeness was apparent in his incorporating a lift into Terry's chair which enabled him to raise himself and look people in the face, overcoming his eye-level restricted vision.

By the time he was 17, Terry could type 27 words a minute, play an electric organ, get books from shelves, and serve tea. He was writing his own short stories and attending business classes at Huntingdon technical college. His electrically operated wheelchair/car, the "Silver Shadow", was displayed at the 1977 London Exhibition of British Genius. Len and Hazel Wiles's love and ingenuity, and Terry's courage and resilience had heroically risen above devastating handicaps.

Author Marjorie Wallace wrote about the Wiles family. Her book – "On Giant's Shoulders" – won universal admiration for their courage.

Legal Battles

It was obvious that Len and Hazel Wiles were exceptional people, and that most parents were going to need a lot more expensive help in bringing up the most desperately crippled thalidomide children. Even Len and Hazel needed more money than they could earn to spend on Terry.

It was also obvious that liability must lie with the companies that had developed and marketed the drug. Chemie Grünenthal's blatant attempts to wriggle out of the observed link between thalidomide and peripheral neuritis had led to very serious criminal charges being brought against some of its senior staff. They were not to be spared their civil responsibility to the victims – for ten years the company was compelled to hand over its entire profits to the thalidomide children.

If Richardson-Merrill had faced an equal proportionately large number of suits, the inadequacies of their application to the FDA for licence would probably have swung feeling strongly against them as the $2.5 million awarded by the Carrick jury indicated. They were lucky to have relatively few victims to settle with.

In Sweden, the Association for Parents of Thalidomide Children united 105 of the victims' families, and they jointly took legal action against Astra, the Swedish pharmaceutical company who had marketed the drug. Astra settled out of court in September 1965, agreeing to pay continuing grants for the children's lifetimes. Should all 105 victims live to the age of 75, the cost to Astra would be in excess of $14 million.

In Great Britain, the issue of compensation for thalidomide victims was to drag on for ten years before a settlement was reached.

The Battle with Distillers'

The magnitude of the disaster looked capable of bankrupting even a giant liquor and chemicals corporation. It was not irresponsible of the Distillers' Company to mount a rapid damage-limitation exercise to protect their employees and shareholders.

Distillers' denied that they bore responsibility for the terrible effects of Thalidomide as they said they did not know or have any reason to suspect what the drug might do. They maintained their denial throughout but many felt that whatever they said, they should have accepted their moral responsibility at the outset.

Enoch Powell, then Minister of Health, assured Parliament that no responsibility lay with Distillers'. His department told a Bristol teacher, who wrote to them concerning her handicapped daughter in 1961, that there was no reason to suspect the drug (sold by Distillers' as Distaval) could have the side effects it had. The press accepted Distillers' company handouts and issued similarly anodyne reports. After all it was not as if they had been harassing critics with private detectives like Grünenthal.

20 thalidomide children were at Chailey Heritage, where the centre had a special school, a Lady Hoare sheltered workshop, and access to the famous artificial limb-fitting centre at Roehampton. When their parents learned that Distillers' were denying all negligence and responsibility, and that counsel's opinion was that a claim for injuries sustained before birth was unlikely to be upheld by the courts, they formed the Society for the Aid of Thalidomide Children. In Glasgow, Dr R. W. Smithells, who would become Britain's leading medical authority on thalidomide cases, formed the Kevin Club, named for a thalidomide child. These two organizations became the main representatives of the children's and their parents' interests in Britain.

David Mason, who had momentarily felt that his daughter Louise should not be allowed to live, was the son of a Distillers' Company shareholder. it seemed apparent to him that the company intended to put the interests of the shareholders first, and a fight would be necessary. In 1962, the parents brought a suit against Distillers' but the issue of the writ brought the matter sub judice, and the parents were restrained from seeking public support.

In 1968, Distillers' offered to settle with 62 out of the 430 children claiming against them. They were, in effect, accepting that after distributing the drug for three years they might have taken heed of the warnings about peripheral neuritis. However, they still denied all responsibility for children whose mothers took the drug before any adverse side-effects were known to them.

David Mason fought on, bringing the case into the open. The press learned that grossly handicapped children were struggling for aid with the company that had accidentally caused their deformity. They also learned that the company earned £62 million annual profits.

The Daily Telegraph newspaper featured the Thalidomide story. Soon the Sunday Times joined the struggle and became one of the strongest advocates of the thalidomide children's cause.

Louise Mason

Before Louise Mason's birth, David's wife Louise had complained of perpetual tiredness. Her doctor diagnosed anaemia and told her she was pregnant. She was given iron tablets and pills to help her sleep. The first seven months of her pregnancy passed normally.

Then a student at her clinic gave her worrying news. There seemed to be something amiss with the foetus, he said. He could not detect any limbs. A consultant reprimanded the young man, assuring Mrs Mason that her baby's arms and legs were in place.

Labour was delayed. Thirteen days overdue, the obstetrician decided to induce birth. The delivery proved long and difficult, and before Mrs Mason was allowed to know anything about the child she and David were already calling Louise, David was warned that the child was not completely developed – not really ready to be born... her arms and legs were not complete, and... well... there were one or two other things.

David Mason's shocked response may have determined the persistence with which he fought on her behalf subsequently. The child was never placed in his and Vickie's care, but was taken immediately to the Chailey Heritage for skilled professional nursing and upbringing.

When Mr Mason went to see his doctor subsequently, the GP asked him, "Tell me, did I prescribe Distaval for your wife?" The Lancet had carried an article warning about birth deformities related to the drug. But it was too late for the Masons.

Fighting on Alone

It seemed unlikely that further legal action against Distillers' would work. Already 62 parents had been offered their settlement in the face of the apparent legal position that unborn children had no rights. Nonetheless, David Mason's legal advisers noticed a loophole which might just allow him to struggle on. Because Louise had been taken straight to the Chailey Heritage, David and Vickie had never been allowed normal parental custody. On these grounds, David was given leave to appeal.

In 1971 Distillers' gave in. They set up a trust of £3.5 million for the children, and offered each set of parents £1,500. This meant that each family would receive, on average, £8,000. But Distillers' wanted this to be the absolute end of the affair. The offer would only be honoured if it was unanimously accepted by all the families involved. The Masons stood out. Alone.

Their resolve was certainly not because David Mason hoped to make a large personal gain from the case. Like almost anyone else going to law fighting a protracted suit, he was onto a hiding to nothing financially. He was carrying on because of the principle. Mason's legal costs ultimately rose to £10,000. He estimated that the time he devoted to the case cost him £160,000 in business losses, and a further £40,000 because he hadn't time to close a deal on a West-country farm that had thereupon doubled in value. Unlike many of the other parents, David Mason could have afforded the best treatment for Louise himself. He simply wanted Distillers' to accept their moral responsibility.

His altruism was not altogether appreciated by some of the other families, since his refusal to accept immediate compensation meant that they still had to wait and see what, if anything, they would ultimately get. At Chailey, some of the other thalidomide children attacked Louise on the ground that her father was blocking their families from recovering money they needed.

Appealing to the Public

In December 1971, David Mason told his story to the Daily Mail. Soon after that, the courts in Los Angeles decided that each American thalidomide child merited £321,000 compensation. The Sunday Times, whose "Insight" team were an outstanding group of investigative journalists during this period, came out in September 1972 with a huge feature headline: "Our Thalidomide Children: A Cause for National Shame." From then on, the Sunday Times stood in the forefront of the campaign to obtain decent compensation for the victims.

Members of parliament took up the case. Although the British government was unwilling to interfere with legal matters, MP Jack Ashley became the children's parliamentary champion, with Barbara Castle giving very effective support in the debate.

At the same time, Ralph Nader, the American consumers' interests campaigner, began to take an interest in what was happening in Britain. He calculated that Distillers' profits and moral responsibility meant that they could be reasonably expected to set up a £60 million trust to be paid into funds for the children over the coming 20 years. He took it upon himself to write to Distillers' chairman, Sir William MacDonald, warning that American whisky and gin sales might be affected if the company was seen to be stingy. He ended the letter: "May there be a reflective Christmas for you and your management."

Louise at Chailey

When Louise Mason first went to Chailey she had to be placed in a moulded flowerpot to support her in an upright position – something she could not do on her own.

At 18 months, when other children were crawling, she was given a low-wheeled plastic platform to get herself about. She had to wear a sponge-rubber helmet to protect her head against her constant falls. To simulate walking, she was given rockers on rigid struts, before she moved to artificial legs. Since she had hands, it became possible to teach her to write and type.

Louise had to have numerous operations: to clear the nasal blockages behind her flattened nose; to repair damage to her face caused by her falls; and to move the position of one of her rudimentary legs so that she could position herself on her prosthetic limbs.

> *"As you know, the scotch whiskies and gins produced by your company are sold in large numbers in the US, especially at this time of year. The fact that the bulk of your highly profitable sales in the US derive from well-known brands of alcoholic spirits serves as a special irony when compared with the horrors of thalidomide."*

RALPH NADER, IN A LETTER TO SIR WILLIAM MACDONALD

A Famous Victory

David Mason was absolutely furious when the news came that Distillers' had upped its offer to £5 million. He refused point-blank. In Washington, he and Ralph Nader held a press conference, announcing that Distillers' had made no response to their letter of protest.

The public's reaction was immediate. Over the next nine days, Distillers' share value fell by £35 million. The free market was speaking. And with the voice of morality.

At the same time the Wrenson chain of shops and supermarkets, with 240 outlets, announced a total boycott of Distillers' products until a settlement in the region of £20 million was agreed. The threat of a serious fall in Distillers' sales and investment loomed. Distillers' shareholders put pressure on the board.

Finally, in 1974, Sir William MacDonald flew to London to consult with his legal advisers. The paltry offer of £5 million was swiftly withdrawn. In its place Distillers' promised to make ten annual payments of £2 million to set up the Thalidomide Trust. The offer was accepted. The battle was over. Prime Minister Harold Wilson topped up this figure with an additional £5 million from the government to offset against income tax.

The victory had to be won by publicity. There was no legal case to suggest distillers' had deliberately deceived the public or misled the Ministry of Health. But a moral view prevailed – to wit: "You were accidentally involved. You are very rich. You must help clean up."

Survivors' Stories

The mixture of triumph and tragedy for the thalidomide children was summed up well be young Patrick Pope, who had once asked his mother to stop his endless operations.

By the time he reached adolescence he had been under the surgeons' hands 40 times. But now he could swim and ride a bike, and had the ambition to become a vet. All the same, like so many other thalidomide children, he was lonely and afraid to mix with his own age group. "I wish to be normal, terribly normal," he said. "But I can't help getting depressed and angry about it."

By the end of the 1970s, numerous success stories were being reported. 19-year-old David Bickers was studying mathematics and electronics and producing his own talking magazine for the blind. This in spite of only having rudimentary finger-like digits for arms.

Jerry Limb won his brown belt for karate after 30 months in training. His rudimentary arms proved effective in blocking blows, and he managed the aggressive kicks. "We don't show him any favours," said his trainer.

Gary Skines worked as a telephone operator, even though he had short flipper-like substitutes for arms.

One hundred thalidomide kids passed their driving tests, in spite of their disabilities. In 1980, Gillian Thomas of Wales passed the Institute of

Advanced Motorists' test. Armless Gillian drove a converted Mini-Clubman, which she steered with one foot by a disc on the floor. Her other foot controlled the accelerator and brakes.

Elizabeth Buckle passed her B.Sc. degree at Durham University when she was 22. Even more surprisingly, perhaps, she also played in goal for her college hockey team. Fellow thalidomide victim Peter Spiers, with an honours degree in classics, became vice-president of Durham Students' Union.

Perhaps the most heart-warming of all the thalidomide success stories given press coverage was that of Elaine McAvoy. She was the first thalidomide victim to become a mother. By 1986, with a seven-year-old daughter and five-year-old son, 26-year-old Mrs McAvoy demonstrated to the world how well a loving mother with no arms could cope with the physical demands of caring for her children. She had developed highly skilled legs and toes. Indeed, she boasted that, "There isn't anything I cannot do." The pictures of her cuddling her daughter Sara proved that she, like 70 other thalidomide mothers, was perfectly capable of giving a child proper love and nurture.

Louise Mason

When she was 12, Louise was allowed to sit up at night and watch her father on television. Animals were important in her life. Despite having no legs, she had mastered riding. She also kept newts and goldfish. At that age she hoped for a career working with animals, training domestic pets to perform tricks.

She was an adventurous person. Her disability didn't stop her from going caving, and once abseiling, strapped to a stretcher.

In the end, Louise found work as a computer operator. She also found a husband who shared her interest in animals, and had some awareness of the difficulties of being handicapped.

Partially sighted John Medus worked at a boarding kennels. He and Louise married in 1987, and supported themselves successfully, with the Thalidomide Trust supplying essential extras like Louise's wheelchair, and a telephone for her specially adapted car, since she would have been quite helpless in the event of a breakdown.

In 1988 their first daughter Emma was born. Louise decided to have an epidural caesarean so that she could remain conscious throughout labour, and later remarked that the only thing that hurt was having a drip in her jugular vein, because she lacked the limbs that would normally be used.

Louise proved adept at handling Emma, even though she needed a special hook to hold between her teeth and insert into a loop in the baby-carrier to pick her up. Louise often held her child by bunched Babygrow fabric between her teeth, like a cat picking up a kitten. Mrs Medus trained for her unorthodox mode of child handling. "She'll have to get a lot heavier before that's impossible," she remarked, "since I can drag a half-hundred-weight sack."

Difficult Cases

The 1990s saw publicity given to some thalidomide victims whose lives had been more chequered. Armless and legless Janette Mottley first made news in 1986 when she was about to become a mother. She was unmarried, though she hoped to marry her lover when he completed his divorce. Janette, stuck in an electric wheelchair which she operated with her chin, was unable to wash or dress herself, and would never have Elaine McAvoy's prospect of fully caring for her child. She taught herself to negotiate a feeding bottle between her chin and shoulder, and had a pram attached to the front of her chair.

Five years later, Janette's mother Sheila published her own autobiography. Sheila had been 20, unmarried and pregnant for the third time when her doctor prescribed Distaval. Janette was just another huge complication in her life. Sheila refused. She went on the streets to feed her children, giving up prostitution only after a stretch in Holloway Prison. Janette learned art and sewing, holding brushes in her mouth. Then in college she rebelled against her lot. Her sister was on heroin. Her brothers abandoned the family, resenting all the attention that had been given to janette. Only Janette's baby seemed to bring things together again.

This desperation is echoed in another case. In 1994, 32-year-old Heather Bird went on hunger strike at her drab sidestreet bungalow in Motherwell. Two other thalidomide victims shared her protest. They feared that the Thalidomide Trust was running out of money and the vital aids that kept them going would be cut off. Heather had resented training in dull repetitive crafts in her teens, and now resented the 35% tax paid on grants she received. Her courage had made her live, but her existence brought her limited fulfilment.

McBride Returns to the Fray

In 1972, Dr William McBride went public with a new claim. He declared that three deformed babies had been born in Sydney after their mothers took the anti-depressant drug Imipramine during pregnancy. One of the children, aged two-and-a-half, was shown on television playing with toys.

This news rather startled the medical establishment. Imipramine was a drug with a highly specialized action on noradrenalin, one of the mono-amine neurotransmitters which provide chemical links between nerve cells. Imipramine prevents noradrenalin from being reabsorbed into the cell which first released it, thereby enabling its mood-altering action to continue. It was only prescribed to clinically depressed patients, and had been in use for twelve years. It had attracted a mere three complaints in Australia throughout that period. Moreover, the manufacturers included a warning with the pills that they should not be taken in early pregnancy.

McBride complained that the warning was on loose paper. A pharmacist might discard it if he was filling a prescription for less than the full contents of a box. Dr McBride wanted a distinctive cap with a special warning to be fitted on every pill bottle that might go to a patient.

The Pharmacy Guild remarked that such warnings were primarily technical and for the use of doctors only. The case of Imipramine proceeded no further. If there ever was any real danger of its having teratogenic side effects, this seemed to have been nipped in the bud.

The Committee on the Safety of Medicines

One positive result of the thalidomide disaster was the establishment of a Committee on the Safety of Medicines in Britain. It was recognized that the American food and Drugs Administration had fully proved its worth over thalidomide, and it was a thoroughly acceptable restriction on trade to make manufactured drugs pass through the inspection of such a government watchdog body.

Unfortunately, Britain's committee was never given quite such stringent powers as its American counterpart. (It has always been a curiosity of British culture that, while less avidly devoted to the principle of free enterprise than the USA, Britain has consistently has less effective restraints on the growth of monopolies and the overweening use of competitive commercial power against smaller rivals.) In fact, the Committee on the Safety of Medicines, like a number of other British government watchdogs, seemed at times to take the ideal of sang-froid a little too far, issuing anodyne reassurances. Many observers have felt that they ought to let their caution err on the side of consumer protection rather than guarding zealously against any unwarranted restriction of trade.

Their report that Imipramine need not be withdrawn was sound enough. The drug was marketed in England as Toframil or Berkomine. There was no British report of any increase in deformed live births over the period it had been in use. There had been some congenital deformations in babies born to women who had taken Toframil, but these ran at a rate of 1% – 2% of live births: – exactly the rate of deformity found in nature.

Thalidomide Trust

In 1993, Britain's oldest thalidomide victim, Freddie Astbury, founded the Thalidomide Trust Action Group. 34 years old, with four children, Mr Astbury was finding it hard to make ends meet. he received a regular £100 in disability grants, and the Department of Social Security paid his mortgage. Discretionary payments from the Thalidomide Trust topped this up. (They paid amounts from £1,000 to £24,000 to victims, relating the grants to the degree of disability. The larger sums usually went toward buying appropriate housing.)

Mr Astbury could drive, but could not afford a car. His telephone had been cut off. Then he heard that the Thalidomide Trust might be insufficiently funded to continue grants for the whole of the victims' lifetimes. It was, in fact, expected to run out in about ten years. Mr Astbury wrote to Prime Minister John Major, and started the Action Group with other concerned victims, initiating its activities with the hunger strike that he, Heather Bird in Scotland, and Kim Morton in Belfast undertook. The Action Group was also perturbed by the news that thalidomide was back in the pharmacopoeia.

Sauramide

Continued research on thalidomide had shown that its teratogenic effects were even more frightening than might have been thought at first. One tablet alone was sufficient to cause congenital malformations. It also transpired that thalidomide acted in some way on the immune system. In the age of AIDS this was of great interest. Clinical trials were started in 1991 to see whether it could be used in cases of AIDS, multiple sclerosis, leukaemia and Beckett's syndrome. They were, of course, strictly controlled. Sauramide (as it is now called commercially) is not available to GPs or the general public, and those hospital consultants who use it do so only with great caution and when all other remedies have failed. But the seriousness of the conditions for which it is being tested makes the degree of known risk acceptable.

Hereditary Teratogeny?

In 1993, Georgina Harrison was born in Peterborough with thalidomide-like deformed hands and feet. Her father had been one of the original thalidomide children. While he and his wife had two other perfectly normal children, their distress and anxiety were understandable.

British doctors were immediately reassuring. There was absolutely no evidence that thalidomide malformation could be carried genetically. Laboratory and animal tests had all proved negative.

But the alarm bells rang worldwide because Dr McBride again took up the issue, and wrote to the British Medical Journal suggesting that the drug might damage genes in ways that could be passed on to future generations. By this time, however, Dr McBride was himself under a cloud.

DEBENDOX

The Debendox saga forms a curious coda to the thalidomide disaster. In 1975, David Mekdeci was born in Florida with a deformed right arm and caved-in chest. His mother was sure that one of the many drugs she had taken during pregnancy must be responsible. Soon after David's birth she asked the FDA for information about them A phone call from an FDA informant, who insisted on anonymity, advised her to concentrate on an anti-nauseant drug marketed in America as Bendectin, but known elsewhere as Debendox.

Debendox had been developed by Dr Raymond Pogge, Richardson-Merrell's director of medical research from 1950 to 1960, and approved by the FDA in 1956 after an application with a mass of favourable outside clinical trial reports from a Dr Ray Nulsen. But Richardson-Merrell was still struggling after its difficulties with thalidomide and another drug.

The Scandals of the Early Sixties

Richardson-Merrell's management in the late fifties and early sixties were ambitious for their company. To this end they promoted two new drugs.

The first to be exposed was Triparanol, put on the market in July 1960 and trumpeted as the first absolutely safe anti-cholesterol drug which did not require the patient to make any change in his diet. Patients very swiftly began reporting side-effects such as hair falling out. Within a year, in an unprecedented move, the FDA inspectors had gone on to the premises following information about laboratory practices received from a Richardson-

Merrell employee. Triparanol was withdrawn from the market in two days. Two years later the company was fined $80,000. Additionally, one vice-president, a laboratory director and a pharmacological researcher were all given six months probation after pleading "No Contest" to six charges. This was serious commercial as well as medical malpractice, and ultimately cost Richardson-Merrell a reputed $200 million in damage suits.

The company's other disaster was the purchase and marketing of thalidomide. A report prepared by Doctor Pogge describing a large number of favourable tests that had been made on the drug was published under the name of Doctor Nulsen. As a result, a report prepared by the company's own director of research appeared as an entirely independent and disinterested scientific paper. Now, the two men's names were linked again over Debendox.

McBride Returns

The Mekdeci case was greatly strengthened by evidence from William McBride. He reported that in laboratory tests he had found eight baby rabbits with deformed limbs after their mothers had been given Debendox. This seemed to him a statistically significant number, and he believed Debendox was potentially teratogenic.

Despite this powerful support, the jury finding for the Mekdecis only awarded them £20,000 – a tiny sum in the light of normal medical negligence cases at the time. The judge ordered a re-trial, and in the run-up to those proceedings, it transpired that looking for potential weaknesses, Richardson-Merrell had hired a private detective to investigate Dr McBride's work, reputation and standing. This certainly made the company look bad, and encouraged MPs Jack Ashley and David Ennals to press the British government to investigate Debendox and restrict its sale. The government declined, citing work done by Professor Smithells which compared the proportion of births of deformed babies to women who had taken Debendox with a matching control group who had not. This indicated there was a very slightly lower chance of giving birth to a deformed baby after using Debendox in pregnancy!

Richardson-Merrell cited this work too. They were bedevilled by experimenters doing nasty things to rats in laboratories with their drug, and had to make clear that controls had not been used in these animal experiments. They also pointed out that over 300 times the normal human dose had been given to produce adverse effects!

The Mekdecis actually lost their second trial, but the worldwide attention they had drawn to Debendox had depressed sales severely. In 1983, when a Washington couple won $750,000 damages on behalf of their daughter born with a shortened right arm bearing only two fingers, Richardson-Merrell threw in the towel and withdrew the drug. The company management took great pains to make it clear that they were striking off a safe and useful remedy to morning-sickness simply because they couldn't afford the on-going litigation.

Debendox in the Clear

Proof that the company were right came too late. Studies in England, Northern Ireland and Australia all confirmed that the drug had no teratogenic properties whatsoever. More shocking still, Dr William McBride was proved to have faked his evidence. The charge was first made in 1982 by his young assistant Dr Philip Vardy. After an inconclusive investigation Dr Vardy was sacked.

Six years later an older colleague, Dr Normal Swan, looked back at the early research material and realized that the figures had indeed been doctored. The wrong number of rabbits and the wrong dosages were described in the published work. This time a tribunal found there had been scientific fraud, and Dr McBride was lacking in scientific integrity. Although McBride protested that he was being smeared by the jealous drug companies he was forced to resign from Centre 41.

In 1991 McBride admitted that he had changed some data "in the long-term interests of humanity" and had allowed himself to depart from "proper scientific practices".

In 1993 the New South Wales tribunal declared Dr McBride guilty of four of the sixteen charges they had investigated and called the whole affair a "sorry saga".

VALIUM

The search for a safe and perfect tranquillizer seemed to have arrived at the rainbow's end in the late 1950s, when researchers began to look at the properties of a group of chemicals known as the Bensodiazopines. These had been discovered by a Polish chemist in the 1930s, but not as yet put to medical use.

It was found that they relaxed muscles and calmed the mind. Laboratory tests showed no adverse side effects. It also seemed difficult to take sufficient quantities for an accidental overdose.

Librium went on the market in 1961. It was followed a year later by Valium. Sleeping pills like Mogadon and Halcion came from the same group of drugs. However, it was with Valium that the absolute top-selling drug of the next twenty years had appeared. The little yellow 5-mg tablets went to hosts of users. More seriously anxious patients enjoyed the 10-mg tablets.

Valium was absolutely non-toxic. That was its great appeal. One researcher joked that the only way you could kill a guinea-pig with valium was by amassing a huge heap of the pills and burying the creature. Given 100 tablets, the little animal just took a very long sleep and woke up apparently refreshed and none the worse for wear.

"Don't worry. They won't do you any harm," Heather Jones was told by her doctor in 1971. "You can take them all your life if you wish." With ten years constant use in the market behind them and no fatalities reported he seemed entirely justified. Joan Jerome's doctor thought them so safe she casually referred to them as her "Smarties".

Millions of satisfied patients took them no no ill effects. It appeared that this drug, at last, was really safe and non-addictive. At times of great stress and trauma, it was possible to take the pills and carry on calmly with one's work, reducing the dosage steadily over days, weeks or months as one felt less need for them, and ultimately giving them up and returning to normal life. Only 20% of patients took the entire course of pills prescribed for them. The remainder realized that they were no longer under stress, and not wanting to become habituated to anything unnecessary, or disliking the very slight wooziness incurred by taking them unnecessarily, either threw them away, or kept them to use a quarter of a pill on any random night when traffic or noisy neighbours were disturbing enough to prevent sleep. For many people Valium was a godsend. The vast majority of all users took valium for less than a month and used less pills than the doctor had ordered.

Habitual Users

Given the drug's evident safety, there were those who felt that the permissive outlook of doctors like Heather Jones's might be interpreted as downright encouragement to go on valium for life. People in peculiarly stressful jobs, or long-running difficult domestic situations, or (as they felt) cursed with short tempers and unnecessary irritability, settled down to make the daily dose of valium a part of their regular routine. It wouldn't do them any harm, so they might as well enjoy stabilized stress-free living for as long as the good Lord left them on this all too frustrating planet. Some enthusiastically advised others to make their lifelong commitment to valium. Others in high-pressure and competitive jobs lifted themselves through periods of demanding overwork with stimulant amphetamines, calming themselves back down for rest and relaxation with benzodiazopines.

A life alternating between "uppers" for hard work or zestful all-night parties, and "downers" for rest, became the exhilarating background to the "Swinging Sixties".

For some reason, twice as many women took valium as men. One suggestion was that because the women's liberation movement had just started, patriarchal doctors quietly decided to calm these harridans down. That seems grossly improbable. It is far more likely that women were succumbing to the accumulated pressures of traditional social patterns which depressed them under what Betty Friedan had labelled "The Feminine Mystique". This took place in an economic climate where more women were in employment – some finding great fulfilment in their work, others taking on dull, unfulfilling jobs out of necessity to supplement their family income.

It wasn't an easy time to be certain what a feminine identity should be. And women executives in business and the media faced constant pressure from men who resented or feared their competition, or were constitutionally incapable of appreciating their real worth. For such women, the strain of continuous demanding work and frequent frustration was best met by the little pill that was able to put it all into perspective.

Men were more likely to become habitual valium users when they passed middle age and saw that their youthful ambitions would never be realized, and yet there was still a decade or more of increasingly unwanted work stretching ahead of them. Older women, too, used valium to relive themselves of some of the anxieties that were inevitably brought on by aging in a fast-moving, youth-worshipping culture.

The Uppers Alternative

Some doctors were more likely to prescribe uppers for depressed housewives, especially if they were putting on weight. A side effect of the amphetamines was that they depressed the appetite. So a woman who was bored as a housewife and miserable about her middle-aged spread could be given Benzedrine or Dexedrine in the confident expectation that she would lose weight and enjoy the energy and vitality to cope with her life. There were a few doctors who thought they might well arrive at putting the majority of their middle-aged female patients on lifetime courses of amphetamines. But only a few.

"Bennies" and "Dexies" were sold on the streets as "Speed". They gave the partying, drug-consuming young a high, and so could obviously be dangerously habit-forming. Thankfully, the lavish over-prescription of amphetamines never reached the heights achieved by valium.

The End of the Valium Splurge

For many British doctors, the first warning that the benzodiazopines posed some serious dangers came with a report from the Committee on the

Safety of Medicines in January 1988. This was very late. For a long time, columnists commenting on the "drug culture" of the "alternative society" had remarked that the biggest group of heavy drug-users were not hippies, but depressed housewives given running prescriptions of tranquillizers by their doctors.

The first major book describing the possible effects of habitual valium-taking had appeared eight years earlier, but the victim was not a bored housewife – she was an active and successful television producer.

Barbara Gordon's Story

Barbara Gordon's first experience with valium came when she fell off her bicycle as a student at Vassar and slipped a disc. The hospital gave her valium in its capacity as a muscle-relaxant. Like others, she found it useful, non-addictive and free from adverse side-effects. Not that drugs held real fears for her – like many kids of her generation, she had popped speed, LSD and even heroin for fun, and had not lapsed into an addicted junky.

After graduating, she built a career in television, ultimately becoming a very successful scriptwriter and producer with CBS. She specialized in documentaries, and so was well-informed about a wide range of current problems, never imagining that she was going to become a spectacular exemplar of one that was as yet unsuspected.

Her work was competitive and demanding. Her boyfriend and family were pressing her to marry, yet she felt that this would be a mistake. For years she kept the pressure under control by taking valium. However, she noticed that the drug became less and less effective as time went by. To overcome insomnia and recurrent feelings of tension she increased the dosage, until she was taking her 5-mg tablets six times a day. The apparent "side-effect" after years of heavy dosing seemed to be the recurrence of the very symptoms the drug was supposed to suppress. The natural tendency was to go on and increase the dose.

She consulted her doctor, who offered to transfer her to Thorazine. Barbara decided that she wanted no part of becoming dependent on another drug. She would simply give up the valium altogether. Her doctor did not discourage her. Few people at this time were aware of the dangers of instantly giving up valium after years of habitual high dosage.

The instant effects were frightening. She suffered a burning sensation in the head. Generalized anxiety changed to raging panic attacks. She became agoraphobic to the extent that she wanted to hide in bed all day. She lost interest in sex, and started throwing tantrums. Not surprisingly, her relationship with her boyfriend suffered. He was at first extremely caring and nurturing. She seemed have regressed to a childhood way of behaving, and at times welcomed this. But he did not or could not sustain it. He wanted her to go back on the valium and become the person she had been before and they had a fight. Yet she was so unsure of herself that when he accused her of becoming paranoid, she wondered whether this wasn't all just hallucination.

Soon her condition was so serious that she was moved into a mental hospital. She was diagnosed cyclothymic – subject to wild and irrational mood-swings. She was put on the anti-depressant Sinequan. When she was discharged she realized that the deep doubts she had about marrying her boyfriend were justified and she subsequently broke off the relationship.

Meanwhile she was still unfit for work. The first psychiatrist she saw put her on the anti-manic depressive salt Lithium, and finally the very Thorazine that her GP had originally recommended to replace valium.

She found it difficult to find a psychiatrist she could trust, but accepted the insistence of one that she should go back to hospital for monitored medication to bring down her valium withdrawal symptoms. She was horrified to find herself placed in a ward with violent schizophrenics. It was a young female psychiatrist, using the traditional analytical method of gently leading her to remember childhood traumas, who seemed to do her more good than the various cocktails of drugs. She was discharged after a few months, although she still had occasional panic attacks.

A year after her original breakdown she was put on megavitamins, and with the help of a therapist struggled back to facing life and recovering her job. Though she now faced the serious stigma of having been a "mental patient".

Barbara's book "I'm Dancing As Fast As I Can", describing her experiences, came out in 1980 and immediately hit the headlines in America.

The warning had gone out. Prolonged high doses of valium become ineffective and lead to very dangerous withdrawal symptoms.

English Experiences

In the early 1980s, two Englishwomen recounted similar sufferings to Barbara Gordon. Heather Jones had started taking the "perfectly safe" drug in 1971, cutting back her dosage after two years, but increasing it again when she lost a baby. Within five years she was taking 15 mg a day, and experiencing personality changes. She began to suffer extreme moodswings and sudden rage. She also endured intense agoraphobia which put a serious strain on her marriage as she could not bear her husband's absence at work. Anxiety and depression, the very symptoms the drug was supposed to alleviate, became her familiar mental state. She was, as she later described herself, "a prisoner on prescription." For two years doctors experimented with various drugs until finally, like Barbara Gordon, she too entered a course of traditional psychotherapy which enabled her to recover her health.

Joan Jerome took valium for ten years, finally reaching a daily dosage of 20 mg. By that time she was also using other drugs to counter her increasing insomnia, irritability and anxiety. In 1980 she learned that a medical review committee report had questioned whether benzodiazopines were as safe as had been imagined. Two years later she went into hospital and became the first pure tranquillizer addict to be placed in a ward with junkies and winoes to be weaned off her addiction.

Today valium is only prescribed in small doses for very short periods.

Valium: The Key Dates

1962: Valium is marketed
1972: Valium is regarded as totally safe after ten years use and no fatalities
1980: Committee on Safety of Medicines gives first hint that valium may not be safe

MORE TROUBLES WITH TRANQUILLIZERS

The benzodiazopine group of drugs faced more challenges in the wake of the valium scandal. In 1987 the press reported that some doctors were trying to blame the drug for provoking sexual fantasies in women, which led to false charges of molestation! At the same time, Professor Malcolm Lader of the Institute of Psychiatry conducted a study which suggested that people taking normal dosages might become disturbed if they took them over an extended period of time.

When the good professor's work had been digested, it opened the floodgates of litigation. In 1990, the Legal Aid Board in Edinburgh gave permission to six people to sue the makers of Ativan. Soon the six had swollen to 450. By the beginning of 1991, sufferers who blamed valium and other benzodiazoprines for their condition had joined in, and the number of would-be litigants rose to 3,000. Mr Justice Ian Kennedy quickly set a deadline date for any further applicants joining this group case against benzodiazopines, and the numbers shot to 5,000.

The Halcion Case

First and foremost under attack was Halcion, the world's most widely prescribed sleeping pill. Its peculiar benefit was that it was fast and short-acting. Patients could expect to fall asleep within half an hour of taking it. But its effects lasted only six hours, and they awoke clear-headed and ready to go. This was a manifest advantage to insomniacs who had to work early and handle machinery.

British doctors, nevertheless, tended to prefer the rather longer-acting Temazepam, and in 1991 it seemed they were justified when Flo Grundberg's prosecution for murder in America was dropped after psychiatrists blamed Halcion. Flo's plea was followed by a number of others, and abruptly in October, the Department of Health banned it from Britain.

The BBC current affairs programme "Panorama" aired a show called "The Halcion Nightmare", during which it alleged that American drug manufacturer Upjohn's application for a licence had misled the regulators. It seemed that a good 24% of users complained of side-effects.

In America the FDA moved more cautiously. A committee of experts examined the drug for six months, and reported that it was safe. Meanwhile, in Britain the mass claim against the manufacturers failed, at an enormous cost to the Legal Aid budget – and considerable advantage to the lawyers.

Upjohn won £60,000 from the BBC when they sued over the Panorama programme, and a further £25,000 from one of the expert witnesses. The witness, however, won a countersuit and got £50,000 back. Upjohn's robust defence of its submissions had gone too far, and libelled the professor by challenging his competence and integrity.

Upjohn gave their damage awards to Save the Children and Help the Aged. But the real winners were the lawyers. The BBC and their witness each owed legal fees in excess of £1 million. This was a medico-legal mishap because whether or not Halcion is safe – it is still banned in Britain but available in America – a huge amount of money has been thrown down the drain of legal costs for an unsatisfactory conclusion.

The Killers Who Blamed Their Medication

Flo Greenwood of Hurricane, Utah, fired eight bullets into her 83-year-old mother. Two psychiatrists testified that she was "involuntarily intoxicated" by the Halcion she had been prescribed, and she never even had to face a jury.

William Freeman, a 44-year-old policeman of San Antonio, Texas, "became bizarre about six months after he began taking Halcion," his lawyer claimed, "and it got worse until he was plain crazy." He shot his best friend, former colleague Donald Hazlewood, with a rifle. Freeman was sentenced to life imprisonment, but appealed, citing the British ban, and sued Upjohn.

51-year-old Anne Mundell in Scotland drugged her journalist husband Matt and stabbed him in the neck after he told her he was leaving her for another woman. Her lawyers decided to look carefully at her possible ground for appeal after the Halcion ban, since she had been prescribed the drug.

Joe Wesbecker went to his former employers', the Standard Gravure Printing Works in Louisville, Kentucky, armed with semi-automatic weapons. He killed eight workers and wounded 12 more before killing himself. The new (1989) wonder drug Prozac was found in his blood-stream, along with other anti-depressants. he had been prescribed it recently, and his family sued the makers, Eli Lilly.

Rebecca M. Stoots shot her doctor in the neck. Since he didn't die, she was only convicted of aggravated assault, and was sentenced to 10 years imprisonment. She, too, sued Eli Lilly claiming that Prozac had been responsible for her violence. Her case collapsed, however – she had previously shot her former husband in New Mexico and stabbed another woman in California!

....

CELEBRITY SPOT

EVELYN WAUGH

Before the development of sophisticated sedatives like the barbiturates and the benzodiazopine group, Victorian and Edwardian gentlemen took other chemical cocktails to encourage sleep and soothe their nerves. Toward the end of his life, Evelyn Waugh made the shattering observation that he had almost given up drinking, and now only consumed about seven bottles of wine, three of spirits and one of paraldehyde every week. The last, a preparation of oxidised alcohol, was a sedative and sleeping draught.

Selina Hasting's 1994 biography of the writer revealed that it replaced his previous sleeping draught, potassium bromide. This antiquated sedative – the bromide reputed to be put in army tea to curb the lusts of the licentious soldiery – is notoriously inefficient unless used in very precise dosages. Waugh had used it liberally, often chased with gin and creme-de-menthe. When he suffered an episode of distressing auditory hallucinations (described in his novel "The Ordeal of Gilbert Pinfold"), two doctors immediately agreed that he was suffering from "bromism" – poisoning caused by excess use of bromides.

After the publication of the Hastings biography, several commentators observed that Waugh's florid appearance and evil temper strongly suggested chronic bromism for much of his life. They wondered whether overuse of his sleeping drug had permanently injured his personality as well as his short-term mental health!

OPREN

Opren was not a tranquillizer and it did not lead to any difference of opinion between Britain's Committee on the Safety of Medicines and America's Food and Drugs Administration. Opren was a painkiller that was especially useful to sufferers from arthritis. Opren was withdrawn worldwide in 1982, which meant it had enjoyed a remarkably short market life.

It was launched in Britain in 1980 by Dista, a subsidiary of the American pharmaceuticals manufacturer Eli Lilly. Opren was marketed with a flurry of advertising, employing James Burke, the "pop-science" television personality.

Seemingly Opren was a real breakthrough. Arthritis – especially rheumatoid arthritis and osteo-arthritis in the old – can be appallingly painful. It can seriously interfere with walking or using the hands. It can make it agonizing for the sufferer to even turn over or alter position in bed. However, arthritis often strikes people who otherwise boast absolutely sound constitutions. Hearts, lungs, arteries, Blood-pressures – all the things which leave old people in danger of strokes or heart attacks when they weaken – may be in perfect working order. Therefore, doctors dare not prescribe dangerously addictive painkillers derived from morphine – they're not, after all, in the business of creating geriatric junkies.

Aspirin is useful, but not the perfect solution. Many people cannot take it because it upsets their stomachs or bowels, and very large doses create a risk of internal haemorrhage. Steroid drugs offer another alternative, but they can also carry alarming side-effects. In particular, they may increase the risk of osteoporosis, the agonizing and crippling skeletal weakening to which old ladies are particularly prone.

Opren relieved the pain of arthritis spectacularly well, and there was no doubt that thousands of sufferers genuinely felt that it was, to use its marketing slogan, "The Sign of Success". The beaming elderly lady holding up a capsule in one of the advertisements undoubtedly represented the happiness felt by many, as the pain which had cut back their freedom to enjoy life was blissfully relieved.

The Paris Conference

The first warning that all was not well came in the spring of 1981. Eli Lilley organized a conference in Paris, and two British specialists in geriatric treatment then revealed that they had independently come to the same conclusion about Opren – that it might be dangerous for some old people.

The problem was that elderly kidneys and livers tended to eliminate the drug very slowly. It was not clear that the drug would continue to be harmless as it piled up in the body. In extreme cases, there seemed to be a possibility that Opren might become a cumulative poison. Dr Ronnie Hamdy of St John's Hospital in London decided it was "potentially harmful", and stopped prescribing it for his patients. Dr A. Kamal felt that risks of adverse side effects might be seriously increased if he went on giving the drug to his patients. Both men published their conclusions as learned papers, and passed them on to Eli Lilley.

In the summer, Eli Lilley told officials at the Department of Health that studies of old people were raising some questions about Opren. A few months later they handed over Hamdy and Kamal's papers, accompanied by some studies of their own which apparently pointed to different conclusions. Nevertheless, Eli Lilley recommended that dosages should be reduced for elderly patients – specifically those over the age of 75.

The Department of Health was put on the spot. Lowering the dosage would decrease the efficacy of the drug's pain-relief. And it was old people who were particularly in need of it. furthermore, the two sets of studies submitted appeared to be in conflict. More research was needed – the Department of Health wrote back to Eli Lilly that they new recommendation was "inappropriate."

The Deaths

The fatal blow for Opren came from Ulster. Dr Hugh Taggart, consultant geriatrician at the Belfast City Hospital, was surprised to have six elderly ladies come under his care, one after the other, suffering from jaundice. It is not an epidemic disease, but it is not sufficiently common for chance to bring in so many cases at once.

Dr Taggart concluded that there must have been a drug his patients were taking that was seriously attacking their livers. The jaundice quickly proved fatal, and though the authorities refused to let Dr Taggart carry out autopsies on the first two victims to check his theory, they yielded when a third died.

The post mortem proved that Dr Taggart was right. Pathologist Joan Allardyce confirmed that the livers of all three victims showed a "remarkably similar" type of drug-induced jaundice.

When two more of the six died, Drs Taggart and Allardyce reported their findings to the British Medical Journal. They reported that there was one drug common to all six patients. It was Opren.

The Bizarre Symptoms

By the spring of 1982, geriatricians were starting to notice some rather extraordinary symptoms which seemed to result from Opren retained in the bodies of elderly patients. It could affect their hair. Bald men suddenly found tufts of hair sprouting on their domes. Women found whiskers growing on their faces. Both sexes might find hairs springing out from their arms, fingers and toes. Additionally, their nails starting growing with unwelcome rapidity – some found their nails starting to come loose.

Two doctors in Norwich found that eight out of ten patients over 70 suffered unacceptable side-effects. Another study of 300 patients over the age of 47 found that 200 of them reported side-effects, and 100 had to be taken off the drug.

One of the most common complaints was dermatological. Patients described a burning sensation in the skin after a few minutes in direct sunlight. Longer exposure might cause blistering. Whereas the werewolf-like growth of hair and nails only affected one in 20 Opren users, the sensitivity to sunlight seemed to strike half of them.

A quarter of them also endured stomach and bowel pains, nausea or heartburn, just as though they had gone on with unacceptably high doses of aspirin.

Bringing Down Opren

Dr Taggart's letter to the BMJ prompted other doctors to consider Opren in relation to their elderly patients. It seemed that 25 Britons had probably died as a consequence of their taking the drug.

This was a tricky time for Eli Lilly. The drug had been pioneered in Britain. It was about to get its licence for distribution in America under the name of Oraflex. But Eli Lilley itself was coming under FDA scrutiny, following the allegations from a disgruntled former employee that information about the side-effects of two of their heart drugs had not been reported.

Licensing was also not proceeding smoothly elsewhere. GMBH, the German subsidiary of Eli Lilley, had been refused permission to distribute Opren only a month after the great 1980 launch in England. They asked the parent company in Indianapolis for more data on the dangers entailed in taking Opren, so that they would be able to put forward a good case for an acceptable "risk-to-benefit" ratio.

Swedish authorities also refused to accept Eli Lilly's reports on Opren. The Swedish Ministry of Health felt that too few animal tests had been done using too few animals and giving them too small doses: under half the recommended human therapeutic dose. Other tests were thought by the authorities to be "too simple".

Australia, too, gave Opren the thumbs down. Britain had accepted it on a basis of 4,400 trials in the USA. However the FDA was hearing questions about those cases. A report of side-effects mentioned in an early Lilley submission had not been repeated in a later submission.

Close scrutiny of clinical trials by five doctors showed that they had reported 173 cases of side-effects. Eli Lilly had only passed on 65 of these to the FDA.

Eli Lilly explained these apparent discrepancies. As more information had come to light it became apparent that the early reports were "no longer alarming". Indeed, it didn't look as though the FDA inspectors had picked up a major scandal when they reported that there had been "substantial under-reporting" of side-effects such as toenail growth and indigestion. These side-effects sounded like "acceptable risks" if the concurrent benefit was relief from extreme arthritic pain.

Opren was granted a licence in the USA on April 19 1982, even though five American life-threatening cases were associated with its side-effects. By this date there had also been FDA information about the 25 Opren-related deaths in the UK. Oraflex only lasted six months – by October the number of deaths attributed to Opren had risen to 61 and the drug was withdrawn worldwide.

The Worst Case

Up to 1980, Mrs Grace Grasham of Thorpe Bay, near Southend-on-Sea, was a fit and healthy old soul. She was a good gardener. She regularly walked three-and-a-half miles. She had never suffered a major illness. And her mind was keen and alert.

Then, when she was 81, she was struck down by sciatica. The sciatic nerve between the pelvis and thigh is the largest in the body. If neuralgia affects it, the results are concomitantly painful. The sudden onset of sciatica is capable of instantly transforming a robust old lady into a miserable old woman. Like arthritis, however, sciatica is not in itself life-threatening. The patient may be doomed to years of unhappy life, as acute pain restricts movement and causes constant distress, while the rest of the body functions as efficiently as ever. A strong and reliable painkiller is precisely what the doctor orders.

In February 1981 Opren had been available for four months. The makers said it was relatively free from side-effects. Mrs Grasham's doctor started her on a course. Six days later, having taken 12 of the 30 tablets prescribed, Mrs Grasham felt sick to the stomach. Severe diarrhoea followed. The next day she complained of a burning sensation of the skin – she developed a severe rash, which she said made her feel as if she was on fire.

By the evening this covered her whole body. Her doctor, suspecting that she was allergic to the drug and that her kidneys were failing, rushed her into hospital the following morning.

The pain was by now making her confused, and within hours of entering hospital she had lapsed into a coma. In moments when she came round it was clear that she was suffering terrible pain. This was not surprising – her skin was falling off in great patches.

There was little anyone could do about this terrible spontaneous flaying. The hospital tried to keep Mrs Grasham's raw flesh protected by spraying her with a compound intended to stick skin back in place. Mrs Grasham was unable to swallow, and struggled against her frightening disease for four days before she died.

Dr Oliver Norman, her GP, had been a personal friend, and he had no doubt it was Opren that had caused her terrible decline and sudden death. He sent in the yellow card which drug manufacturers supply for adverse reports on new drugs. No action was taken.

Dista, Eli Lilley and the Department of Health could all be criticized for the delays between the first warnings about Opren and the final positive action of withdrawing it. It was on the market for 17 months after Dr Norman's report; 15 months after Drs Hamdy and Kamal had issued their warnings; eleven months after those warning reached the Department of Health; and six months after Dr Taggart wrote to the BMJ.

A drug that could induce jaundice and kill old people was hardly a painkiller of choice!

Who Decides Liability?

Not all arthritis patients were grateful for the care exercised by the licensing authorities. A 74-year-old man wrote to The Times:

> *"I think I should be permitted the choice of living the rest of my life in relief from arthritic pain, if I feel prepared to accept the risks of taking Opren."*

Doctors might well have wondered whether he knew just how painful jaundice may actually prove. Writer Ernest Hemingway once compared it to being kicked continually in the testicles.

And the case of Mrs Grace Grasham might have given anyone pause for thought.

Legal Action

In the 22 months Opren was on sale in Britain, 500,000 prescriptions were written. Within four years, campaigners were alleging that 4,000 people had suffered severe side-effects, and around 100 had died.

Eli Lilly preserved a discreet silence. To make any apology or offer any opinion might prejudice the court actions threatening against them Their discretion outraged victims and their survivors. Mrs Grasham's daughter Kathleen, a headteacher, had become one of the leading lights in the campaign to recover damages from the manufacturers and the Department of Health, and she protested strongly:

> *"To date Eli Lilly has shown no remorse regarding its calculated acts which have allegedly brought about the deaths of some 100 UK citizens."*

Eli Lilly, of course, could not oblige her. To express remorse would amount to a confession of guilt. To agree that it had "calculated" actions resulting in the deaths of innocent people might amount to manslaughter. In fact, the company actually felt that many of the cases being brought forward were unrelated to Opren.

It was agreed that in a very few isolated cases the drug caused serious disturbance to the kidneys or liver, with results alarmingly similar to diabetes or even cancer. But Eli Lilly challenged many of the claims about sensitivity to sunlight.

The scientific position argued by the plaintiffs was that in certain cases Opren was carried to the nerve endings, where its action with sunlight caused the severely painful reaction. There was no doubt that the victims who had come forward were suffering severely.

57-year-old Mrs Joy Davis, a boatyard manager from Twickenham, had at first imagined that she was suffering from simple sunburn, though this had not happened before. But when it recurred she had blisters and a feeling like nettle rash over her face and hands. She had to give up sailing and carry an umbrella whenever she ventured out into the sun.

Some old people had to stay indoors behind drawn curtains whenever the sun came out. Others found that a single flare-up would take weeks to go down. Most gave horrid descriptions of their feelings – it was like being scalded; like being scratched till they bled; or like having acid spilled on them.

Eli Lilly's defence was that there was no direct scientific proof that these skin disorders were related to Opren. In some cases they believed that patients who were already suffering from skin disorders were probably wrongly ascribing their worsened condition to the drug.

Too Many Plaintiffs

The British courts had never been confronted with a situation where so many plaintiffs wanted to bring suit against one set of defendants. (Dista, the Department of Health and the Committee on the Safety of Medicines were named in the suits along with Eli Lilly). Thalidomide had only involved 400 or so victims. But the Opren Action Group had written to 1,000 and the numbers were growing all the time. Ultimately 1,500 people would be claiming some sort of compensation.

It was beginning to look as if it could take up to ten years to get the legal proceedings completed. Yet many of these were elderly people, who might not even live that long. It was recognized that the American practice of a "class action" would have to be followed. A small number of suits would be tried as representative cases – the others would remain on ice until the trial suits had settled and provided a bench mark for out of court settlements to be made.

Mr Justice Hirst described it as "unthinkable" to go through the entire rigmarole, time and expense of repeating evidence hundreds of times about the defendants' alleged negligence in testing the drug, or selling it, or licensing it for sale. One case should determine the degree of responsibility, if any. Then settlements could be made with the other claimants.

It seemed as it if it would cost a fortune in Legal Aid until in 1987 the Appeal Court reached a crucial decision which looked likely to put many of the plaintiffs out of court. My Lords of Appeal upheld a High Court ruling that when a large number of claimants were "riding on the backs" of a select few legally aided cases going through the courts, everyone must share in the legal expenses. As these were likely to amount to an absolute minimum of £3,000 apiece, all those claimants who were not entitled to Legal Aid – roughly a third of the total – seemed bound to give up their actions.

The Fairy Godfather

Within a month their cases had been reinstated. Financier and property magnate Mr Godfrey Bradman stepped forward and offered to shoulder the costs of any claimants who would have otherwise been unable to pursue their case. He agreed to underwrite their legal fees up to at least £2 million.

When this was reported to the claimants' counsel, Mr Louis Blom-Cooper QC, and he reported the matter to the judge, Mr Bradman still hoped that his anonymity might be maintained. Mr Justice Hirst, however, while acknowledging "the providential intervention of the Fairy Godparent, if I may so call him or her," had still to insist that this benefactor's identity should be known to the court.

Mr Bradman was a co-director of the socially concerned pressure group Citizens' Action. His involvement brought in the group's leading spokesman, the experienced campaigner Mr Des Wilson, onetime founder-chairman of Shelter, the housing pressure group, and in 1987 the president of the Liberal Party. Mr Wilson announced that he would be opening hostilities with a full-page advertisement in The times, and his intention was to shame the company into settling quickly.

An Eli Lilly spokesman protested that they were a responsible and caring company, and sincerely regretted side-effects which occurred to people taking medicines, whether the medicines were rightly held responsible or not. But he insisted that no pharmaceutical company on earth could compensate a wide variety of people complaining about a wide variety of symptoms until full medical reports had been received.

"I find it incomprehensible that a company of such wealth continues to try to justify itself when, irrespective of the level of proof, it is clear that a vast number of people, all of whom took Opren, have suffered side-effects."

Lawyers vs Litigants

With the full range of plaintiffs back in the fray, Eli Lilly moved to close the proceedings. They offered a secret settlement, rumoured to be worth about £2,000 to each claimant on average, and costing the company a presumed £2.5 million in compensation with another £4 million or so set aside to cover the legal costs. Once again, the lawyers were the big winners.

However, there were strings attached. Eli Lilly wanted this to be the final end of the affair. The plaintiffs must not reveal what they received, and they were not to continue legal actions or public campaigns against either the company or Opren.

David Mason had resisted just such pressure from the Distillers' Company, but the memory of Mason and Nader campaigning to hit sales and cut share values was something Eli Lilly devoutly and explicitly wanted to avoid recurring. The company was infuriated by suggestions that such a campaign might be waged against them.

The claimants were unhappy with the deal, but were left with little option. The scale of the compensation had been worked out in discussion with their own lawyers. Rodger Pannone, the solicitor acting for them, cautiously called the offer "realistic". He pointed out that proceeding to trial would push the costs up immensely, and could well mean that it was four years before the claimants saw any money. And after all that, he thought they could only hope for "modestly more."

Mr Justice Hirst sounded as if he had had quite enough of this interminable proceeding. He warned the claimants that the settlement would break down if a majority did not accept the offer. (This was, however, a clear advance on Distillers' insistence that the thalidomide claimants must be unanimous before anyone received any money at all.) The judge also offered an even more alarming admonition when he warned those on Legal Aid that if they refused the offer against their lawyers' advice, their aid might be withdrawn.

The power of lawyers to make and enforce settlements their clients didn't much like, without actually going through the procedures of a trial, had been majestically demonstrated. It did not delight most of those involved.

> *"The long and vastly expensive fight has resulted in a settlement offer. I must emphasize it is legal; but today the poor, the sick and the old can see exactly where they stand in regards to British law."*

KATHLEEN GRASHAM, DECEMBER 1987

Much where they had stood in the 19th century, in fact, when Disraeli remarked that the Poor Law declared to Europe that poverty in England was now a crime: and a judge allegedly remarked to a poor bigamist who could not have even contemplated the vast expense of a Victorian divorce, that "the law was open to all...like the Ritz Hotel."

Mrs Drury's Reservation

One of the claimants publicly refused the settlement on interesting grounds that had nothing to do with the actual money involved. "After all this time, when our standard of living has been so badly affected, the compensation is almost totally irrelevant," said 65-year-old Mrs Anna Drury. She objected to the way the whole case was shrouded in secrecy – and not merely because she was forbidden to discuss the amount of money she might be awarded. She felt that shareholders' interests were being allowed to outweigh the search for truth, about how the drug had come to cause fatalities.

"I will be instructing my solicitor not to take the money or any other settlement offer until the company discloses the constituents of the drug," she told the press, "because I want research in this country to find a way of stopping the serious side-effects." She had a point.

Opren Fizzles Out

By March 1988, 98% of the 1,350 claimants had accepted the settlement. Lilly Industries took the chance to reassure their 2,300 employees that they were not working for some irresponsible well-poisoner. The public had been "misled by certain press reports," the management informed the staff, and they still believed they would have won "the vast majority of cases" had they come to court. Specifically, they challenged the claim that they were responsible for the photosensitive skin conditions. Some patients, they believed, had been taking other drugs which caused them. Some had the conditions long before they took Opren, or developed them so long after they had discontinued the drug that it could no longer be accumulating in their systems. Some had come in with conditions that were not drug-related at all.

Lilly Industries told doctors severely that they had warned them about some side-effects, and therefore should not be held responsible for their patients. The British managing director acknowledged that the publicity was "not pleasant".

Des Wilson hit back calling it "incomprehensible" that "a company of such wealth" went on trying to justify itself, when a vast number of people had clearly suffered side-effects. Indeed, it was odd that photosensitive conditions should have emerged in the limelight so suddenly after the marketing of Opren if the two things had really been unconnected..

The remainder of the story was just wrangling about how costs and compensations might be divided among multiple litigants: wrangling that, once again, could only really interest and benefit lawyers who, in the end, reduced to case to balancing global legal costs against likely damages.

Joe Lilly

Faced with the threat of protracted legal proceedings and the potentially bankrupting experiences of huge costs and massive damages, manufacturing executives may look superficially like caricatures of grinding capitalist Scrooges. So it is perhaps worth noticing that the late Joe Lilly, heir to the Eli Lilly business, was in practice closer to the benign philanthropic capitalist Cheerybles. In his home town of Falmouth, Massachusetts he was a notable public benefactor, contributing largely to the community's resources and charities, and personally endowing a valued convalescent home.

> *"It's a horrifying thought, but perhaps it needs another thalidomide disaster to bring about effective monitoring systems."*

> PROFESSOR DAVID FINNEY, EDINBURGH UNIVERSITY

> *"We are a responsible and caring company and we sincerely regret side-effects when they occur to people taking medicines, whether or not they are attributed to the medicines. We are not unfeeling about these things."*

> ELI LILLY SPOKESMAN

LARGACTIL

One of the strongest and most efficient tranquillizers ever invented is Largactil. It works directly on the thalamus, depressing activity in this part of the brain which regulates and stimulates physical and emotional responses.

It has a rapid and decisive calming effect on people who are over-excited or violent, and is one of the most useful additions to the pharmacopoeia for mental patients. But caution is required because of its side-effects, which have on rare occasions proved lethal.

Michael Shirkey was 10 years old when he suffered serious brain damage in a car accident. It became necessary for him to be put under permanent hospital care. Two years later he attacked a fellow patient – an elderly man who died. Michael was clearly a case Largactil, and was immediately put on the drug.

Michael himself died two years later, in 1980, when he was still only 14. On January 19 he complained of being cold. He was always complaining of cold, and the male nurse attending him paid little attention, simply giving him an extra blanket and leaving him as usual, locked up for the night. Michael kicked it off in his sleep.

Five hours later, when nurses unlocked the room and came in, Michael was unable to stand. His GP was called, and diagnosed hypothermia. Michael was rapidly transferred to a General Hospital for emergency treatment, but it was too late – he died soon after arrival.

His nurses had not been warned that the thalamus also controls body temperature. Largactil users who complain of cold are not merely being oversensitive to the weather. Their medication can actually cause their bodies to fall to subnormal temperatures with dangerous – in Michael's case fatal – effects. While few people expected nurses to be informed about all the side-effects of all the drugs their patients took, Michael's parents reasonably complained that the institutional system should not have allowed the boy to be unattended and disregarded in a locked room for five hours when heavily sedated. One might add that it would seem reasonable to assume that doctors who prescribe drugs with dangerous side-effects should ensure that attendants are advised to guard against them.

A year later, 26-year-old Mrs Julie Head died in a south-coast psychiatric hospital, where she had been admitted because it was feared she was suffering from schizophrenia. She was given Largactil, and died five days later from lack of white blood cells. Unlike hypothermia, this is a very rare side-effect of the drug, but it was known to be possible. The case prompted the "Church" of Scientology to spearhead complaints about her treatment. This, however, was largely because the cult (which incidentally lacks either scientific or spiritual authentication) disapproved of Mrs Head receiving any psychiatric treatment in the first place.

Entero-vioform and Quixalin

Tummy upsets and mild food poisoning are distressing at the best of times, and can seriously mar holidays in strange places where travellers are not accustomed to the local bacteria. For this reason there have always been a number of cures for the "collywobbles" on the market – the most entertaining, perhaps, being Dr J. Collis Browne's Chlorodyne, which in its old formula used to include a marvellous tiny-printed leaflet in which traveller after traveller vouched for the most astonishing range of sudden diseases in howling wildernesses being instantly cured by the handy bottle of chlorodyne in the first-aid kit. Most of these users were content to take it as a remedy for mildly upset tummies or hangovers.

Entero-vioform was a more modern remedy for irritable bowels, and many tourists automatically took a bottle before going abroad. So it was quite a shock when the makers, Ciba-Geigy, admitted in Japan that it could cause sub-acute myelo-optic neuropathy: a disease of the nerve-sheaths in the eye. 10,000 Japanese patients suffering seriously defective eyesight from this claimed to have taken Entero-vioform.

Manufacturers E. R. Squibb & Sons had earlier suffered adverse publicity over their rather similar medication, Quixalan.

In 1976, a 36-year-old woman was in a Middle-Eastern country, where she was unable to get kaolin, (finely powdered china clay), the favoured mild treatment for diarrhoea. So she took Quixalin. It soon became clear that she was suffering from some nerve disease. Her first symptom was tingly feet. Then walking became difficult. Finally, she became effectively blind.

Squibb & Sons defended themselves vigorously against the charge that Quixalin had cased the woman's condition. She had made herself ill at a party, they said, by drinking Seddicke: the illegal moonshine spirit sold among expatriates who broke that country's strict Islamic prohibition of alcohol.

However, they admitted that animal tests as far back as 1962 had shown that Quixalin could cause blindness in rabbits and calves.

••

CELEBRITY SPOT

SAMUEL TAYLOR COLERIDGE

Best-known of all victims of medically caused addiction was Samuel Taylor Coleridge. In his day, laudanum – the alcoholic tincture of opium – was often the well-stocked household's painkiller or sleeping-pill of choice: by today's standard, aspirin and Nytol rolled into one.

Coleridge's health was affected by bad food and harsh conditions at his boarding school. He suffered from neuralgic headaches and rheumatism. In 1796 he started to take laudanum for it, with devastating consequences. The writing of Kubla Khan – by his own account an opiate-stimulated vision – encouraged him to think there was artistic value in drugging himself. By 1800 he was firmly addicted. Ten years later his friendship with Wordsworth was damaged by his increasing enslavement to opium. The belief of many people at the time was that sheer willpower and strength of personality should prevent habituation. (Laudanum was even included in "Godfrey's Cordial", the 19th century's favourite soothing medicine for infants!)

Coleridge's capacity to produce sustained and responsible work was steadily curtailed, and it was not until the end of his life that Highgate surgeon James Gillman managed to reduce his consumption of opium and restore him to regular writing, though his later work never matched the output of his twenties.

••

ACCUTANE

The misery of acne spoils the lives of many adolescents. Teenagers are not convinced that the spots will clear up and go away when they get older, and anyway know that those blessed with clear young complexions are going to get chosen first in their competitive pursuit of dates and sweethearts and steadies. They are all too likely to buy any old snake-oil offered them that purports to clear up the condition. So it seemed good news when the Swiss pharmaceutical firm Roche introduced a new, modern product, promising to do something really effective about the hormonal upheavals that produce pimples and zits.

British authorities were immediately cautious. They stipulated that the product – marketed as Ro-Accutane – could only be prescribed by specialist dermatologists. In 1988 it seemed they had been wise. The FDA suddenly announced that between 600 and 1,300 babies had been born, either mentally retarded or with severely deformed features after their mothers had taken the product – which was sold in America by Hoffman-La Roche as Accutane. Some of the deformities described sounded more like medieval travellers' tales than congenital malformations – ears growing out of babies' chins, for example.

Hoffman-La Roche protested strongly that only 62 cases had been reported. But the FDA insisted that in future the product must carry a photograph of a deformed baby on the label to scare off pregnant women. Britain could feel rather smug, for once. Ro-Accutane already carried warnings of possibly horrific side-effects on its packaging, and female patients were obliged to sign consent forms confirming that they were not pregnant before they could be given the drug.

Septrin and Bactrim

Another unpleasant feature of growing up for young women may be cystitis. Often colloquially described as "honeymoon cystitis" because its appearance often coincides with the onset of an active sex life, it is not a very serious illness. But the symptom – a burning sensation while urinating – is acutely unpleasant.

Hoffman-La Roche again produced a suitable antibiotic to cure this. They called it Bactrim. The generic name of the drug was co-trimazole, and it worked by the double action effect of two quite different antibiotics – the sulphur-based sulphamethoxazole and the compound trimethoprin. The widely hyped suggestion was that the combination should be twice as good as either taken on its own. Wellcome also produced a brand-named version: Septrin.

In 1987, a 31-year-old man who had taken Bactrim for an infection of the urinary tract died with ghastly symptoms reminiscent of those which had killed Mrs Grasham when she took Opren. His body burned and blistered – his skin fell away.

The Sunday Times, which has monitored the drug and medical situation keenly in the public interest ever since playing a key role in resolving the thalidomide scandal, realized that a very similar fate had befallen 18-year-old Justine Gibbs in 1988, after she had taken Septrin for cystitis. Justine's death had been identified as resulting from the very rare conditions Lyell and Stevens-Johnson syndromes, contracted because she was allergic to sulphamethoxazole.

Septrin and Bactrim have been on the market since 1969. They are among the world's most commercially successful drugs. Septrin, in fact, is the top-selling drug in India, routinely treating illnesses as severe as typhoid and as mild as the common cold. Given all of which, it might well seem that the rare chance of a rare allergy which may trigger a very rare condition is an acceptable risk. Too many millions of lives are saved and illnesses cured to justify pulling the drug off the market because of the occasional mishap. In fact, the Committee on the Safety of Medicines reported a figure of only 1.42 deaths for every million prescriptions of Septrin and Bactrim.

But the Sunday Times also found out that a great many specialists believed that trimethorprim taken on its own was equally efficacious, and there was no need for the sulphamethoxazole which was largely responsible for the side-effects. The paper argued that, with 3 million prescriptions for co-trimoxazoles written annually in the UK, five lives were being put unnecessarily at risk every year. Not, then, a great disaster like thalidomide. But evidence of our increasingly keen awareness that drugs and medications need to be treated with caution.

So... Prozac?

No seriously harmful consequence of taking the drug Prozac has been established. Chemically fluoxetine hydrochloride, it was developed deliberately to affect the neurological pathways of the little understood amine serotonin through the body. Like adrenalin – usefully controlled by the sedative imiprahine – serotonin is known to be important in affecting moods.

Prozac, developed by combining the work of several separate research chemists at Eli Lilly, went on the market in 1987 and quickly proved a very efficient sedative with very few adverse side-effects and very little chance of being taken in accidental overdose.

It attracted nationwide attention across America with the publication of Charles Kramer's book "Listening to Prozac" in 1993. Kramer, a psychiatrist, found an amazingly wide range of positive effects from giving his patients Prozac. It alleviated obsessive-compulsive disorders, panic anxiety, eating disorders, drug habituation, poor attention span, and a host of other symptoms. In fact, Kramer felt that Prozac had showed him how many mental conditions really rested on the chemical balance in the body, rather than the kind of adaptations to experience proposed by classical psychoanalysis and much of modern-day psychology.

Kramer coined the term "cosmetic psychopharmacology", suggesting that by taking useful drugs (especially Prozac) people might be able to give themselves the sort of personalities they and their society found preferable. Only "pharmacological Calvinists" and philosophers who thought "suffering ennobles" would object, he believed.

A short period in which the media enthusiastically suggested that everybody might soon be taking Prozac for life and comin' up roses was swiftly recognized as being irresponsible. Although two attempts to blame Prozac for the creation of murderous personalities failed, it was realized that nobody has yet taken Prozac continuously for ten years.

COSMETIC CATASTROPHES

The word plastic comes from a Greek word meaning *"to mould"*. The surgeons's original task of tending to wounds might be enhanced if he could mould substitutes for small organs that had been cut off, and so, surprisingly, plastic surgery is one of the oldest forms of surgical art.

In 600 B.C., the Indian guru Susruta left an account of his technique for replacing noses and ear-lobes cut off in military action (or in some cases as a punishment for adultery). In the 17th century, travellers' tales from India recounted unlikely operations in which fakirs stuffed clay under the skin of deformed noses and moulded into seemly shapes.

19th century plastic surgeons were astonished when they discovered Susruta's Sanskrit description of his practice.

There was no doubt that, 3,000 years before European plastic surgery began to take important steps forward, Susruta had been using exactly the recently discovered technique of bringing down the flap of skin and tissue from the forehead to mould a new nose.

RHINOPLASTY

The surgical reconstruction of noses is one of the oldest and most important forms of plastic surgery.

The great European syphilis epidemic of the 16th century, with mercury as its only treatment, caused a great many men to suffer nasal degeneration. Surgeons initially built prosthetic false noses using gold and copper alloys. It was the Italian surgeon Tagliocozzi who devised the technique for grafting flesh from the arm, which would be bound to the nose while the graft healed. This was the first important piece of European plastic surgery.

Restoring the wounded soldier to an acceptable appearance was obviously a praiseworthy activity. Removing the marks of sin from the faces of depraved lechers was quite another. Or so thought those Puritans who contentedly noted that even the scars of small-pox were a great deterrent to vanity.

Plastic surgeons have always had to defend their art against those who see it as godless. Their argument that it is only reasonable to improve on such "mistakes" of the Creator as harelips and cleft palates often found favour. But few would criticize the surgeon who can improve the devastated features of a soldier scarred on the battle field. The most significant advances in cosmetic surgery were made during the two World Wars: Sir Harold Gillies made great steps forward in rhinoplasty and the replacement of ears; Sir Archibald McIndoe did as much for the burns and facial injuries suffered by fighter pilots.

But the very name "cosmetic surgery" suggested that this technique might be used as an advance on the morally suspect "powder and paint, that makes a girl look what she ain't". Plastic surgeons, humanely recognizing that some people suffer undue psychological distress from what they wrongly believe to be ugly features, or from the sad effects of ageing, often accepted commissions to render beautiful what God had made simply okay.

Cosmetic surgery was almost halted in its tracks by the disaster associated with Robert Gersury. Indeed, the entire practice of plastic surgery was threatened by the results of his treatment.

Gersury (1844–1924) was born in Prague, and made a number of important contributions to the growing art of plastic surgery, discovering effective folds and tucks to improve the disposition of re-ordered flesh.

He also took an interest in experiments at the Bilroth Clinic with paraffin wax, used as a filler in resected joints where bone or cartilage had been scraped away. The inert vaseline derived from petroleum had been discovered in 1830, and it proved to have the merit of melting down to a smooth liquid that could be injected, and firming up again into a malleable solid that yielded like flesh and fat and resembled their texture.

Gersury started using it to fill in blemishes. It seemed as if he had discovered the gift of eternal youth – paraffin wax ironed our wrinkles. It also filled out old necks that were growing webby and softened hands.

There seemed little limit to the wonder substance's ability to replace the lineaments of age with the smooth features of youth. However, it took some time for the drawbacks to show up. And what a drawback – paraffin wax wandered. It permeated the tissue and became almost irremovable from its new and undesirable site. Wrinkles came back in the original places, and the unfortunate patients were left with unsightly lumps and bumps on other parts of their faces and necks.

Plastic surgeons were kept very busy trying to remove "paraffinomas". All too often this proved quite impossible without leaving a scoop in place of the lump.

This utter disaster almost destroyed the growing art of cosmetic surgery. Gersury is remembered with a shudder in the profession, although the over-enthusiasm of his colleagues should bear as much responsibility for the tragic tale of paraffin wax.

••

CELEBRITY SPOT

KAY KENDALL'S NOSE WAS MCINDOE'S MISTAKE

Actress Kay Kendall went to Sir Archibald McIndoe after the war asking for a shapelier nose. The fashionable ideal at the time was a straight and dignified Greek nose. McIndoe was horrified when the bandages came off and the swelling went down to see that he had given his patient a tip-tilted nose – generally despised as "snub" in the 1930s and 1940s.

Miss Kendall, however, wisely perceived that it very much enhanced her appearance for the sort of sophisticated light comedy in which she excelled. She insisted on retaining it.

Sir Archibald McIndoe's mistake set a fashion. For the next thirty years, the retroussé nose with its permanently youthful appearance became the model of choice for women undergoing rhinoplasty. Not till the 1980s was there some return to requests for the longer and more dignified down-turned probosces.

••

CELEBRITY SPOT

THE DUCHESS OF MARLBOROUGH

Visitors to Blenheim Palace have their attention drawn to portraits of American-born Gladys Deacon, second wife of the 9th Duke of Marlborough.

Once described as "the most beautiful woman in the world", she suddenly stopped having her portraits painted and withdrew to a house near Banbury where she lived a reclusive life under the name "Mrs Spencer". The palace guides do not, unless specifically asked, give any more details about this lady's sad life. After "Sunny" Marlborough, the popular 9th Duke, dissolved his loveless dynastic marriage with Consuelo Vanderbilt, Gladys Deacon became his lover, and in 1921 they married. Unfortunately their love did not survive domesticity, and in 1931 they separated. Three years later "Sunny" died. The widows Duchess found herself a free woman with a grand title, but with the onset of middle age beginning to threaten her magnificent looks. Not knowing the dangers, she took the paraffin wax treatment for rejuvenation.

The Duchess of Marlborough suffered one of the worst cases of "paraffinomas". It was the disfigurement of the unremovable lumps that led her to shut herself away from the world until her death in 1977.

....

The Fight for Beauty

Despite the hostility of puritans and the scandal of paraffin wax, it was pre-dictable that nothing would stop a market promising an eternally youthful appearance. Cosmetic surgery was given a tremendous boost by the rise of the film industry with its alarming capacity to screen a close-up of a face magnified tens of times above its normal size. Similar magnification had made the most winsome Brodingnagian giant maidens seem hideous to Gulliver.

The studios had recourse to beauticians and make up specialists, and ordered simple cosmetic interference with the natural appearance of their actresses, like raising the hair-line to emphasize a smooth brow and frame the eyes appealingly. The actresses themselves had recourse to cosmetic surgery as soon as they realized that there were increasingly real and safe ways of eliminating wrinkles. The great advances made by plastic surgeons during wartime could be adapted. Skin that could be released from its normal anchorage to stretch over an area of burn might also be released, stretched, cut off and restitched above the hairline, simply to make it look younger and more elastic again. The face-lift was born.

People used to painting themselves to represent other people, now had the chance to be permanently, visually unmatured. High profile patients like Marlene Dietrich made widely known the eternal glamour available from the surgeon's knife. Actresses hoping for a career into old age, playing ever maturing parts, needed either the profound inner beauty of a Lillian Gish to compete with the neatly lifted and tucked compeers, or had to be willing to wring melodramatic triumph from hideous harridan roles, like Bette Davis as "Baby Jane".

The Full Facial

CORONOPLASTY

FOREHEAD MOULDING

A lift will stretch out creases. Injections of toxin botulin will freeze muscles for several months which, it is hoped, will cause frown lines to fall away. Collagen (purified animal protein) can be injected into frown lines between the eyebrows to fill them. Set aside £2,000-£3,000 if you want all this done.

BLEPHAROPLASTY

EYELID MOULDING

Bulging or bagging of upper or lower eyelids can be removed. In the case of the upper eyelid, blepharoplasty has a very respectable plastic surgical history, being needed to help those whose vision was impaired by drooping eyelids. Surplus skin and fat are removed, and to avoid scars, operation and stitching is done from the inside. The cheapest form is to incorporate a small lift to take out "crows'-feet". Be prepared to spend £2,000 or more.

RHINOPLASTY

NOSE MOULDING

The historic facial surgery. Genuinely necessary in some cases to help impeded breathing. Usually, however, a "nose job" is for people who want real or imaginary hooks, bulbs or lumps removed, or a bigger or smaller hooter. Size cannot be varied enormously either way, but coupled with reshaping, a tiny increase or dimunition may satisfy the patient immensely. It's going to set you back about £2,500.

OTOPLASTY

EAR MOULDING

Another operation with a respectable history, since it was clear from an early date that children suffered teasing if they were "bat-eared". Though Clark Gable made do with spirit gum when filming, pinning back the "lugs" is the commonest ear job, and with a local anaesthetic can be one of the cheapest at £1,500 or less.

CHEMICAL PEEL

FACIAL STRIPPING

The outer surface of the skin is stripped from the face with a mild and sterile corrosive solution. This removes spots and blemishes of old age. It also reduces wrinkles. For the entire face the cost could be up to £2,000.

MALARPLASTY

CHEEKBONE MOULDING

An implant is placed via the mouth into the cheek to give the desired angle and effect. This operation can cost anything from £750 to £3,000.

PERMANENT MAKE-UP

This is, effectively, tattooing. Pigment in the skin may reshape lip outline or replace bald eyebrows. It can even be used to apply a little eyeshadow. The process will set you back about £250 a time, but it may need redoing every four years or so.

COLLAGEN IMPLANTS

Although used in coronaplasty, collagen implants are much more common in work on and around the mouth. Collagen can remove deep nose-to-mouth sneer lines, and give a "kissing-pout" or "bee-stung lip". A full mouth treatment will cost around £1,500, but it is likely to need renewal.

RHYTIDECTOMY

FACE-LIFT

For the removal of wrinkles, the skin around the face and jawline is loosened, pulled tight, and then stitched into a new position. The surgery will cost at least £3,000, and should be effective for between seven and ten years.

MENTOPLASTY

CHIN-MOULDING

Weak chins can be strengthened with an implant or part of the jawbone sliced and slipped forward. This process usually costs between £1,000 and £3,000.

Facial Drawbacks

All surgery carries a risk of some sort. If facial surgery goes wrong, the results vary from the trivial to the devastating.

Risks of a Growth Medical Industry

The popularity of plastic surgery among those who can afford it is undeniable. Two million Americans every year have their appearance improved "under the knife", and the number is constantly rising. In contrast, Britain has an annual estimated 85,000 cosmetic surgery patients.

The majority of these cosmetic operations are privately performed. American medical insurance does not cover cosmetic surgery unless the face has been injured, so the patient must elect to undergo treatment at his or her own expense.

In Great Britain, the National Health Service provides treatment only after injury or if psychiatric reports declare that it would be strongly beneficial. Even in the cosmetically generous Dutch health service, an inspectorate checks that alternative measures have been attempted before any drastic irreversible surgery is approved. Such restrictions open the field to "cowboy" private surgeons. They will not be completely untrained or unqualified. They have to be licensed medical practitioners before they can take a scalpel to someone's face, or they would be liable to assault charges. However, they do not have to be properly trained plastic surgeons.

Every doctor undertakes some simple surgery as part of his training. Even in days of increased specialization, we expect a GP to be able to meet certain emergencies: set a fracture; deliver a baby; maybe even deliver by caesarean section if unanticipated labour complications begin. So if a doctor wishes to maximize his earnings, he may take a short course, and offer simple cosmetic operations. In this field, the public would seem to be overly trusting. Many patients who would never consider going to anyone but a specialist surgeon for a heart bypass seem to have no fears about going to a small, new private clinic after assurances from unqualified salesmen about the excellence of their beauty treatments.

The results are best shown in stark estimates about US practitioners. There are nearly 4,000 properly qualified plastic surgeons in the USA,

3,000 of whom practice in California. Yet a further 27,000 people practise "cosmetic surgery" in that state alone! Some of them are specialists who reasonably feel that their field makes them the obvious practitioners for certain types of cosmetic work. Dermatologists, for example, are clearly good people to treat skin problems and give collagen injections or chemical peels if they are indicated.

The official bodies of plastic surgeons are deeply concerned by the sudden emergence of "cosmetic surgeons". many feel that the term is itself completely unreal – all surgery heals or mends something; it cannot be merely cosmetic. Most are appalled by the emergence of "surgeons" who have taken very short courses at fly-by-night colleges, and exhibit diplomas or board certificates which are virtually worthless.

And so the horror stories of failed cosmetic surgery emerge from the work of the ill-trained professionals.

The Risks to the Face

BLEPHAROPLASTY

During the healing period the upper eyelid may prove impossible to close completely. This may cause the cornea to dry, requiring eyedrops. Loss of vision has also been reported, though it is, fortunately, extremely rare.

RHINOPLASTY

The nose may not turn out the expected shape – not everyone is as lucky as Kay Kendall in finding the mistake a blessing. Scar tissue may form inside the nose causing blockage and the need for a second operation.

OTOPLASTY

Apart from faint and unobtrusive scarring there are hardly any risks.

CHEMICAL PEEL

The skin will be sensitive and may appear swollen and shiny for a time. It is likely to end up a lighter shade than it was before, and pores may appear enlarged. Scarring and infection are possible, though.

MALARPLASTY

The implant may slip out of place, but can be removed. The operation can be reversed if the result is felt to be unsatisfactory.

PERMANENT MAKE-UP

As with any form of tattooing, there is a small risk of infection.

COLLAGEN IMPLANTS

The implant may be reabsorbed faster than expected, necessitating a repeat operation. There is also a small risk of allergic reaction. Of the cheaper alternatives, silicone (now banned in the US), can wander; Gore-tex can become infected.

RHYTIDECTOMY

Temporary tightness and numbness. The face must be protected from the sun for several months. There may be infection or haematoma (blood under the skin). In very rare cases nerves may be damaged, creating a horrifying lopsided appearance.

MENTOPLASTY

As with malarplasty, the implant may slip out of place. This is reversible if it fails, as the implant can be removed.

Two Bad Nose Jobs

In 1981, the Sunday Times started looking at the dangers of improperly conducted private cosmetic surgery. They learned that the BMA had received information about a 25-year-old girl whose rhinoplasty left her nose looking worse than before. The clinic tried again and made matters still worse. The girl had been sent to a mental home because of intense depression about her looks.

A 52-year-old housewife, giving her name as Glenys, went to a cosmetic "consultant", who sent her to a private clinic for her long and bulbous nose to be shortened. The surgeon left two bumps on one side and a dent on the other. The wound was infected and suppurated.

Said Glenys, "I feel so terribly distressed about it. Before, it was my nose and I had to live with it, but now it's ended up like this and it looks much worse. I feel such a stupid old fool."

Without admitting liability, the Medical Defence Union agreed to pay Glenys £1,900.

••

CELEBRITY SPOT

VALENTINO'S NOSE

When the silent screen's romantic superstar Rudolph Valentino died suddenly and unexpectedly in 1926, his family in New York were appalled to think of all the Hollywood money and glamour which had spilled over to them drying up. They decided that one of his brothers must replace him and become an actor and national heartthrob.

The best looking of the other Valentino boys was Albert Guglielmo. The trouble was, he didn't have the elegantly refined nose that had wafted Rudolph on clouds of feminine desire from tea-dancing to the tents of The Sheik. Albert Guglielmo had a bit of a bottle nose. Undeterred, he went for rhinoplasty.

The first attempt left him with a narrower nose. But it stuck up in an unaristocratic snub.

A second operation tried to give Albert's nose extra length and dignity by shortening his upper lip. This simply gave him a fixed smirk with slightly exposed teeth, while leaving his nose still up-tilted, and too short.

Albert went back for renewed surgery. A wax implant was put in his nose to fill it out to give it dignity. Unfortunately the wax ran off to one side. Albert now had a lopsided, bulbous nose. And it was still too short.

The surgeons tried again. They cut off part of the septum, hoping that a steeper angle would make Albert's nose look longer. What they succeeded in giving him was a hook.

Albert Guglielmo Valentino bravely went through three more operations to try and get his nose to look classy and sexy. After the seventh time he gave up, and the Valentino family resigned themselves to the fact that plastic surgery couldn't create a second Rudy.

••

Crooks with Facials

Several of the notorious American gangsters of the 1930s underwent plastic surgery in the vain hope that their changed appearance would sidestep the

"WANTED" mug-shots circulated nationally among police departments. They proved notable failures.

"Doc" Barker, of "Ma" Barker's gang of kidnappers and bank robbers reported to John Dillinger, "Public Enemy Number One", that his brother Fred and the brains of the Barker gang, Alvin Karpis, had successfully had their faces altered and their fingerprints obliterated by plastic surgery.

"Doc" was wrong on both counts. Dr Joseph P. Moran of Chicago undertook the operations. Karpis, who would live on in jail to become mentor and guitar tutor to Charles Manson, was always nicknamed "Creepy" because of his sinister appearance. Minor plastic surgery failed to make any serious improvement, nor had it made him unrecognizable to law officers.

The fingerprint surgery was even less successful. It actually proved fatal. To Dr Moran, that is. He sliced off the gangsters' fingerpads – an appallingly painful operation. However, when the wounds healed, they found that the fingerprints had returned, clear and unchanged. Dr Moran was rubbed out and thrown into a lake!

John Dillinger

John Dillinger was the most famous crook to try plastic surgery. His published description included three moles between the eyes and a cleft chin. Dillinger's lawyer, John Piquette, approached Dr Wilhelm Loesser. Loesser was assisted by the very capable young Irish doctor, Hugh Cassidy, when he operated on Dillinger on May 27 1934. Dillinger's moles were removed. His cleft chin was filled with a skin graft. And he was given a face lift – his cheeks being cut from ear to jaw and tightened with kangaroo tendons.

The facial proved very risky for Dillinger. Under the ether used for his anaesthetic, he choked on his tongue and turned blue. It took artificial respiration to revive him after Loesser had fished his tongue out. At the same time, Dillinger and the clown of his gang, Homer Van Meter, had the doctors attempt to erase their fingerprints. They brandished guns as they warned Loesser that he'd better not cause the pain that Moran had inflicted on Barker and Karpis. So Loesser treated them with acid, and wisely disappeared without waiting to find out whether their papillary ridges would return when the skin healed.

They did. In fact, both operations failed in their main purposes. Dillinger's dark good looks remained identifiable – his last photographs show him looking the same as ever, but with small scars at the corners of his face left by the operation. In July of the same year he was betrayed to the FBI and shot down as he left a cinema. J. Edgar Hoover made it very publicly known that Dillinger's lawyer and surgeon had both been jailed for obstructing justice, and that the surgery aimed at wiping his dabs had not succeeded.

The attempt to erase fingerprints had proved such a dismal failure that 300 points of similarity between Dillinger's grafted and ungrafted fingerprints could still be noted. 16 per finger would have been enough to satisfy the courts.

....

CELEBRITY SPOT

RONNIE BIGGS

British "Great Train Robber" Ronnie Biggs was the last criminal to have highly publicized facial surgery. After his escape from Wandsworth Prison, he and his fellow escapee Eric Flower were spirited away to Paris where a package deal for their flight to Australia included plastic surgery to be carried out by "the best cosmetic surgeon in France".

The nominal cost of the surgery was an outrageous £20,000, which had been extorted by underworld middlemen. Biggs and Flower were to have their noses altered, and then face-lifts. Flower's prominent hook nose was reduced, to his great satisfaction. Although as he said to Biggs when he came out of the operating theatre, "Don't let anyone tell you it don't hurt."

Biggs found the pain of the plastic surgery excruciating, this was because the surgeon began chipping at his nasal bone before the anaesthetic had taken effect. During the healing process he was only able to breathe through his mouth, and could not laugh without extreme anguish. The face-lift proved even worse. For 36 hours after the operation the pain was so severe that

Bigg's minders had to dissuade him from attempting suicide by jumping from the window.

Flower was extremely satisfied with his enhanced appearance. For Biggs, although the slight shortening, straightening and narrowing of his nose didn't alter his appearance radically, nevertheless, along with the temporary rejuvenation of the face lift, the surgery saw him safely through customs and immigration and away to Australia. By the time Biggs finally surfaced in Rio, Brazil, however, he looked much as one might have expected an older Ronnie Biggs to look.

* *

"Nobody would even recognize you now"

ERIC FLOWER ON SEEING BIGGS AFTER SURGERY

The Collagen Question

The "Paris Lip", created by French surgeon Thierry Besins, has become so popular in France that there reputed to be walk-in clinics where women can change their lips as quickly and easily as they might change a broken shoe-heel. The operation injects collagen in the outer lip only, shaping it as a "Cupid's bow" without puffing it out.

A larger implant is possible, however, creating a kissing pout. This operation carries risks. The National Hospital for Aesthetic Plastic Surgery, a highly thought of institution in Worcestershire, had to undertake repair work on a woman whose collagen implant from another clinic had given her a mouth that looked like "a car tyre, doubled then clamped on her face".

Another woman answering a magazine advertizement for "Paris Lip" at a reputable London clinic felt that the salesmanship at her consultation was rather high pressure. She was not allowed to meet former satisfied patients – it would have been "unethical". Her operation was a failure. The collagen was inserted unevenly, giving her an upper lip swollen on one side. "I couldn't go out for weeks," she said. "It looked as though I had gone ten rounds with Mohammed Ali."

The clinic rebalanced her lip. But it cost her another fee.

Nose and Chin

Julie, a 37-year-old housewife, suffered both pain and disfigurement after spending £2,500 to have her nose and chin reshaped in 1987. The surgeon's consultation seemed perfunctory to her, and when she came round from the anaesthetic she had two black eyes and could neither breathe through her nose nor swallow. The surgeon sold her antibiotics for £10 and discharged her. When she telephoned subsequently to complain that she was still in pain, and it was clear that her nose and chin had not been improved, her calls were ignored.

The National Health Service replaced her wrongly positioned chin implant, but she had to start saving her money all over again for a further operation to correct her nose.

> *"I suspect that women often want something done because they don't feel good generally. Lips are also sexual. Women might imagine it would make them more alluring. But look at Julia Roberts who was born with full lips – it didn't do much for her love life."*
>
> IRMA KURTZ

An Unusual Death

A facial operation which usually has no side-effects is ear-pinning. But a young English schoolgirl died when surgeons were correcting her protruding ears.

Although she was never teased about them, the teenager had always been self-conscious about her ears, and grew her hair to cover them up. When she was seven she learned about the operation, and pestered her parents to let her have it.

Originally it was intended that she should have a local anaesthetic, but when she arrived at the hospital it turned out she was due for a general anaesthetic. The girl and her mother discussed the differences with the anaesthetist, and opted for the local anaesthetic. At the last minute, however, there was a further brief conference, and the girl changed her mind. It was to be a costly decision.

Her breathing stopped toward the end of the surgery. She need emergency resuscitation, but the anaesthetists were unable to use the stand-by emergency equipment in the theatre. Although it was in perfect working order, it was so old-fashioned that none of them had ever used anything like it. The teenager was given emergency respiration and rushed to an intensive care unit at another hospital where she fell into a coma.

Five days later she died. Her brain had been starved of oxygen when her lungs collapsed.

The girl's death was not caused by the plastic surgery, but by the inadequate anaesthetic equipment that accompanied it. David Gault, a London plastic surgeon, commented that protruding ears could be corrected very quickly and easily in the first few days after birth, when the ear cartilage is sufficiently malleable to be remoulded without surgery.

The Sleepless Eyelid

Linda Ovar revealed her wretched experience with blepheroplasty to a live television audience. She had wanted her upper eyelids lifted and her "crows'-feet" removed. So her surgery combined lifting the upper facial sides with her eyelids.

She came round from surgery to find her face swollen and "Chinese-looking". For four months she was only able to close one eye when she slept.

Thereafter the hair at the sides of her head fell out where the lift had been stitched, and scars and baldness were exposed unless she wore her hair long. The top of her head was completely numb.

Her "crows'-feet" have been smoothed out and her eyelids are unbagged. But Linda Ovars passionately wishes she had never had plastic surgery.

CELEBRITY SLot

LYNNE PERRIE

Actress Lynne Perrie, long a star of the seemingly immortal British soap opera Coronation Street, had a satisfactory face-lift which helped her through the difficult mid-career stage, when an actress may seem too old for ingenue roles, but too young for character parts. Ms Perrie made no secret of the fact, and was only mildly annoyed when the tabloid press erroneously post-dated the event to the year when she left "The Street", as though she needed some consoling for that simple career move.

Indeed, in 1996 Ms Perrie revealed in a daytime televised discussion of plastic surgery, made for Central and Carlton TV, that she intended to have a repeat operation to keep up the good work in her sixties. Her appearance confirmed that the work had been good, but she also revealed that a collagen implant in her lips had failed. She had developed an allergy to the cow's-hide protein extract, and had to have it removed.

Presenter Sue Jay remarked casually, "Yeah, I remember you with those puffy lips" – an unfortunately ambiguous comment in context, as it was not clear whether she was remembering with sympathy the swelling caused by the allergy, or recalling with distaste that to her eye Ms Perrie's implanted lips were not an improvement on nature!

Disfiguring Discolouration

A truly dreadful case of cosmetic medical failure is that of 75-year-old George Sangster. When he went for treatment, Mr Sangster had three moles or freckles on his face which he felt were disfiguring. He went to a private clinic whose Harley Street address suggested reputability. He was not aware that this was simply one branch of a chain of cosmetic clinics whose management have been described by former employees as devoting more time to training staff in high-pressure salesmanship than in understanding the genuine problems of clients. Mr Sangster made an appointment with a consultant, who sold him an ointment for the blemishes. The ointment turned Mr Sangster's face a deep greyish-brown, giving him something of the look of a cold and unwashed southern Indian or Sri Lankan. Naturally the clinic took steps to try and remedy this disaster. However, they continued to charge Mr Sangster as they went on to make bad worse.

Their efforts to restore him to his natural colour succeeded only in spreading the discolouration further across his body, and introducing on his hands and face, particularly in the area of the neck, some pink spots. These stood out luridly against the black, with very sharply defined edges and a startling vermillion hue. Mr Sangster understandably felt that he presented a ridiculous spectacle, and he was too embarrassed to leave his house and be seen out on the street.

For the privilege of enjoying this humiliating condition he had paid the clinic £11,000! Considering his case for Carlton TV, the Cook Report team noted that the cost of a simple blemish-lightening cream on the National Health would have been £5.25. Indeed, at Mr Sangster's age, if his GP believed that he needed the moles removed for his psychological well-being, he need not have paid a single penny.

Bitten By A Shark

Mr Sangster suffered his incompetent treatment in the Harley Street of the 1990s. In the 1980s, university researcher Jennifer King was carrying out a study of doctor/patient relationships. This took her to the surgery of a private practitioner in the Harley Street neighbourhood whose alleged incompetence at the cosmetic surgery he offered was being mercilessly attacked in the Sunday Times.

As it happened, Ms King had three moles that she disliked, and decided to use the opportunity to have them removed. The notorious practitioner took the moles off all right, but he left some scarring that, Ms King told the Sunday times, "looks like I've been bitten by a shark."

The newspaper's reports on her cosmetic surgeon would suggest that metaphorically she had indeed been so bitten!

Call This A Success?

"Sue" didn't know that the surgeon she went to for a nose job had disfigured five previous patients. She only knew that with her bandages off, she wasn't looking at an improved nose: she was looking at a missing nose!

Her boyfriend burst into tears when he saw it, and later left her because she became persistently bad-tempered. Sue was afraid to go out. She sat at home and drank heavily.

After a year, her surgeon agreed to repair his botch. He put an artificial bridge in Sue's nose. Within six weeks, it collapsed. Sue found another surgeon. He put in a new implant which looked all right. For ten weeks. Then it, too, collapsed.

Sue's next operation was extremely unpleasant. It took place in a private north London clinic which used "twilight anaesthetic" inducing a drowsy semi-conscious sleepiness without the risks of a full anaesthetic. Sue was too drugged to make a protesting sound, but not drugged enough to stop her feeling every cut, every needle, every stitch. After the operation the clinic had no overnight bed for her and she was sent home to look after herself. And it didn't work.

Sue's fifth operation was the most disastrous of all. Her nose became infected, and her implant started forcing its way painfully out through the infected area. Sue turned in desperation to an independent cosmetic surgery advisory network, and was directed to Edward Latimer-Sayer. Although he is not a trained plastic surgeon, Mr Latimer-Sayer has general surgical training and four years experience of general surgical practice. He cured Sue's infection with antibiotics, and then re-operated on her nose.

Five years, six nose-jobs and £15,000 after Sue first decided to have her appearance improved, she really was improved.

> "There are numerous cases of members of the public being misled by unscrupulous cowboys who run some of the private cosmetic clinics. These victims are easily swept under the carpet because of their embarrassment and shame. Animals have better protection than people."

ANNE CLWYD MP

CELEBRITY SPOT

MICHAEL JACKSON ...AND HIS FORE-RUNNERS

In Marlene Dietrich's case it had seemed understandable that for career reasons she wanted to remain sensational as a glamourous beauty at an age when all her contemporaries had gracefully yielded to the ravages of time. Phyllis Diller, too, boasted that at the age of 72 she felt and looked like "a red-hot 50-year-old."

In the past the movie star Cher has lent her name to an advertising campaign for the Jack La Lanne health spas. "I owe my body to La Lanne and La Knife," she claimed in the advertisements. In the 1990s, however, Cher went to a leading reputable British plastic surgeon for a certificate stating that she had only ever had work done on her nose and breasts. This in hand, she garnered a whole new round of publicity, causing the surgeon to note wryly that his £70 fee had proved a startlingly good investment for her.

Some psychologists noticed that as new techniques were developed for beautifying the face and body, so some patients seemed impelled to try as many of them as they could.

Of course there are those for whom, particularly in the entertainment world their looks are their livelihood. Individuals such as Marlene Dietrich, Phyllis Diller and Cher have had a reputation for using plastic surgery to enhance their looks. Another who has acquired a reputation in recent years is Michael Jackson.

Perhaps it is this, as well as his reclusive lifestyle that has contributed to the singer's strange quality of agelessness. Certainly he has changed since the days when he was the chubby youngest member of the Jackson Five.

BEAUTIFYING THE BODY

After the face, the body. Various treatments are on offer which will promise, and sometimes effect, a lovelier shape: sylph-like or buxom, to taste. And, as the case of Michael Jackson suggests, men may also want some of these treatments.

Most men want little surgical done to their faces other than removing bags from the eyes or pinning back ears. The narcissism of 1980s culture showed up more in men imitating Ronald Reagan and dyeing their hair than in huge recourse to plastic surgery. Baldness is, of course, a perennial problem. Actors may feel they have to do something about it, or lose desirable roles. Frank Sinatra, Ray Milland and George Burns all resorted to the toupee. Other men have become enthusiasts for hair transplanting. Enough anxiety seems to be generated to suggest that anyone who succeeds in devising a guarantee reversal of baldness will become as rich as the wealthiest cosmetic surgeon.

In the meantime, many men would welcome treatment to reduce a beer belly or enhance a manly chest. If Michael Caine could allow surgical artifice to check his middle-aged spread, why shouldn't other men.

So, working down the body, the main treatments available for men and women are as follows:

MAMMOPLASTY

BREAST REDUCTION OR BREAST AUGMENTATION

Breast reduction is more often necessary for health reasons than for vanity. Tissue is removed from the breasts, and the skin is tightened and lifted. If the centres of gravity have been sharply changed, the nipples are grafted back in appropriate situations. If you need this operation because of fatiguingly weighty breasts, you probably should be able to get it on the National Health. Otherwise allow in the region of £3,000.

In breast augmentation operations, the breast is enlarged by inserting envelopes of silicone gel or saline fluid under the skin or pectoral muscle, or by grafts or injections of fat from elsewhere on the patient's body. Men, too, may have small inserts put in to simulate large pectoral muscles. This operation can cost anything from £1,000 to £4,000.

ABDOMINOPLASTY

"TUMMY TUCK"

After childbirth, this operation can help to remove stretch marks and flaccid folds of skin. Surplus skin and tissue is drawn down and cut off; the navel moved up and skin and tissue stitched back tightly. Prices can vary greatly, but average at about £3,500.

LIPOSUCTION

The wonder fat removal operation of the 1980s. Fat is sucked out from under the skin by vacuum pressure, usually from the waists, hips, or thighs. It can cost up to £2,500, depending on how many sites are treated. An experimental new version with an ultra-sonic tip to melt the fat as it is extracted might cost a little more.

LIPOSCULPTURE

Fat removed by liposuction is purified and injected back in depressions and wrinkles where a filler mould is wanted. A small insert tube makes this especially effective for wrists, ankles, necks and double chins. This is the basis of hand surgery, plumping out ageing wrinkled claws with fat at a very favourable cost of £700.

BOTTOM LIFT

Like a face lift, this process can make sagging skin taut, giving an impression of firmness. Lifting can probably be carried out almost anywhere large enough on the body. Marlene Dietrich was said to have been lifted everywhere that was possible in order to achieve her "world's most glamourous granny" status. Prices for this treatment average at around £3,000.

PENILE ENLARGEMENT

Fat is injected into the penis to increase girth. Part of the penis normally held in the abdomen is released and extruded to increase length. Remarkably, this has been performed free on the National Health. However, you should prepare to spend £5,000 on creating a mighty organ if your GP doesn't agree that you'll go bonkers without it!

CELLULITE REMOVAL

Unbecoming subcutaneous deposit on the thighs can be removed by fine liposculpture vacuum process, or broken up by current injected from fine needle electrodes. A one hour session will usually cost about £800. How many sessions you need will depend on how much cellulite you're carrying.

And the Dangers

BREAST REDUCTION

May leave anchor-shaped scars across the breast, although women who want relief from the weight of excessively large breasts do not usually find this too high a price to pay. Grafted nipples may not take, falling off and leaving a nippleless breast.

BREAST AUGMENTATION

Inserts may slip or leak with worrying after-effects. Some areas of the injected fat may calcify, confusing scans and manual checks for tumours. Equally, gel inserts do not help mammography. Any surgery involving muscle may leave it weakened, so men imitating Tarzan with pectoral inserts run a small risk of actually emerging weaker, if looking stronger than before.

TUMMY TUCKS

The only risks are those you carry with any form of surgery – infection and possible thrombosis.

LIPOSUCTION

The basic risks have been well described by practitioner Jan Starek, who has carried out thousands of successful liposuctions. The shock is as severe as a third degree burn, but this may not be immediately apparent as there is only a small puncture in the skin. A lot of blood is sucked out with the fat, and more drains into the channels left by the fat. A blood transfusion is absolutely necessary if more than 3Œ litres of fat are taken. The procedure is dangerous to patients with heart conditions, high blood pressure or diabetes. In fact, patients should be "not just fit, but utterly fit."

LIPOSCULPTURE

Any error in the removal or repositioning of fat may cause lumps, dents or ridges. Women have been known to end up with asymmetrical or twisted thighs, far more unsightly than their original "saddlebags".

BOTTOM LIFT

All lifts carry the same risks of possible infection or, at the very worst, severance of nerves with consequent numbness and possible asymmetry.

PENILE ENLARGEMENT

For lengthening, a tendon has to be incised that is dangerously close to important nerve and blood vessels. The results are not such as most men would find impressive or necessary, though subjectively they may be extremely satisfying to the patient. Most men would probably find the thought of a scalpel in the penis and a stuffing of fat in that sensitive and intimate organ thoroughly off-putting. It seems an extraordinary price to pay for such vanity. As with collagen, the fat may be rapidly absorbed elsewhere in surrounding areas, indicating the need for a repeat treatment.

CELLULITE REMOVAL

There is some risk of unsightly dents or ridges if cells are sucked out.

Three Terrible Tummy Tucks

Margaret Trusler was 59 years old when she went to a private clinic for a tummy tuck. Like 25% of all plastic surgical patients, she needed the treatment to clean up the mess left by a previous operation that had failed.

In fact, two reputable plastic surgeons had examined her and refused to treat her.

Ms Trusler was a nurse, and might have felt confident that she would be able to spot any incompetence on the part of her surgeon. She had no suspicion that the surgeon operating for the clinic would not prove satisfactory, and never anticipated that her own expertise would be needed to save her life. The tummy tuck proved the wisdom of the two surgeons who had refused to attempt it. Ms Trusler went home with a wound that proved deeply infected. It was necessary for her to return to the clinic for two further operation.

After the second, she recognized danger signs which, as a nurse, she was trained to spot. It was clear to her that a pain in the leg was a blood clot – a thrombosis, which if not removed or broken up would travel up to her heart and kill her. This common and unavoidable post-surgical mishap is something for which all medical staff ought to be on the alert at all times. It seemed to be quite unconsidered by the staff at this private clinic. Margaret correctly diagnosed her own danger and ordered her own treatment.

Mrs Rose Zappone was not quite as lucky. Given an abdominoplasty by the same clinic chain, she too developed a deep vein thrombosis after surgery. Hers, too, was unrecognized by staff who should have been looking out for such a thing. At the age of 45, Mrs Rose Zappone died quite unnecessarily.

In Orange County, California, Joyce Palso wanted a tummy tuck. To begin with, she prudently called the California State Medical Board and the American Medical Association, to ask whether her surgeon was competent. He was, in fact, so grossly incompetent that there were 11 lawsuits pending against him, and the state medical board was trying to revoke his licence to practice! Not one word of this was told to Joyce Palso!

Blithely unaware of her dangers, Joyce went in for her tummy tuck. The operation was conducted with so little finesse that Mrs Palso suffered a heart attack, and then, while the medics were trying to cope with that inconvenience, a stroke. It seemed absolutely impossible that she could survive. Her son was so certain that she was dying that he bought a cemetery plot. Thankfully, good treatment brought Mrs Palso round and she recovered. It is hardly surprising, though, that she was highly indignant with the State Medical Board and the AMA: "There are no controls. It's just dollars and cents," raged Mrs Palso. "I just praise the Lord I'm still around!"

"The National Hospital of Aesthetic Plastic Surgery was set up in Worcestershire to correct faulty cosmetic work after administrator John Terry had noted the appalling practices of some of his former employers."

Confessions of a Private Clinic Administrator

"We invested £20,000 persuading one man to train as a cosmetic surgeon. He nearly lost one patient. We had nipples sloughed off, or patients saying, 'I feel very number here.'

———————————————————

Yes, we'd think. The surgeon probably caught a facial nerve with the forceps. "When we could correct the surgery, we would. But most of the time we never saw our patients again."

JOHN TERRY, NOW PROPRIETOR AND ADMINISTRATOR OF THE NATIONAL HOSPITAL OF AESTHETIC PLASTIC SURGERY

••

BREAST SCULPTURE

••

There are a few serious, if rare, conditions that might encourage anyone to place their hopes in the hands of the plastic surgeon.

A very few women have the misfortune to be born with breasts of markedly different sizes, and understandably may feel acute embarrassment about their appearance. Equally, a few women may suffer from misaligned breasts, with nipples so obliquely angled that they feel it to be a deformity.

The overwhelming majority of young women are blessed with bosoms that will automatically please some men. Although exceptionally large breasts may seem peculiarly desirable to some men, the totally flat-chested, looking like boys with rather prominent nipples, also have their many admirers. However, either of those extremes may seem like an embarrassment or humiliation to the woman so blessed. Truly enormous breasts may, in fact, be a genuine handicap. One has only to think of the Dutch health service's agreement that free surgery should be granted to any woman whose nipples hang at the level of her elbows, to realize the folly of the pornographic dream of "boobs like footballs".

Old age and child-bearing take their toll on almost every bosom. Some will shrink – most will become to some degree pendulous. Because our culture normally covers the breast and expects it only to be revealed in situations of intimacy with erotic overtones, this natural ageing is likely to cause a level of distress that would not be felt by women in tribal societies where breasts are habitually exposed, from infancy to the last stages of old age.

In the past, clothing and padding remedied real or imagined mammary deficiencies. Supportive stays and jumps lifted bosoms to the Junoesque cleavage demanded by victorian and Edwardian evening gowns, long before Caresse Crosby invented the brassiere as an automatic enhancer. When, as in the 1920s, a boyish flat-chested look became fashionable, tight bandaging successfully flattened the full bosom for those to whom it mattered. When a woman wanted a fuller figure than nature had given her, prosthetic "falsies" were available to give her the desired public shape.

But around the middle of the 20th century, the breast became an erotic and fashion fetish. "Sweater girls" were extravagantly admired. Large breasts were seen as essential assets for glamourous actresses of the Marilyn Monroe, Jane Russell, Jayne Mansfield generation in ways that had never been the case for Clara Bow or Theda Bara. Women's so-called "vital" statistics were really all about the fashionable overhang of bustline above waist and hips, and nothing to do with excellent anatomical proportions.

Frankly, western society has come to put a wholly unnatural emphasis on the erotic importance of bosoms, so that only very mature and well-balanced women could always feel totally confident that they were properly endowed.

Plastic Surgery and the Breast

In 1903, the first attempts were made to improve breasts by letting the surgeon rather then the dressmaker shape the outline. Robert Gersury adapted his paraffin injections to the breast, successfully filling out some which had lost volume and started to flatten back against the chest.

Paraffin wax was even less successful in the breast than it had been in the face and neck. sooner or later, Gersury's implants almost inevitably slipped out of place. Sometimes they slipped almost in one piece away from their original location, creating extraordinary extra breasts without nipples, further down the thorax or abdomen. Once again, Gersury's invention created a mass of corrective work for other plastic surgeons.

This experience, coupled with the normal puritanical suspicion that all aesthetic surgery is catering to vanity, might have meant the end of breast implants. But the latter half of the twentieth century saw a huge increase in a new condition which invited sympathetic awareness of healthy women's feelings of disfigurement. Cancer was identified as a disease suitable for modern surgical treatment. Radical mastectomy, to remove cancer of the breast, left growing numbers of women feeling that they had been hopelessly disfigured. Plastic surgeons willingly investigated new techniques for building up new breasts for such women.

First Attempts

Like susruta 3,000 years ago and Tagliacozzi in the 16th century, the surgeons of the early 1950s turned to the best and most natural material for moulding breast replacements: the patient's own flesh. With the advantage of knowing that this was least likely to be rejected by the body, they moulded grafts of flesh and skin, taking lozenge shaped pieces from the buttocks.

These grafts proved to be imperfect, tending to shrink or harden. The outline under a dress might still be loosely satisfactory, but the same effect could more easily and safely be achieved by padding and prosthetics in brassieres. The whole point of surgery was to let a woman feel comfortable with herself in her bath or with her husband in bed.

Foam sponges were tried next. These, too, were prone to solidify and encourage solidification of the surrounding flesh.

In France, pioneering surgeons came up with a water- or saline-filled balloon of specially treated rubber. These were a definite improvement. However, although the breasts did not turn solid, the balloons did not hold their size and shape permanently, either. Over a varying period of time – sometimes as little as a matter of hours – they simply went down. It was normal to assume that they would ultimately have to be replaced. Where similar implants are used today, they are referred to as "inflatables"; a curious evasion of their true characteristic as deflatables!

In the late 1950s, Japanese surgeons started experimenting with silicone. This could be injected like Gersury's paraffin wax, and did not appear to wander around creating unsightly lumps in the wrong places. So just when the mid-20th-century fetishistic belief that the only good breast is a BIG breast took firm hold, it seemed that science had found the way to enhance the bustline of any woman who could afford the treatment.

Carol Doda

At 24, Carol Doda was a pretty, shapely cocktail waitress in San Francisco. The year was 1964. Society was becoming "permissive". Certain bars in San Francisco wanted to go beyond the extraordinary American habit of dressing up cocktail waitresses of all ages in inappropriately sexy clothes. They wanted their waitresses topless. They wanted young female dancers. Topless dancers.

Carol Doda wanted to become a topless dancer. But she was not satisfied that she had enough "top" to attract properly admiring glances. So she had the silicone treatment. Twenty injections transformed her attractive bust into a "44 Double-D" cup spectacle that attracted widespread media attention.

Carol's new bust could be seen as a joke, or an adventure, or an Awful Warning. It made her famous, and one must hope it made as much money for her as it did for her sponsors. The publicity given to Carol Doda, in and of itself, probably did much to stimulate many of the 2.6 million women who have followed her example since, and magnified their bustlines with internal implants.

Silicone Injections

By the time Carol Doda had her silicone injections, the treatment was already suspect. Just as aesthetic optimists had leaped too readily at Gersury's miracle flesh sculpting, so doctors and patients had been too eager to assume that silicone avoided all the problems of paraffin wax.

It didn't. It may not have wandered lumpily, but it wandered. It wandered around the body leaving traces in various organs. In very unfortunate cases this might lead to infection or necrosis of the skin. But essentially no one was sure exactly what the presence of loose silicone might do to vital organs. While there are some doctors who still believe that silicone is one of the most inert substances that can be introduced, and the least likely to cause secondary problems, others were seriously doubtful about possible long-term effects.

From 1963, a year before Carol Doda underwent her breast enhancement, the plastic surgery profession was looking for ways of encasing silicon gel implants rather than simply injecting the stuff raw. After the massive publicity given to Carol's transformation, the FDA opposed raw silicone injections, conclusively banning them in 1991.

Solid Implants

The feverish search for a new and safe way of padding out the breast from the inside had more to do with mid-century narcissism and its "boobs and beauty" culture than with the crucial needs of mastectomy patients. Almost any woman might at some time or another feel a twinge of doubt about her breasts as she contemplated the conflicting ideals of a superslim Twiggy or a busty Dolly Parton. It was American ingenuity that came up with an answer.

Plastic surgeon Thomas Cronin devised the first really successful implant. His silastic prosthesis used the principle of the French "inflatable", but filled the interior with silicon gel and created a stronger exterior envelope. There were still a few cases of leakage, however. Solvents in the gel sometimes seeped out, and the area around the implant might become sore and inflamed. And while Dr Cronin's prosthetic didn't limply deflate, it was liable to some contraction which, combined with the natural changes in patients' breasts, meant (and means) that an implant may need to be replaced after about fifteen years.

Industrial research, particularly by Dow-Corning, refined the exterior until High Performance Silastic II was produced, creating an implant so strong it could be stamped on or pounded with a hammer to convince would-be patients of its safety. By 1980, most of the bugs had been ironed out, and the operation was sufficiently common that the Journal of the American Medical Association was able to give a sort of currency to the most extraordinary legend about breast implants.

Silicone (almost) Rides Again

In 1992, Dr James E. Fulton of Palm Beach, California, started using liquid silicone for facial treatments, much as Gersury had used his paraffin wax. Fulton injected industrial liquid silicone to fill acne pits, deep blemishes and wrinkles. The U.S. Justice Department promptly stepped in to point out that liquid silicone had not been approved for medical treatment, and its injection was a breach of the Food, Drugs and Cosmetics Act.

Exploding Breasts, Crawling Swimmers and Handicapped Golfers

Dr William M. Baker told the JAMA that an airline stewardess had reported to him her feeling that something funny was happening to her breast implants when an aircraft she was in suffered a decompression incident at 8,500 metres in the air. She was the more concerned as she enjoyed experimental decompressed flying, and wanted to know what heights she could safely risk.

The JAMA observed that according to the laws of physics, if her plane had fully decompressed at 8,500 metres, the lady's implants would have expanded to three times their normal size. However, it also noted that all commercial airlines pressurized their cabins, so there was no risk to the general travelling public.

Nevertheless, the rumour started to circulate that implantees should beware of flying in high altitude planes, as there was a danger that their implants might swell up and burst!

Drs N. Levine and R. T. Buchanan reported the experience of a 46-year-old physical education teacher and competitive swimmer whose implants increased her from a "32 A" bra size to a "34 B". She felt sleeker and more buoyant in the water, and her backstroke times were unchanged. But in the 2,000 yard freestyle her time rose from 42 minutes 15 seconds to 53 minutes. It would seem that her new twin keels were dragging in the water rather than giving the buoyancy and smoothness she felt subjectively.

Dr B. Lissner reported that a patient's golf handicap increased after her implants were fitted.

Despite these possible drawbacks, however, all three patients were perfectly satisfied with their operations.

Diminishing Problems in an Expanding Industry

In some patients there was still a tendency for the implant to create irritating scar tissue. Experiments with foam-coating ultimately gave way to the discovery that a ridged or patterned surface was the most reliable way of reducing the problem. The foam-coating was liable to cause encapsulating – the build-up of hard tissue around the implant, giving a rock-like and painful breast. Some of those who suffered from this have been described as ending up with breasts that looked and felt like grapefruit.

Polyurethane coating seemed to reduce the contraction problem. However, massive doses of polyurethane induced cancer in laboratory rats, and, always concerned with possible carcinogens, the FDA had polyurethane coated implants withdrawn in 1991.

One deeply angry patient, asking for her name to be withheld, wrote to The Times in 1994 complaining that her polyurethane foam-coated implants had turned rock hard and were most uncomfortable within months of her double mastectomy. She wished she'd "never heard of the damn things."

The majority of patients were satisfied with their operations and delighted with their new breasts, although about 30% reported side-effects ranging from desensitized nipples to swelling and congestion of the breasts that made sleeping difficult. Some women observed, without necessarily complaining, that their implants led a separate temperature life of their own, and felt cold while the body was warm. Occasionally husbands or boyfriends were also able to detect the difference in temperature.

Apart from the occasional wandering implants that produced asymmetrical breasts, the most significant dangers seemed to come from accidents that might occur in any surgery, but which were accentuated in cosmetic cases because of the lack of restrictions on the private practice of plastic surgery.

Saved by the Breast!

Nude dancer Dora Oberling had reason to bless her implants for more than the professionally useful "36 D" size they gave her. In 1993, her ex-boyfriend Bernard Fortune called her out for a conversation between acts at the Mons Venus Club in Tampa, Florida. The two sat in Mr Fortune's car and started quarrelling. (Since Mr Fortune was 75 years old and Miss Oberling 30, their relationship was more than likely to have been doomed from the outset.)

Finally Mr Fortune pulled his .38 calibre pistol, pointed it at Miss Oberling's heart, and shot her. Miss Oberling, like some Superwoman, responded to the deadly assault by stepping out of the car, going back into the club, and saying, "give me a cigarette – my breast is burning."

Miss Oberling was lucky. The bullet had entered the top of her breast and penetrated the implant, which steered it away from her ribcage and heart, to pass cleanly out of the bottom of the breast. Mr Fortune was charged with aggravated assault.

Surgical Disasters

A 41-year-old housewife, who gave her name to the Sunday Times as "Yvonne" in 1981, had a horrifying experience when her breasts turned septic after she received silicone gel implants. It became clear that her operation wounds were infected, and she went to her GP to have them dressed. One month after her operation she was in his surgery having her dressings changed, when the implant in the right breast fell through the suppurating wound and onto the floor.

The GP sent her on to a consultant who removed the implant from her left breast, and reported that he found it lying "in a sea of pus". The private practitioner with Harley Street offices who had implanted the gel bags in Yvonne was completely impenitent. He had taken £700 for his fee, and did not feel that either his operating or his follow-up consultation need be questioned. Indeed, he said it was "totally Yvonne's responsibility and her fault," because she did housework after the operation!

Yvonne had the power of the press on her side: the Sunday Times was campaigning fiercely at the time to stop her surgeon from practising. But eight years later, Jodie Bullock of Los Angeles took on a local TV station as well as a west coast doctor. Jodie saw a programme about breast implants in 1985 which said that Dr Stephenson was one of a mere handful of qualified and skilful West Coast doctors able to carry out the process, which it described as "new, safe and painless."

Jodie Bullock claimed that the programme lied. The process was not new, and it certainly wasn't painless. Jodie claimed to have been left with scars, severed nerves and muscles and permanent physical and emotional injuries. The detectable language of the American malpractice lawyer in that final phrase, coupled with the legal oddity of suing the television station, creates the impression that Ms Bullock's sufferings need not necessarily have been as great as Yvonne's.

Weird Uses for Silicone Implants

When breast implants are planted elsewhere on the anatomy, the reasons are likely to be strange. In 1992, police at Bogota airport were struck by the awkward gait of a woman boarding a flight to the USA, and they pulled her in for a strip-search. Nothing illegal was found about her clothes or person, but there were recent operation scars on her buttocks – the results of cosmetic surgery, she claimed.

An X-ray told a different story. Surgeons opened up the bouncing botty, and found a pound and a half of heroin instead of silicone gel in her implants.

Earlier that same year a trainee Japanese Sumo wrestler underwent three hours of surgery to have an implant placed on the top of his head. He had to raise his height by just over an inch to reach the statutory minimum of 5 feet 6 inches for wrestling in public. Having a breast implant put under his scalp was a great improvement on the old way of compensating for short height – to get a colleague to whack one on the head with a stick until a bump of the requisite size had been raised to take to the measuring authorities!

The Panic

In 1991, breast implants became a hot new item as a large pressure group insisted that they carried serious dangers which were often overlooked and of which patients were rarely warned.

It had long been feared that the implant would impede normal mammography: X-raying or scanning women's breasts for cancer. Simple manual checks for lumps in the breast were not made easier by the presence of one big implanted lump of heavy-coated gel.

Writer Sybil Goldrich had a double mastectomy in 1983 when she was 46. She lived in Beverley Hills, the great centre of cosmetic surgery. She was told she was a perfect candidate for implants, and happily accepted the operation. Things began to go wrong from the start. Sybil Goldrich came round from general anaesthesia with fever and a rash, and was in bed for the next six weeks. The medical team thought this was an allergic reaction to Betadine, the sterilizing solution they had used. (Years later it would be decided they were wrong. It was the implants.)

When the fever subsided, Ms Goldrich's implants started acting up on their own. They hardened painfully. They started wandering. One went up – the other went down. Ms Goldrich was faced with ugly asymmetry when she looked in the mirror. One of the implants even tried to force its way out of her body through the nipple graft that was part of her reconstructive surgery.

Three attempts at corrective surgery failed to solve the problem. Finally, in 1984, Ms Goldrich had her breasts rebuilt with tissue taken from her own abdomen, and at last ceased to have painful or ugly breasts.

Four years later, however, Ms Goldrich had to have a hysterectomy – tests showed that there was silicone in her uterus and ovaries. They could be removed, but silicone remained in her liver. Nobody was sure what the long-term effects might be. Nobody could doubt that the source must have been the artificial implants.

Ms Goldrich joined other dissatisfied patients to form the Command Trust Network, a clearing-house for women who had problems with breast implants. By 1991 the trust had records of 8,000 unsatisfactory cases. The most worrying were those in which cancer seemed to be linked to leakage of silicone into the body. However there were not enough of these to offer proof positive that silicone was carcinogenous.

Similarly uncertain was the claim that leaking silicone affected the immune system, leaving women liable to crippling rheumatic and arthritic conditions. Many plastic surgeons and manufacturers insisted that all this evidence was merely anecdotal and unscientific. The side-effect of wandering silicone is still uncertain. Of the two million women who had undergone breast enlargement, a mere 3% ever asked to have their implants removed, and half of those decided against it after taking medical advice.

With cancer in the background and the immune system under renewed threat in the age of AIDS, the FDA took cautious action, setting up an enquiry into the possible dangers of implants and imposing controls on the advertising of implants.

Many women started law suits against implant manufacturers. Many surgeons switched from silicone implants to saline-filled sacs – the "inflatables" which were still certain to deflate over the years.

The Deflation of Silicone

At last, in the spring of 1992, the FDA reached its decision. Silicone gel implants were banned for general enlargement, though surgeons would still be able to use them for mastectomy patients. The deflatable inflatable had won the day.

The trickle of women suing Dow-Corning suddenly turned into a rush, even though the company had ceased distribution of silicone implants when the controversy started. Once it became evident that there could be massive damages coming down from the courts, Dow-Corning filed for bankruptcy on behalf of its implant-manufacturing subsidiary.

Australia, too, banned the gel implants, but British plastic surgeons insisted that this was a needless panic, and the government declined to prohibit their use.

Women were understandably anxious and confused by this disagreement among the medical profession. Some who had undergone several replacements and corrective surgery insisted that it was all well worth it and fell within the acceptable risks of any surgical procedure. They objected that their sisters would now be unable to enjoy the benefits they had received.

Others, however, were unnerved, and had their implants removed. One observed glumly that once her operation had been undone, her breasts were back where they had been before, only now they had lines all over them.

Perhaps the gravest mistake in the whole episode was the excessive recourse to surgery for a socially induced anxiety. By the time of the ban, breasts had received more implants than any other part of the human body – a good 2.6 million. Only corneal lenses (curing cataracts) were in serious competition, and they fell a comfortable half-million behind. Vital implants like heart pacemakers simply weren't in the running!

Last Word

One unexpected profession is firmly hostile to the practice of artificial breast enlargement. Undertakers would be more than happy to see all breast implants go. Unfortunately they won't cremate with the rest of the body – they leave a pile-up of thick melted goo in crematorium ovens.

The Case of Jenny Jones

Comedienne and presenter Jenny Jones had her breasts enlarged in 1981, and went on to television success, first with an act called "Girls Night Out" which ran from 1989-91, and then with her own Chicago-based syndicated talk show.

In 1992, while the FDA ruminated on implants, Ms Jones decided to devote a programme to the topic and tell her audience what she had suffered. Six operations and five replacement implants of different kinds were only the start of it. Her breasts had completely and permanently hardened. They were lopsided, and scar tissue showed up around the nipples. A silicone ridge was apparent in her right breast. And both were completely without feeling.

Finally in December 1991, Ms Jones discovered that she had suffered silicone leakage into her body tissues. "I hate my breasts right now," she said. "But the sad part is that you can't undo this."

MALE INSERTS

Official statistics attribute 100% of breast implants to women patients. Actually this possible jocularity is not 100% true.

Transvestites may have false bosoms surgically sculpted to give them the startling androgynous appearance of a healthy penis and scrotum on an otherwise female body. Transsexuals will include breast implantation among their catalogue of recreative surgery, though in law they remain men in the UK. The numbers of "shemales", however, are miniscule compared with those of genuine women who want larger breasts.

An equally miniscule handful of men have opted to have their chests reshaped with small inserts to simulate Herculean pectoral muscles. As in the case of self-feminizing males, the numbers are too small for dramatic disasters to be recorded.

The operation that really is for men, and men only, does not entail an artificial insert. Penis enlargement is carried out with fat or tissue drawn from the patient's abdomen, or simply by, in effect, pulling the penis further out of the body.

Penis Envy

Sigmund Freud's extraordinary delusion that every woman wishes she were equipped with a penis as soon as she discovers the existence of this delightful male appendage, might well have been a cover for the genuine penis envy felt by men who believe themselves to be underendowed. Like women who imagine their breasts to be unacceptably small, men who long for larger penises are usually mistaken in feeling they fall outside an acceptable normal range which will appeal to many women. As physicians routinely point out, erect penises are not as a rule very different in size. Most will measure 4-6 inches. The normal detumescent organ, by contrast, may be anything from a full 5 inches to something more like an inch and a half, but quite capable of swelling to a good four-inch erection.

There are exceptional cases of very long penises. The late pornographic actor John Holmes and the living model "Long Dong Silver" are cases in point, though the latter's pictures are so extraordinary that some form of trick photography has been suspected. In John Holmes's case, homosexual men rather then heterosexual women were excited by his mighty organ. Hence his transition to making homosexual films, from which he was unfortunate enough to contract AIDS.

Penis envy, then, is something men feel, and feel with reference to other men. And, like women wanting big breasts, they are the victims of a cultural fetish. Not all societies think a large penis is attractive. The ancient Greeks thought it vulgar and hideous. Their idealized nude statues invariably show men with quite small penises. Slaves, clowns and satyrs in Greek comedies were fitted with extravagant leather phalli denoting their ludicrously low status. The men walking around with huge uncontrollable erections as a result of the women's sex strike in Aristophanes' Lysistrata are risible and unattractive.

Cosmetic Penis Enlargement

Just as there can be abnormally large penises, so there is a rare condition, "micropenis", in which the organ is as small as a little finger. Men cursed with this condition need to be very skilful to satisfy women sexually, and may find that many women miss a certain pleasure from penetration in any case. Quite properly and understandably, plastic surgery does what it can to assist men suffering mental distress or sexual problems from micropenis, and uses grafts or fat implants to try and remedy the problem. For nearly fifty years, reputable urologists and plastic surgeons have done what they can to help men with truly abnormally small penises.

True impotence – an absolute inability to achieve or sustain an erection – is another condition for which a prosthetic insert in the penis may be indicated as a treatment.

But it is only in the last few years that purely cosmetic penile enhancement has been marketed. /the intention is to enlarge a penis to gratify its owner when he looks at himself in a mirror, or wonders about fellow-sportsmen admiring his assets in the locker-room or shower. There is no market for having unattractively long penises shortened. Penis-enlargement patients themselves unanimously admit that they are not under pressure from wives or girlfriends to maximize their manhood. It seems to be very much a male hang-up with regard to other males.

The Method

Modern penile-lengthening draws on the fact that about a third of the length of the penis is hidden inside the body. The surgeon opens the pubis to expose this hidden root, then severs the suspensory ligaments that hold the penis upright during erection. This frees the organ so that the submerged third can be extruded from the pelvis and stitched into a more prominent position, often with a flap of skin from the pubic area brought round to cover the wound. Some doctors hang weights from the penis for a time to encourage a lengthened position.

The usual effective result is that about an inch more penile length can be observed in the flaccid condition. There is no change in the erect length, but the severed ligaments mean that the angle of erection slips down by about 15°, which can make it look more prominent.

Penile girth may be increased by grafts of tissue from the buttocks, or, increasingly, by insertions of fat extracted from the abdomen for liposculpture. The problem with inserted fat is that up to 70% of it can be fairly quickly absorbed back into surrounding areas of the body, and top-up operations may be necessary. The general enhancement is likely to be about an additional inch in circumference: something which might make a small difference (for either better or worse) to a sex partner's penetrative pleasure.

In the case of either lengthening or widening, the penis will be too sore for intercourse for at least a month. If both are carried out at the same time the period of post-operative celibacy is likely to extend to nine months.

Dr Long and Dr Dick

It should, perhaps, come as no surprise that modern penile lengthening started in China. The old Chinese erotic novel "The Before-Midnight Scholar" opens with its hero giving himself a horrifying enhancement by inserting a quartered dog's penis into four deep slits cut along the shaft of his own organ.

"We're just at the beginning of what I think is going to be a very popular surgery."

DR BRIAN NOVACK

The pioneer of genuine penis lengthening was the inventive modern Chinese surgeon, Dr Long Dau-Chou. Dr Long has been in the business of penis enlargement since 1984, and devised the process of extruding more of the root in 1992.

Dr Brian Novack, a Beverley Hills plastic surgeon, went to China to work with him a year later and brought the process back to America. A Hollywood urologist, Dr Melvyn Rosenstein, went into partnership with marketing man Ed Tilden. An advertising campaign carried the ideal of the bigger and better penis all over America. Rosenstein had inserted penis implants professionally since his student days in 1977.

Rosenstein was operating up to 14 times a day at anything from £4,000 a time. Before long he was carrying out an estimated 150 penis enlargements a month and had completed 2,000 – 70% of all those in America. He was nicknamed "Dr Dick" in the press and reputed to be a millionaire, and suing Tilden for misrepresentative advertising.

Perhaps equally importantly to Rosenstein, he also fell out with Tilden over advertising and who had the right to their would-be lucrative client list a dispute that led to litigation between them.

Tilden had claimed in advertisements "Most Patients WILL Double in Size...DREAMS DO COME TRUE." This was the language of the quack and Rosenstein did not like what he saw as an exaggeration of the operation's benefits.

It dragged penile enlargement surgery down to the level of the glass cylinder and vacuum pump advertised in girlie magazines aimed at men who hoped that the sensation of the penises expanding to fill the vacuum in the cylinder would mean a permanent enlargement.

Penile enlargement attracted critical comments from various individuals within the medical profession.

What They Said

"You can't make an erect penis longer than it is. You can only create the illusion of length through these techniques. If you want a longer penis you can save yourself $4,000 by putting it on a wooden block and slamming it with a hammer."

DR D. S. DANOFF, BEVERLY HILLS UROLOGIST

"For the most part, nobody in their right mind would support it."

DR F. GRAZEN, CALIFORNIA BOARD-CERTIFIED PLASTIC SURGEON

"You're cutting a ligament that's very near important blood vessels and nerves. This is a potential danger. And the vast majority who have the surgery are very unsatisfied because their expectations are not met by the results. I would not do it without psychiatric clearance. There may be adverse psychological reactions after the operation."

DR E. D. WHITEHEAD, PROFESSOR OF UROLOGY, MT SINAI, N.Y.

"It must be remembered that this operation originated in China, where the average Chinese man's genitals are smaller than the average British man's. Therefore post-operative expectations are lower in China and higher here."

DR TONY ERIAN, GUY'S HOSPITAL

"The emotional and psychological implications of the perceived abnormality of the penis go far beyond the ground that other types of cosmetic surgery tread on. If your ears don't match, there may be a good reason for surgery. But for something lurking out of sight most of the time, who are they doing it for? These men need psychotherapy, not surgery."

DR P. NADIG, PROFESSOR OF UROLOGICAL SURGERY, UNIVERSITY OF TEXAS

"It's not the panacea patients imagine and not all doctors have skills necessary to provide optimal results."

GARY GRIFFIN, PALM SPRINGS AUTHOR AND PUBLISHER OF NEWSLETTER ON SURGERY

"The operation is debatable."

DR CLIVE GINGELL, CONSULTANT UROLOGIST, SOUTHMEAD HOSPITAL,
BRISTOL

"... bizarre...."

DAVID CONGDON MP, HOUSE OF COMMONS SELECT COMMITTEE ON
HEALTH

PENILE ENLARGEMENTS

The Drawbacks

Despite advertising claims, length is unlikely to increase more than about
an inch, and that is only when the penis is flaccid. Increased girth is
extremely likely to be reabsorbed rapidly, requiring another operation

The glans cannot be enlarged in any case. Circumcision may be essential
to avoid infective inflammation or if the foreskin cannot contain temporary post-operative swelling. Pubic hair is likely to grow on the newly
exposed base of the shaft, requiring regular shaving.

The post-operative recovery period is liable to be accompanied by soreness, scabs, scars, problematic skin flaps and gross swelling. One patient
who underwent lengthening and widening at the same time told The
Guardian that his penis swelled to the size of a coke can, keeping him
housebound for three weeks because he couldn't get into his underpants.
He concluded:

*"The pain and swelling were awful. It isn't something I would repeat.
Although my penis is longer when flaccid by two inches, I've noticed no
change in erect length. The doctors keep saying I'll notice new erectile*

length at nine months, but I'm not convinced. Apart from the blistering and some scarring, I feel that the widening part of the operation went better, even though it's not as thick as I thought it would be."

This patient had been enticed by advertising which promised normal sex within three weeks. In fact it was out of the question for nine months.

Some patients have suffered from impotence and permanently impaired sexual performance after the operation. Dr Erian of Guy's Hospital believes that it should never be undertaken by a urologist or plastic surgeon alone: team backup from a neurologist and a psychiatrist is essential for the patient's well-being. And that's just in cases where the operation has proved satisfactory!

Satisfied Customers

Like women with enhanced breasts, men who are satisfied with their enlarged penises seem very satisfied indeed.

One of the most ecstatic of Dr Rosenstein's satisfied customers unusually claims that his longer genital organ has proved itself to be instantly exciting to women: "They look at me," he claims, "and think, 'wow! where did that come from? It's like the Loch Ness monster!"

As anecdotal proof of his visual aphrodisiac appeal he tells how he was "fooling around" with a girl after his operation, and she unbuttoned his pants, only to turn white and jump back as his mighty member fell out. According to this satisfied customer her immediate reaction was, "No way is that going inside me!" But then she wondered whether it was real... and one thing led to another!

It is probably relevant that Dr Rosenstein has claimed that his operation adds two inches to flaccid length, and an indeterminate "some" difference to an erection, rather than the one flaccid inch which other doctors have achieved. One can't imagine that the first two Britons to have the operation on the National Health would have evoked gasps from any woman less sheltered than a Victorian maiden. Each had a flaccid two-inch penis – not as small as some men who feel no need for enhancement, as plastic surgeon Brian Tanner pointed out. But they felt themselves to be small – Tanner's addition of one inch to one man and half an inch to the other made them feel much happier with themselves. A San Fernando Valley fireman was very positive about his operation. "It's made a huge difference in my whole overall attitude. I feel so confident now," he said. "I'm still getting used to it. But I definitely feel better about myself. It's an internal thing."

A patient of Dr Novack's in his mid-thirties had circumference and length increased by about an inch apiece. Having been warned, he was not surprised when his extra inch of girth was largely reabsorbed after the $5,000 operation. he went back for more fat insertion, and was satisfied that this time it "took better," cheerfully contemplating going back for a third helping: "I'm more comfortable both outside the house and inside the bedroom," he commented. "It does wonders for your mind. Size matters. I know it sounds ridiculous, but we're men, and that's all there is to it."

Melvyn Rosenstein would not be at all surprised by the accounts given by these men. The operation is, he agrees, a matter of improving self-image – for some its mental worth is equivalent to ten years expensive psychiatric treatment.

Doubtful Cases

A 43-year-old Mauritian who underwent the operation in 1993 had a different agenda. He was quite explicitly trying to deal with both childhood traumas and mild culture shock. His wife was perfectly satisfied with his five-inch erection and the couple had three children. However, the man remembered his family teasing him when he was a boy. A female relative had also interfered with him sexually. On coming to England at the age of 21 he found himself unable to approach women with any confidence. His marriage had been arranged, and he really had rather a lot of problems to be cleared up by an extra inch of flaccid penis.

He was pleased with his new appearance, but eight months after the operation he had not returned to satisfactory relations. He lost both interest and his erection quickly after penetrating his wife. If he ejaculated, he found that he suffered "painful muscle spasms" at the base of the glans.

Miami urologist Harold M. Reed reports that of the five hundred penis enlargements he has carried out, only two patients found their erections were inhibited and one suffered a serious nerve injury.

The worst victim of surgical penile disaster was, however, a patient of Dr Rosenstein.

Trauma Under the Knife

Of the six patients who started malpractice suits against Dr Rosenstein, charges against which he denies liability, 34-year-old Ronald Nance, seems to have undergone the greatest suffering. Television viewers in England and America watched in horror as the big builder dissolved into tears relating his appalling experiences. Nance wasn't particularly under-endowed to any practical purposes. But being a large man he felt that his averagely sized genitals looked disproportionately small. He accepted Dr Rosenstein's salesman's pitch, and flew from San Jose to Los Angeles for the one-day surgery that would increase his length and girth.

At home that night he was in agony, unable to even urinate through his swollen penis. Dr Rosenstein booked a return appointment to make all well. But with the first incision, Nance says, "all the fat that they had added to my shaft spewed all over him and he had to cut the rest of the skin off."

It took a double row of stitches to suture the wound, but they came out when Nance got home. Dr Rosenstein allegedly recommended putting a Band-Aid over it! Unsurprisingly, this didn't hold everything in – Nance was back on the surgeon's table another three times, ultimately having his penis stapled together.

When the wound finally healed, Nance found that most of his shaft had disappeared back up into his abdomen, and his penis was now shorter than it had been to begin with. It was covered with scars and, he said, "my circumcision looks like a tyre blow-out."

His life was in ruins. He was impotent, and could only get an erection by injecting testosterone into his penis. He even asked a doctor to cut his penis off, it distressed him so much. His girlfriend, who had begged him not to have the operation, had left him. His savings were gone. And he still owed Dr Rosenstein £13,000.

Dr Rosenstein is a skilled board-certified urologist with, it is said, 2,000 penile enlargements to his credit. However, for the very reasons that men may seek his operation, a one-in-2,000 failure rate may seem just too high to risk ending up like Ronald Nance.

LIPOSUCTION

Devised by a French doctor Gerard Illouz, this technique looked as if it would be the answer to a "fatty's" prayer. Instead of the struggle with diets and exercise – and the consequent hunger, fatigue and mental distraction – liposuction promised to take the fat away, just like that, all in one go, quickly and cleanly under anaesthesia on the surgeon's table.

Fat for Scrap

"You can go to any state fair and see that there's another 40 million tons out there ready to be sucked out."

Where Does It Go?

"Some people simply left it out in the alley for the garbage collectors, and some tried to flush it down the toilet."

PETER VOGT, PLASTIC SURGEON

But the patient may still be thoroughly dissatisfied with the resulting appearance. If the tunnels left by the excised fat do not fill in smoothly, the body surface may be ridged or pitted, rather like an orange skin, or thick crepe soles on men's summer shoes. It may also exhibit an unsightly lump or dip where too much fat has come out in a vast globule, or a piece has stayed in place.

If the skin was too old or stretched to recover full elasticity there is the risk that it may hang baggily, or show lines like post-natal stretch marks. In some cases of abdominal liposuction, it may seem to the patient that the baggy skin has left an undiminished waist-line. Unfortunately, the new abdomen, unlike the previous smooth, plump tummy, can no longer be decorously displayed in a two-piece swimsuit or over bathing trunks. It hangs flaccid and ugly over the belt, like a beer belly on a geriatric dinosaur!

A major drawback in all such surgery is that repair operations may leave scars, and don't always succeed in creating the desired form. All of which is a very poor return for the inevitable intense pain which follows the operation immediately, not to mention the longer period during which heavy bruising has to subside. It may be that il faut souffrir pour etre belle, but there's no satisfaction in enduring the suffering without enjoying the beauty.

"Anyone with an M.D. can advertise himself as an expert in liposuction."

DR EUGENE COURTISS, PLASTIC SURGEON

Early Liposuction: Early Problems

The majority of candidates for liposuction when it was first introduced to America were women. More of them wanted fat taken off their hips and thighs than off their middles.

"The typical candidate for liposuction," a surgeon remarked, "is fat, forty-ish and feminine." However, gradually over the decade men began to take to the operation. They were more interested in losing spare tyres, love handles and incipient beer bellies.

By 1988 a US Senate Committee heard that eleven deaths had been reported as a direct result of liposuction. As a tiny 0.1% of all operations this would have been well within the realms of "acceptable risk" had this been a serious life-saving procedure. But these deaths had occurred to otherwise healthy patients, which raised a small question about the technique.

A gynaecologist based in Houston, Texas caused a great deal of anxiety. He had become a liposuctionist after taking a weekend course sponsored by the American Society of Liposuctionists. When two of his patients died from infections developed after their liposuctions, he was accused of killing them and his medical licence was revoked. Two years later his whereabouts was unknown, and other liposuctionists protested, feeling that his case had been blown up out of all proportion.

But those weekend courses worried trained plastic surgeons. Said San Francisco surgeon Mark Gorney. "Why would we want an individual to be trained for five years in general surgery, or seven years in plastic surgery, if we could take a weekend quickie course?"

Failures

In one sense liposuction never fails, in that it always removes a quantity of fat. Since the body has a finite number of fat cells which do not increase we can only grow fatter by enlargement of our existing cells. A spare tyre that has been liposucked away will not return. You don't have to stay on your diet to keep your new figure.

"Liposuction has revolutionized facial sculpture"

DR MICHELLE COPELAND, MT. SINAI, NY

"Once liposuction removes these cells, they don't return."

DR FODOR, SANTA MONICA, CA

"This is absolutely not a treatment for obesity."

DR GREGORY HETTER, LAS VEGAS

"Further complications and overuse of suction lipectomy are foreseen."

AMERICAN SOCIETY OF PLASTIC AND RECONSTRUCTIVE SURGERY

But the patient may still be thoroughly dissatisfied with the resulting appearance. If the tunnels left by the excised fat do not fill in smoothly, the body surface may be ridged or pitted, rather like an orange skin, or thick crepe soles on men's summer shoes. It may also exhibit an unsightly lump or dip where too much fat has come out in a vast globule, or a piece has stayed in place.

If the skin was too old or stretched to recover full elasticity there is the risk that it may hang baggily, or show lines like post-natal stretch marks. In some cases of abdominal liposuction, it may seem to the patient that the baggy skin has left an undiminished waist-line. Unfortunately, the new abdomen, unlike the previous smooth, plump tummy, can no longer be decorously displayed in a two-piece swimsuit or over bathing trunks. It hangs flaccid and ugly over the belt, like a beer belly on a geriatric dinosaur!

A major drawback in all such surgery is that repair operations may leave scars, and don't always succeed in creating the desired form. All of which is a very poor return for the inevitable intense pain which follows the operation immediately, not to mention the longer period during which heavy bruising has to subside. It may be that il faut souffrir pour etre belle, but there's no satisfaction in enduring the suffering without enjoying the beauty.

Thigh Problems

Liposucked thighs can give their owners complete satisfaction. Tiny hair-stylist Jennie Venner of Virginia Beach, Virginia had dieted down to a miniscule 6 stone 8 pounds, but could not get rid of her immense saddle-bag thighs and hips. Heavy thighs ran in her family, but, "Mine were like battleships!" she complained.

Liposuction took 4 pounds off the offending area, and after two days in bed with her legs up, Jennie was able to return to work. Thereafter she was entirely delighted with a femural appearance which did not deteriorate even when she gained nearly three stone during pregnancy.

Patricia Cockayne was not so lucky. A fitness enthusiast. she swam daily and exercised regularly in her local gymnasium and at a weekly aerobics class. However, no matter how much she worked out she still couldn't do anything about her heavy flaccid inner thighs. The flapping flesh on her firm well-tuned body annoyed her, and she investigated what could be done about it. When she consulted a private clinic, their impressive recommendation of the benefits of liposuction persuaded her to have her waist and hips slimmed down. The waist and hips gave her no problems. The thighs did. When the bandages were removed, she found them lumpy. They were asymmetrical, and she had no doubt she had looked better before the fat was removed. The clinic agreed, giving her a repair operation to level off the lumps. It failed. A third operation left her apple-sized lumps surrounded by folds of hanging skin. She evidently had some quite intransigent lumps of fat that just wouldn't be sucked out, so the surgeon offered to use the knife and "lift" her thighs, trimming, stretching and re-stitching the loose skin.

The operation left large marks with huge stitches in her groin. The wounds became infected and suppurated. When the stitches were removed, the wounds broke open again. Patricia was finally left with heavy scarring which may well be with her for life. Her private life was devastated, because she was too embarrassed to make love. Her social live suffered because she felt she couldn't face going out. Flaccid inner thighs would have been better to say the least of it.

Irene Taylor, on the other hand, was actually given flaccid thighs by liposuction. In her mid-forties she decided to do something about the heavy thighs she felt were disfiguring, and started saving for the operation. It took her six years to put aside the money, but increased happiness with her own body would have made it worth it.

Like most liposuction patients, she went for treatment never doubting that the doctors knew what they were doing – the process sounded simple.

Alas, when she saw the results she was horrified. In taking out the fat, liposuction took out all the elasticity and resilience from her thighs. It seemed to Irene they were as big as ever before, only now they drooped in saggy bags instead of standing out in puffy jodhpurs. Eileen fell into depression. Like many depressives, she started over-eating for consolation. She put on nearly 20 pounds, and her baggy thighs ballooned again. Where they had formerly been 18 inches in diameter, they grew to nearly two foot across. So much for liposuction as a visual reducer in Irene's case.

Why the Failures?

Plastic surgeon Peter Vogt of Minneapolis offered a possible explanation to USA Today for the reasons these disaster cases sometimes happen. Fat, he pointed out, is not evenly distributed throughout the body. It is, for example, obvious that we all tend to put on weight in different places. Some of us find that an extra cream bun makes the waistband tighter. Other put on in fatter faces and double chins. An internationally famous Czech model has suggested that drinking lager gives her larger breasts instead of a beer belly. The sad fact is that some people can't pig out without paying for it in a broader beam.

When the surplus fat cells have been sucked out, Vogt suggests, extra calories looking for cells to enlarge have to go where they find them remaining. This could presumably lead to cases of localized enlargement if fat remained in the liposucked area, as well as the heavier ankles, chins and arms Vogt proposed.

The American lipoplasty society, however, has categorically denied the myth that liposuction encourages larger breasts. And on this we should probably trust them, since breast enlargement as a side-effect would be more likely to win sales than lose them.

Liposucked Tummy Troubles

Fat pulled out from the waist and neck is likely to leave more shock and pain than fat extracted from hips and thighs.

Office manager Sally Aveni of Austin, Texas was quite satisfied with the removal of her double chin and the saggy tummy she picked up after child-birth. But she had not been prepared for the degree of post-operative pain she experienced. Mrs Aveni's pain lasted a week – the bruising took three months to disappear.

"It was like I got hit with a Mack truck. My whole torso got black and blue. So did my face, around the chin."

SALLY AVENI

In 1992, Mr and Mrs Rajeev Syal decided to have their waistlines reduced by liposuction. 38-year-old Mrs Syal was the more enthusiastic of the two. They had three children, and she found that no matter how much she exercised and dieted, she couldn't keep her tummy down. When she looked into possible treatments, liposuction seemed the most feasible. As a bonus, the surgeon she consulted pointed out that her double chin could be removed at the same time.

The operation was carried out in June. Mrs Syal was surprised by the post-operative pain and discomfort which made sleeping impossible and eating difficult. The feeling of puffiness in her chin made her doubt that there was any real reduction there. But it was her liposucked waistline that caused her most distress. Three months after the operation, with her bruises faded for nine weeks, Mrs Syal complained that her skin had lost all its elasticity and she just hadn't regained a slimmer shape at all. "If I hold my stomach in it looks wrinkly. If I push it out, it looks just as it did before," she complained. When people complimented her husband on his new shape nobody seemed to notice that she had also slimmed down. The few friends to whom she showed the operation site were horrified. She had no optimism about ever wearing a bikini again.

Although Mr Syal assured her that he thought she looked very nice after the operation, nothing could alter the fact that while he was very contented with his new waist, she hated hers. Mr Syal may have added insult to injury when he remarked complacently, "Now, when I put my swimming trunks on, if there is some attractive girl looking at me from the other side of the pool, I won't think she is looking at my flab but at my figure."

Pain followed by numbness accompanied by no apparent change in her figure – these are the complaints of a 50-year-old patient who prefers to be known as just Barbara. Small at 5 foot 2 inches and weighing just eight-and-a-half stone, she was dissatisfied with her sagging breasts and tummy.

Barbara found a real cowboy clinic. Instead of a local or general anaesthetic they gave her an injection of the tranquillizer Valium. When she screamed with pain as the cannula was forced into her abdomen, the surgeon said calmly, "Top her up with more Valium." Barbara longed to pass out during the two hours of frightful pain that constituted her operation. When the clinic discharged her they told her to take out her own stitches the following week!

A year later, Barbara's figure seemed completely unchanged to her, and she had no feeling in the skin below the navel.

£2,500 had been spent in doing harm rather than good.

From Suction to Sculpture

In 1990, Dr Marco Gasparotti travelled from Italy to the USA to introduce his new technique of liposculpture. Predictably, it caught on with all the speed and acclaim of Dr Illiouz's liposuction.

Liposculpture, as the name suggests, puts the extracted fat back to use in the body, smoothing out ridges and wrinkles, or remoulding areas that are not to the patient's satisfaction. To ensure the use of mouldable fat it employs weaker suction in a light cannula operating very closely under the skin. This works more favourably with older patients whose skin has lost its elasticity. It enables surgeons to do something really effective about cellulite: the ugly deposit of subcutaneous cells on the thighs which produce a puffy dimpled appearance and are quite impervious to dieting and exercise.

The extracted fat is purified of oils and blood (a lot of which is always lost in liposuction), and can then be softened and injected in places where a smooth surface is wanted. The process has been said by one of its practitioners to have "transformed facial surgery". At the same time, however, its use use for breast augmentation was seen by Beverly Hills plastic surgeon Mel Bircoli as essentially nothing new. He had been using grafted fat implants since 1979, and could not see why the new process of injection rather than grafting was stirring up so much anxiety and protest.

Objections

The underlying objections to liposculpture and liposuction were undoubtedly some of the usual Puritan fears of vanity and idolization of the physical rather than the spiritual body. It was possible to make a rather underhand reference to Dr Illiouz's specialization prior to his invention of liposuction. He had realized the strength and efficacy of vacuum suction through the legal practice of abortion.

There could be an undercurrent of whispering that these fat extracting and moulding techniques had been invented by continental foreigners rather than honest American doctors. But this would not cut much ice with the sophisticated medical profession.

The objection most commonly voiced was that the technique was non-lasting: Dr Gasparotti's injected fat was more likely to dissipate through the body than Dr Bircoli's solid fat grafts. So the effects of expensive liposculpture might last as little as six months.

And the great complaint was the usual complaint. Cowboy cosmetic surgeons sculpted cosmetic disasters.

Liposculpture Problems

"We see many legs full of lumps, bumps, dents and craters after liposuction because some doctors have not been properly trained in this procedure."

So said a spokesman for the National Hospital of Aesthetic Plastic Surgery in Bromsgrove, Worcestershire. The hospital was established by John Terry and his wife Christina in 1978, after twelve years working with plastic surgery administration, largely in hair transplants, had disillusioned John with what he calls "this stinking, deceitful industry."

The Bromsgrove Hospital quickly found that its work followed a familiar statistic. A quarter of their patients needed remedial work as a direct consequence of previous plastic surgical disasters.

Just how bad a failed liposculpture can be was revealed to television viewers in 1996, when 49-year-old Diana Ashton gave The Cook Report an account of her remoulded legs. To begin with, she suffered the all-too-familiar problem of inadequate anaesthetization at the private cosmetic clinic. She was conscious and in pain throughout the operation. When the operation was over, she was simply left seated in a wicker chair to recover.

When she stood up, blood and matter started seeping from 12 holes in her thighs. The clinic plugged them, and bandaged over the plugs so heavily that she could not bend forward. When the bandages came off they revealed asymmetrical twisted thighs and a lump on the knee. Far from having paid for lovelier legs, Ms Ashton had paid for the necessity to wear trousers all the time.

Janet Baker, a teacher from Hampshire, suffered even more because she opted to have a larger area moulded. She paid for stomach, hips and thighs to be resculpted. The "clinic" whose advertisement she answered turned out to be a small terraced house. Liposculpture promises as a convenient advantage that it will be one-day in-and-out surgery, usually under a local anaesthetic. One hour after her operation was over, 60-year-old Ms Baker was packed into a taxi and sent on a seventy mile journey home without the supportive facilities of a proper ambulance.

As soon as she got indoors, she collapsed. An incision on her hip had not been stitched properly. She lost about a quart of blood and passed out. "There was blood all over the kitchen floor," she recalled.

Post-operative trauma wasn't the worst of it. When she looked at the final result she was appalled. "The tops of my legs look like screwed-up paper bags," she said, "and my stomach is lopsided because the surgeon took more off one side than the other."

At least Ms Baker's life wasn't at risk. Kamaljit Marwah went to another clinic in the same private chain for liposculpture and had to be given subsequent emergency treatment in a National Health Service Hospital. It took seven operations and five bedridden weeks to save her life.

Mrs Marwah, a mother of three from the Midlands, had gone to the north for her liposculpture. Nearly four litres of fat were removed, after which she turned blue and had to be taken to a West Midlands hospital for emergency treatment. Her skin was infected, and gangrene set in. Fazel Fatah, her NHS surgeon, stated, "It's quite possible she would have died had I not seen her in time."

"It's Not Our Fault!"

The chain of clinics responsible for Ms Baker's and Mrs Marwah's liposculpture was the same one which had undertaken Ms Trusler's and Ms Zappone's tummy tucks. They cannot be castigated as habitually lethal, since a spokesman told The Cook Report that of their 25,000 patients only one has ever died.

Spokespeople also claimed that the clinics were not at fault over Ms Baker and Mrs Marwah. Ms Baker, the clinic manager said, had not been given enough time to recover. And saline fluid loss – although not blood – was normal. Perhaps the world was to infer that Ms Baker took herself away for her 70-mile taxi journey earlier than the clinic would have preferred.

As far as the press was concerned, the clinics' high pressure sales claims were not supported by adequate staff or facilities, and could easily result in patients being accepted for inappropriate treatment and suffering cosmetic disasters rather than improvement.

To test reputability of the chain's sales techniques, the Sunday Times sent a reporter who was already underweight to pose as a client for fat-reducing liposuction. Far from instantly declining the reporter's custom, the clinic's sales staff offered an assurance that there would be no need for an overnight stay after the operation: up to seven litres of fat could be removed in normal day surgery. Indeed, patients would only be held overnight if they had more than ten litres removed.

Plastic surgeons attached to reputable hospitals were horrified. Four litres is seen as the maximum that can safely be drawn. Anything above that amount is seen as immediately dangerous, and would require an overnight stay. It is unlikely that even a fee-hungry private clinic would be mad enough to extract ten litres. But the unqualified, under-informed calibre of sales staff was certainly highly alarming.

Former sales representatives from another chain of private plastic surgery clinics admitted to the Central Weekend TV programme "Live" that they had no personal medical experience and had been given none by the company. Their training had largely consisted of learning ways to frighten potential customers into thing their appearance demanded treatment.

The Surgical Advisory Service in London offers information to potential patients about cosmetic surgery. In 1995 it reported that it was receiving five complaints a day about liposculpture. The Cosmetic Surgery Network, an aid group for victims of botched operations, has taken on scores of cases after liposuction. Anne Clwyd MP, determined to protect women against the exploitation of their anxiety about their appearance, noted that the chains of instant cosmetic clinics were evidence of yet another free market enterprise in need of state interventionist regulation and licensing.

Bans and Rumours of Bans

1991 saw a new director appointed to America's Food and Drugs Administration. David A. Knessler quickly proved himself so zealous in enforcing bans that the was nicknamed "Eliot Knessler" in memory of the "untouchable" federal agent who harrassed Al Capone's Chicago mob during prohibition.

Knessler placed an outright ban on the medical use of liquid silicone, the industrial lubricant that surgeons were starting to implant be injection to smooth out wrinkles and acne pits. He approved the use of collagen for in-filling acne scars, but he warned that there was no data to show that it was either safe or effective in lip-plumping.

The sale of collagen was not prohibited, but the uses for which it was "approved" were greatly restricted.

As an interesting aside, British cosmetic practitioners sometimes observe with enthusiasm that the protein used in collagen is always prepared from good American or Argentinian beeves. There is no risk, in other words, of contaminating the lips or wrinkles with BSE or "Mad Cow Disease" from Britain's infected herd.

Knessler showed an interest in the promotion of a new chemical skin cream, Retin-A, manufactured by Johnson and Johnson which was derma-tologically approved as a treatment for both acne and the wrinkling caused by excessive sunbathing.

Knessler did not object to the approved use of the new product to treat the relatively short-term condition of acne. He did question its extension to ongoing use on wrinkles, noting that it was itself a photosynthesizer (it absorbed sunlight to promote chemical changes) which might prove car-cinogenous if used over a long period. The Department of Justice was asked to look into the matter, which seemed the more urgent as sunlight itself was by then known to be a major factor in producing carcinomas.

Altogether the climate seemed to have now become one of suspicion as far as new "wonder treatments" were concerned.

Advertising Controls

America's Federal Trade Commission took issue with the misleading advertising used by American cosmetic surgeons. George S. Miler's BelAge Plastic Surgery Center was ordered to withdraw a brochure which claimed that breast implants don't interfere with mammography, and breast-lifting surgery "leaves minimal, barely visible scars."

Donald S. Chevits, a former president of the National Capital Society of Plastic Surgeons described these as "blatant misstatements." Silicone gel implants often obscured tissues, making cancerous growths difficult to detect. Scarring after breast-lifts could be considerable, and patients should be so informed.

BelAge, advertising their ear-pinning operation, said: "Recovery is quick and painless. Many patients require no pain medication and are back to their normal schedule with 'normal' ears in five days."

The rewrite demanded by the FTC painted a rather different picture:

> *"After surgery the ears are covered with a dressing. Usually any soreness or discomfort can be controlled by medication. Within a couple of days the dressing is taken off though some may wear a light head dressing during sleep for a few weeks."*

It was all evidence that the authorities realized that marketing cosmetic surgery must be brought under responsible government interventionist control.

The Case of Dr Elam

One of America's best-known cosmetic surgeons was Dr Michael Elam, whose work in transforming the 72-year-old Phyllis Diller had been trumpeted across the nation by his grateful patient. So it was a considerable shock when in 1990 two disgruntled patients – one of them a former "Mrs California" – charged Elam with fraud, and the California Medical Board stripped him of his licence to practice.

According to the board, Elam had doctored medical records to obtain fraudulent insurance claims for the two patients. Administrative Law Judge Rosalynn Chapman was extremely severe in handing down judgement, branding Elam as dishonest and saying he had no compunction about lying under oath and showed no sorrow, remorse or contrition.

Elam fought back furiously. The charges, he claimed, were part of the ongoing attempt by board-certified plastic surgeons to put cosmetic surgeons out of business and take over all their patients. He pointed out that "Mrs California" had won her title after she had undergone his surgery, so that it really could not have been disfiguring. He intended to fight for his own rehabilitation and the proper recognition of the discipline of cosmetic surgery.

Cosmetic Surgery

The nub of the problem lies in the difficulty of ordering and administering that "discipline". Clearly, general practitioners who go to a single weekend course and instantly set up as full-time liposuctionists are probably a danger to the community. On the other hand, however, general surgeon Latimer-Sayer transferred himself quite satisfactorily to the discipline of cosmetic surgery, and was able to save Sue's nose after other surgeons had damaged it.

As secretary of the British Association of Cosmetic Surgeons, Mr Latimer-Sayer points out that he (and by implication his colleagues) will carry out an average of four face lifts a week. The plastic surgeons who would like them to be debarred from the work probably do no more than one such operation a month. But Mr Latimer-Sayer's organization is very tightly controlled – there are only 20 members, all of which are qualified surgeons.

Mr Latimer-Sayer in turn is concerned about the possibility of doctors with no plastic surgery training whatsoever setting up as cosmetic surgeons. He believes that "sleazy clinics" with unhygienic standards already exist and his association vets applications for membership very carefully.

Most informed medics agree that cosmetic surgery needs to be controlled by a proper inspectorate, codes of conduct and training. But in all countries where the problem is recognized it is immediately bedevilled by disputes as to which discipline should have the final say in licensing cosmetic surgeons – their work overlaps plastic surgery, dermatology, ENT specialization, and even urology.

It is possible that we have not yet heard the last of medical mistakes in this field.

DO DOCTORS KNOW WHAT THEY'RE DOING?

At first, of course, they didn't. They though life was sustained by four vital fluids, the "humours": blood, choler, bile and phlegm. The balance of these fluids in the body determined a person's temperament: sanguine, choleric, splenetic or phlegmatic. (In effect, cheerful, irascible, peevish or laid-back.) An excess of any one of the humours could cause emotional disturbance, and each was though to be somehow directly associated with separate organs in the body, influencing or determining the course of certain illnesses.

The only easily accessible humour was blood. So to alter the balance of the humours, physicians would sometimes order surgeons to bleed patients, otherwise they were more or less limited to offering prayers and incantations, herbs and simples, pills and potions (which might be made from exotic but medically useless components like mandrake root or the dust of Egyptian mummies).

The only reason they were not instantly exposed as incompetent frauds was the "placebo effect". Certain illnesses are so much under the influence of the mind that the very belief that they are being treated leads to palpable improvement. Placebo – a Latin word which may be translated "I will please you" – is the name for a pill or potion that is known to have no real medicinal properties, but which is nevertheless given to the patient to satisfy him that something is being done. Not surprisingly, if people can sometimes feel instantly better after swalling a sugar pill or a little sweetened coloured water, they must equally have felt themselves improved occasionally after forcing down a teaspoonful of mummia.

MEDICINE PROGRESSES

From the sixteenth century onward, medical matters improved. Anatomists began to learn what the human interior was really like. The circulation of blood was discovered, and gradually the proper functions of the mysterious organs were established.

With an improved understanding of anatomy and the general growth of scientific knowledge, new therapies were put to the test. Some of them, like electric shocks or various forms of immersion in hot or cold water, achieved little or nothing. Some, however, like improved ways of measuring body temperature, pointed the way to the future.

It would in general seem unreasonable to criticise doctors for not knowing what they were doing when the knowledge simply wasn't available to them. We may shudder at the physicians who tortured Charles II to death or mock at the best available medical opinion which strait-jacketed and whipped and agitated the unfortunate George III so that it was a wonder the porphyry which affected his brain didn't immediately turn to irreversible psychotic madness, like the poor lunatics in Bedlam whose derisory "treatment" could have done them nothing but harm.

Quite simply, the "mistakes" made by the medical practitioners of the day were part of an inaccurate world picture held by their whole society. The doctors whose ignorance and incompetence concern us the most come from times during and after the 19th century, when scientific method was understood; a number of genuine cures were available; yet still some medical men insisted on working from crazy intuitions; or failed to understand the power of new techniques they were introducing; or mishandled the perfectly effective cures and therapies available to them.

It didn't mean doctors could actually cure people at first. As late as the nineteenth century physicians invented the prescription "TLC" for the "tender loving care" which was often all that could really be offered to a sick person.

••

CELEBRITY SPOT

CHARLES II

On a Sunday night in 1685, the king fell ill. He was 55 years old, and had his doctors but known it, his problem was a kidney disease. Even if they had known and understood it, there was little effective they could have done. So instead, they did what they could.

They darkened his room. They drained off blood from his shoulders with cupping glasses. They scarified his flesh and tapped his veins for more blood. They cut off all his hair and put blisters on his scalp. The coated the soles of his feet with a plaster of pitch and pigeon dung. The blew hellebore up his nostrils to make him sneeze and "clear the humours from his brain". They poured antimony and sulphate of zinc down his throat to make him sick and clear his belly. They gave him strong purgatives and a succession of clysters to clear his bowels. They gave him Peruvian bark to bring down his temperature – almost the only thing they did which might have had a desirable and intended effect. They gave him juleps when he went into spasms and gargles when he complained of a sore throat. They gave him draughts for his thirst, tonics for his heart, and ale with a little thin broth for nourishment.

All this went on for five days. On Thursday night the king's mind was still clear. The following morning they drew another 12 ounces of his blood, and gave him tonics for his heart. He finally expired at noon.

His biographer, Sir Arthur Bryant, remarked, "Three things only they denied him, light, rest and privacy. Nothing else was left untried."

....

CELEBRITY SPOT

ROBERT BURNS

Though Burns had weakened his constitution by following the hard-drinking habits of the gentry who patronized him, he was only 37 when he died, and it seems fair to say his doctors killed him.

His final illness was rheumatic fever, brought on by falling asleep on the roadside after a drunken carouse. His heart was not in as good a condition as it had been, and he was suffering from depression. However, the treatment ordered by his doctors was lethal. He was told to stand up to his armpits in the sea every day. The Atlantic was bitterly cold, and it was a long daily wade to reach the requisite depth.

"It has eased my pains and I think has strengthened me," Burns reported optimistically. However his appetite remained extremely poor, and the regimen quickly killed him.

The Sexual Obsession

Delusions concerning sexual habits and related real or imaginary ills play a large part in the history of bad medicine. They have encouraged unnecessary and useless operations, imbecilic diagnoses of natural conditions as diseases, and general humbug and flummery, which is not surprising, given that the advance of the medico from incantatory leech to scientifically trained materialist occurred at the same time as the evangelical movement began to exert an immense influence on that Christian western culture from which exact science was emerging.

Doctors became scientists at a time when science was establishing itself in the teeth of orthodox hostility. "Was Darwin's grandfather an ape or an angel?", Bishop Wilberforce asked. Disraeli declared himself to be on the side of the angels, choosing intuitional physicking rather than experimentally proven medicine when he patronised a homeopathic doctor, and persuaded the royal family to do likewise.

Doctors depending on the custom of private patients to make a living could not afford to join in knockabout debates on the literal truth of the Bible or the efficacy of prayer as a healing agent. Most had to compromise. Sex was an area of proper medical business in which Christianity itself had suddenly become extremely uncompromising.

Jesus had very little to say about sex as such, being far more concerned with integrity and benevolence. But the founder-theologian of the worldwide church, St Paul, was deeply concerned about sexual morality. He insisted that, along with the prohibition of eating the blood of butchered animals, gentile Christians must adopt rigid Jewish prohibitions of fornication and homosexuality as well as adultery. In language that is often implicitly anti-feminine, St Paul's writings frequently return to his anxiety that Christians should not contaminate themselves with sex.

Still, parsons and clerks quite happily ate gravy for centuries without caring that St Paul would not have approved. The new scientific doctors of the nineteenth century were not asked to declare that blood pudding was unhealthy. Why were they under pressure to support the superstitious delusion that sex is somehow inherently bad?

Essentially it is because from the eleventh century celibacy was imposed on all the clergy. It was commonly held by mystics that complete detachment from all desires and pleasures leads to the highest spiritual experience. It was a commonplace of human experience that any but the greatest mystics denied food and sex will compulsively dream and fantasize about eating and lovemaking. Since most clerics were not mystics, Christian moral theology rapidly took on a lunatic fascination with restricting normal sexual activity, and only doses of hypocrisy kept society sane.

But the new evangelical Christians of the 19th century were determined to extirpate moral hypocrisy. Like the new scientists, they were determined to follow their truth wherever it might lead. They found themselves confronting unscriptural church traditions of supposed sexual morality, like the notion that masturbation is wicked. Unable to exert a healthy Chaucerian laugh at such bogeys, the evangelicals also solemnly tried to restrict all sexual activity to exclusive heterosexual monogamy, to be practised only after the couple had been firmly united by law. They could not possibly correct their mistake if they found themselves unexpectedly unhappy with each other as sexual partners.

Doctors might have told them they were asking the impossible. Doctors didn,t. For not all nineteenth century scientists abandoned their religion or adapted its dicta to the discoveries of science. Some tried to make their science conform to their religion. This was not good for medicine.

William Acton

William Acton was a urologist and venereologist, and a good one. He was kind and humane with his patients and invented an improved catheter which was less painful than its predecessors. He also wrote about prostitution and sexual problems, influencing the Victorian public significantly and providing the corpus of observations which is most often quoted as exemplifying Victorian sexual attitudes.

137

Acton was the son of a country clergyman and the only boy in a family of six girls. From this sheltered background the young medical student went to Paris, where he worked in a hospital treating venereally infected prostitutes.

Understandably he was appalled by the dirt, disease and distress he saw. Equally understandably he jumped to the wrong conclusions. He had, after all, no valid sexual experience himself. His good 19th century Christian upbringing assured him that nice girls didn't, and naughty men shouldn't. And so Acton associated the urban squalor and infection he witnessed with the practice of sexual activity.

He decided that prostitutes entered their profession because they suffered from excessive, unnatural and unhealhty sexual desires. He thought that these desires had led inevitably to the state of disease and squalor he treated humanely. He wished to spare all women such suffering, and so decided that sexual desire in females was certainly dangerous to themselves, and therefore unnatural. Thus arose the first and worst of the mad Victorian medico-sexual mistakes: the notion that women needed to be "cured" of their natural, God-given sexuality.

Unknown to his public, Acton's academic contemporaries did not really regard him as a scientist. He was a doctor: a healer. But he was not an experimenter. He did not tabulate his observations. He did not use the microscope or classify and sub-classify the conditions he described. He just wrote down what he reckoned he'd seen and what he'concluded about it. And the public accepted it as truth and believed the the doctor must be telling them the science of sex.

The academic scientists did not bother to tell the public they doubted Acton's conclusions. He probably didn't seem important enough. And certainly his obsessions, harmonising with evangelical aspirations, would provoke fiercer debate than their importance warranted. Serious scientists had enough on their plate in trying to show disraeli and Bishop Wilberforce that God's creative plan for mankind was a slow evolution, not a conjuring trick with some clay and a spare rib.

SPERMATORRHEA

While women and girls were the worst sufferers from Victorian medico-sexual perversions, men and boys were also under threat.

On no evidence whatsoever, but probably reinforced by parental prohibitions on masturbation and embarrassment at the possibility of his sisters seeing semen stains on sheets, Acton decided that excessive loss of semen was an illness called "spermatorrhea". It almost didn't matter how the excess was lost – by masturbation, by nocturnal emission or by too-frequent copulation, the excessive quantity lost was the main problem.

However, quality did make a difference. Masturbation always debilitated. Nocturnal emission was slightly less damaging. But occasional fornication was more dangerous than involuntary wet dreams, as it might encourage compulsive habitual lovemaking.

Marital intercourse, on the other hand, was compulsory, the excessive retention of semen by a married man being almost as dangerous as any loss of semen from his bachelor brother! Not that married men should go wild and enjoy a lot of sex. Once or twice a week was about right for their health: any more than that, and they too would suffer from "spermatorrhea."

Did Acton recognize the lunatic contradiction in his theary? The preposterous notion that a man will suffer debilitating loss of semen if he copulates the day before he marries, but must dutifully discharge the dangerous substance into his wife twice a week as soon as he has slipped the gold ring on her finger? Perhaps he did. Perhaps he silently thought that unmarried adult men ought to keep mistresses and, for their health's sake, make the necessary semen deposits in them. Perhaps he sadly thought the furtive hypocrisy that characterized so much Victorian sex was an unhappy scientific necessity. For men. They should not, of course, risk the frightening venereal diseases Acton automatically associated with prostitution. Nor – for he was, after all a good and well-intentioned man – should they cruelly encourage the daughters of the streets in that unnatural lust which would inevitably destroy their health.

But still more importantly, they should never, never indulge in the inherently spermatorrheic practice of masturbation. This would lead to debilitation, loss of concentration, spinal weaknesses, poor vision, palsy, drooling and ultimately madness. Almost the only thing that Acton failed to suggest was that spermatorrheics would grow hair on the palm of their hands.

Here an unzcientific use of observation mistook effect for cause. Because certain lunatics and imbeciles lack normal social inhibitions and may masturbate without restraint in front of other people, Acton and his followers in the medical community deduced that the practice of masturbation was the cause of their mental problems. The asylum records of the day frequently list "self abuse" as the cause of a mental patient's illness. And it could make you very mad indeed.

Dr Robert Anderson, the policeman heading the hunt for Jack the Ripper, believed that he knew who the Whitechapel murderer was, and that it was a scientific fact that the habit of masturbation had driven him to his frightful mania!

The long-term effect of this preposterous mumbo-jumbo was a general anxiety about all sexual activity which affected much psychology and most moralizing for 100 years. The short term effect was a good deal of cruelty to little boys, and the invention of frightening devices like spiked penis rings, intended to make erection so painful that masturbation would be inhibited or the sleeper aroused before an erotic dream could culminate.

But little boys were benignly treated at the hands of the sexual obsessives, compared with their sisters.

The Frightening Clitoris

No matter how sexually ignorant the general populace might have been, doctors were aware that the clitoris existed and was the seat of female erotic pleasure. So much the worse for the clitoris. In 1844, Dr Samuel Ashwell, a lecturer at Guy's Hospital, described its dangers.

Dr Ashwell, lecturing at Guy's, was an academic. Despite knowing Acton was no scientist, the scientists had caved in. Acton's dotty delusions about the unhealhtiness of natural sexuality were actually being taught to medical students.

140

The confusion of misplaced moral though with physical health was clear from the outset. Sexual passion was seen as undesirable in itself. Languid amatory behaviour was a dangerous symptom.

Most horrifying of all was the recommendation of torture. The meaningless old idea of bleeding recurred without even an attempt at scientific justification. Who can doubt that the effect of attaching leeches to the vulva, close to the clitoris, would bring sufficiently excruciating pain to eliminate sexual arousal instantly? As for painting the clitoris with dilute acid, the imaginary "efficacy" could only be prolonged soreness. Its desirability only apparent to someone who had madly accepted the notion that quasi-spermatorrheic sufferings would befall women who had the misfortune to experience sexual ardour.

Acton believed that the "healthy" woman probably experienced no passion at all. Ashwell's horrifying proposal went well beyond acton, in recommending that her "unhealthy" sisters be reduced to the same condition by physical brutality.

His word excision was frightening, even though he went on to show that he meant torture rather than mutilation. This comparatively benign state of affairs would not last, however. Within twenty years, mutilation was being practised to "cure" a non-existent diseased condition.

A Dangerous Organ

"Sometimes an enlarged clitoris is marked by exquisite sensibility of its mucous membrane.... It frequently gives rise to sexual passion, and subdues every feeling of modesty and delicacy.... The health soon becomes impaired, constant headaches... sometimes frequent attacks of hysteria. The mind loses all discipline, and the thoughts and expressions assume a sentimental and amatory character while compassion and pity are sought to be elicited from the attendants."

"If the growth is insensible, and relief is sought for its mechanical annoyance... the best way is to excise it.... Excision also is required when the growth is attended with undue sensibility. A few leeches may be applied

near the part.... Hydrocyanic acid in solution will be found very effica-
ceous as a lotion."

SAMUEL ASHWELL

Isaac Baker Brown

In 1866, surgeon Isaac Baker Brown published a book called "The Curability of Certain Forms of Insanity, Epilepsy, Catalepsy and Hysteria in Women". He was reporting on 48 cases under his care at the London Surgical Home, which he had founded in 1858 at Stanley Terrace, Notting Hill as The London Home for Surgical Diseases of Women.

Starting with only 20 beds, it had expanded to 34 by 1861, and its charitable status was unquestioned. The Prince and Princess of Wales even donated 25 guineas apiece to it.

Baker's principle (though not exclusive) treatment for the ailments he diagnosed was clitoridectomy. He simply cut off the clitoris with scissors. He carried out this operation especially on patients whom he suspected of masturbation – which he coyly called "peripheral clitoral excitation".

His conscious motives were sometimes the very best – he believed female masturbation was potentially lethal, and cited the case of a 19-year-old patient he claimed had died from the practice. She had come to the hospital suffering from acute headaches and episodes of blindness. Brown decided that these migraines were the result of masturbation, and didn't look for their real cause, which was evidently some serious problem: a brain tumour or recurring strokes.

For the poor girl was soon found dead by attendants. Brown observed that she exhibited "every evidence of having expired during a paroxysm of abnormal excitement." Let us hope she did – she might have died happy enjoying an orgasm. It seems highly unlikely, however, and there was not a shred of evidence to suggest that masturbation killed her. Brown had failed to investigate a patient's acute symptoms. He had used her death, consequent upon his own incompetence, as pseudo-proof that his theory was correct.

Other cases showed that Brown interpreted female distress at the excesses of the patriarchy as symptoms of illness to be cured by clitoridectomy. Five of his patients were referred to him by their husbands because they wanted to take advantage of the new law of 1857 permitting women to start proceedings for divorce. Brown cut off their clitorises and noted with satisfaction that they all proved docile and returned to their husbands after the operation!

The power of age as well as the power of men was reinforced by the threat and practice of mutilation. A 23-year-old woman was clitoridectomized because "she was disobedient to her mother's wishes". Her disobedience consisted of sending visiting cards to men she liked and spending much time in serious reading!

The Church Times approved of Brown's work and recommended the operation. The medical profession, by and large, did not. The British Medical Journal gave Brown's book a very hostile review. It also brought about the downfall of Brown's English career by reporting that he had placed a large advertisement for his clinic in the London and Provincial Gazette. The Obstetrical Society lost no time in expelling him. To their credit, some members objected to his surgical practices as much as his breach of professional ethics by advertising his services.

The Medical Society of London unanimously accepted his resignation. Brown went to America. Here his appalling ideas enjoyed more success than they had received in England. Clitoridectomy was practised in various parts of the United States, and received favourable mention in medical textbooks. A medical society in Chicago revered the operation as a general panacea for all ills, and produced a Journal of Orificial Surgery from 1890-1925. Halt's standard work, "Diseases of Infancy and Childhood" continued to express itself as "not averse to circumcision in girls or cauterisation of the clitoris" until 1936.

Whereafter, thank God, this evil practice has held no place in approved medicine.

Worst Case

Dr Eyer of St John's Hospital, Ohio proved tenaciously determined to prevent a little girl from masturbating. When she was brought to him, he cauterised her clitoris. As soon as she could, the child reverted to the practice. Dr Eyer brought in a surgeon to create a sort of intra-labial chastity shield. The child's injured clitoris was completely buried in silver sutures. Spiritedly, she went on masturbating through the impediment.

Dr Eyer resorted to the ultimate solution. He completely excised the offending organ. And the poor little thing apparently despaired of enjoying pleasurable genital sensation again.

A Modern Instance

In 1985 it became necessary to prohibit clitoridectomy by statute in England. The practice was not being carried out by ill-advised medicos, but Muslim women.

Although "femal circumcision" has no place in Islamic law and might well have struck the Prophet as absurd or indecent, the spread of Islam to Africa brought Muslims into contact with several tribes who practised various forms of genital mutilation, including labia stretching, male circumcision and clitoridectomy. Since Jewish influence already proposed male circumcision as a religious rite, some Muslims enthusiastically adoped the female "equivalent", which was carried out at puberty in some 30 countries, often without anaesthetics.

An estimated 10,000 Muslim girls were estimated to be at risk in Britain. Even though the British operation was likely to be carried out under proper surgical conditions with anaesthetics, Parliament had little difficulty in determining that no religious or medical justification for it existed. And it was banned.

However, in 1992 the Sunday Times revealed that a London surgeon was still performing the illegal operation. He charged £400, and told the clinics and nursing homes whose surgical facilities he used that he was performing labial repairs.

The Sunday Times reporter masquerading as a would-be patient noted that the surgeon had the honesty to tell her she would lose the capacity for sexual enjoyment. But the continuation of such a practice when its uselessness has been comprehensively exposed shows to what an extent some doctors have been motivated by deep hostility to women and their sexuality.

Two Great Surgeons

••

ROBERT BATTEY

••

Baker Brown was not a surgeon of distinction. Snipping off the protruberant clitoris with a pair of scissors could have been done by a 10-year-old. Robert Battey, on the other hand, was deservedly famous across America.

During the Civil Way he gave distinguished service to the Confederate Army. In 1869 he performed the first ovariotomy, removing the patient's ovary as the only way to excise a cyst. Three years later he removed a perfectly healthy pair of ovaries. he argued that they were responsible for his patient's excessively heavy menstrual bleeding, which he had relieved by creating an artificial menopause.

The operation became famous as "Battey's operation". Alternative names used, however, indicated that the intention might be less than humane. "Female castration" compared to an operation which would hardly ever be performed on men except for the excision of double testicular cancer or the penological disabled of sex offenders. "Spaying" suggested that women patients were as unimportant as so many cats.

Battey Protests

In 1886 Battey went to the Continental Medical Congress and protested about the abuse of his operation. He said that he only ever used it for justified gynaecological reasons, and though it might seem a drastic way of checking heavy menstrual flow, he was now satisfied that it could cure insanity or epilepsy. Nevertheless, in the 15 years since he invented the procedure he had only found 15 cases suitable for treatment.

"Ovaromania"

Other surgeons performing Battey's operation quickly latched on to his invitation to diagnose insanity. "Ovaromania" became a popular (non-existent) disease, remediable by ovarectomy. Its symptoms were that women were "unhappy" or "hysterical".

Female sex organs have traditionally be blamed for mental disturbances which have nothing to do with them: "hysteria" itself is so named because the Greeks believed it was caused by the "hystera" or womb moving around the body!

By 1906, 150,000 American women had been subjected to this useless sterilisation. Their ovariomania was often determined by their proving unwilling to carry out household duties, or their husbands finding them difficult to control. Their average age was 30h.

Victorian Values

Far more ovarectomies than clitoridectomies were performed: deplorable evidence that the stalwart Victorian upholders of marriage and the family could only cope with the institution if women's personalities were severely depressed; and that this mattered far more to virtuous Christian husbands than any real or imaginary threat to the health of their wives that might result from "excessive passion".

Another Wicked Operation

Dieffenbach's hemiglossectomy entailed cutting off half the tongue as a rather radical late 19th century attempt to cure stuttering. Had the whole tongue been excized it would have been a glossodectomy.

This was seriously proposed for other purposes in 1876 by Dr John Scoffern, in The London Surgical Home and Modern Surgical Psychology.

Scoffern advocated the wicked practice of "glossodectomy for ladies that talk too much, tend to appropriate what does not belong to them or who are overkeen on dancing."

Fortunately his advice does not even seem to have been followed. Nevertheless it speaks volumes for male medics' encouragement of the unhealthy state of relations between the sexes that such a volume should ever have been published in the first place.

SIR WILLIAM
ARBUTHNOT LANE

It is a relief to escape from the sexually obsessed misogynists and incompetents to deal with a great doctor. Who was also, incidentally, a great booby. William Arbuthnot Lane was born into a medical family. His father was an army surgeon, and William and his brother both trained at Guy's Hospital. William's tutor, recognising the boy's tendency to opinionated vehemence, tactfully suggested that surgery might prove a better career than medicine. And with Anaesthetized patients who could not answer back, Lane proved a magnificent healer.

Appointed lecturer at Guy's in 1888, he concentrated on abdominal surgery – an expanding and dangerous area at the time. Lane really did have "the heart of a lion and the hands of a lady". His scalpel never slipped, and patients were more likely to enjoy successful abdominal operations under his care than under any other doctor in London. William Lane deservedly prospered and grew rich, becoming a baronet in 1921.

He was quick and imaginative. Once in Grenoble he transformed a glassed-in section of a restaurant into a temporary emergency operating theatre. On another occasion, lacking his instruments, he improvised an operation with a paper-knife.

He also had ideas. One came from the study of working men's skeletons. Lane observed that they adapted to the muscular stresses of their various jobs. And he wrongly believed that this was evolution in action.

His greates contribution to surgery lay in the skeleton, however. Examining dockers who continued to suffer disability after compound fractures had been set, Lane realized that the bones must all go to their exact original places – he invented internal splints for this purpose.

However, his everlasting fame or notoriety came from his dedication to the notion of a "centre of sepsis" resulting from "intestinal stasis" and causing all manner of ills from cancer to consumption. The condition Lane deplored was civilized man's habit of excreting at convenient times and places, rather than voiding anywhere the moment a need was felt.

This reservation of faeces, he believed, made the colon a dangerous sewer inside the body, with putrefying matter constantly threatening health. To cure this he poured barrels of liquid paraffin into his unfortunate costive patients, and invented extremely difficult operations: first to introduce the small intestine directly into the colon; and then to remove the greater part of the colon itself. Ultimately he removed over 1,000!

These skilful operations (like the liquid paraffin) were completely useless, and by the end of his career, all his colleagues knew it. But Lane was a baronet. Lane was unstoppable. He founded the New Health Society in 1925 and for half his life did his best to aggravate Englishmen's permanent anxiety about the presence of digested food waiting to be excreted from their bodies. Calling him Cutler Walpole in "The Doctor's Dilemma", Shaw had him say, "your nuciform sac is full of decaying matter – undigested food and water..."

The Great Freudian Slip

Liberation from the tyranny of Victorian sex-phobia and obsessive anxieties over masturbation would ultimately come through psychology. Especially through the courageous stance adopted by Sigmund Freud, the founding father of psychoanalysis.

He found that sexual anxiety was at the root of many of his patients' complaints, and he said so. He decided that mental health and maturity meant passing from the infant stages of finding primary sensual pleasure in sucking and excreting (the oral and anal pleasures) to the adult stage of enjoying full genital satisfaction. And he said so. He argued that repressing children's natural sexual development in the interest of "morality" would freeze them at an immature stage, with damaging psychological results. And he said so.

He was roundly abused for saying these things. Self-appointed moralists declared that he encouraged amoral irresponsibility. Smart young men scored easy points off him: C. S. Lewis jeered at "Sigismund Enlightenment", and suggested that he so dirtied up all human experience that he would have called a boiled egg "the menstruum of a verminous fowl". The composer Peter Warlock wrote a mildly entertaining limerick that was more a comment on Freud's international fame than on his actual attitudes and achievements:

The young girls who frequent picture palaces Don't care much for psychoanalysis And although Dr Freud Is distinctly annoyed, They cling to their old-fashioned fallacies

In fact, Freud was usually criticised for his supposed permissiveness in wanting young girls to enjoy their natural libido and take a healthy pleasure in young men's phalluses without the pernicious interference of unscientific pseudo-medicine, and a misplaced code of evil ethics. However, through all the public abuse, he stood firmly by his principles until he came to be revered as one of the great thinkers who led European civilisation into the twentieth century. Although this idolisation encouraged the uncritical acceptance of some very unpersuasive ideas, he was undoubtedly the most influential figure in the ultimate downfall of the horrible Victorian sexual code, with its disastrous effects on medicine.

So it can come as a shock to realise that the handsome, able and ambitious young Viennese nerve doctor who began to specialise in treating neurasthenia and hysteria started his career under the thoroughly Victorian conviction that these disorders were usually caused by masturbation or coitus interruptus! He dropped the imaginary disease of "spermatorrhea" from his pathology, but proceeded to replace it with an almost equally imaginary mental cause and effect.

Almost equally imaginary, but not quite. Ultimately, many of his patients' problems genuinely were caused by anxiety about their natural sexuality. By bravely setting out to remove the anxiety, Freud became a liberator rather than an oppressor.

In the early 1890s, however, he was anxiously trying to suppress masturbation with a fervour that Acton might have admired. To his own wonderful creative capacity for exploring his and his patients' minds, and coming up with metaphors for the mental states he believed he observed, Freud added the unfortunate fantasies of sheer crank. An ear, nose and throat specialist who came up with the dotty idea that the non-existent disorders ascribed by Victorian medicine to normal sexual activity could all be cured by treating the nose!

Wilhelm Fliess

Freud became acquainted with young Wilhelm Fliess in 1888. For the next ten years they were to be close friends and intellectual partners. Like many young and ambitious intellectuals they tended to admire each other's epoch-making potential extravagantly, and willingly accepted foolish ideas from each other that in maturity they would quietly reject.

Also, like many other pairs of young intellectuals, they did not go on to joint and equal achievements. For every successful Wordsworth-and-Coleridge, there will be many Tennyson-and-Hallams or Joe Orton-and-Kenneth Halliwells. Fliess, like Hallam and Halliwell, was to be remembered only as the youthful friend of a far greater man.

Fliess nearly dragged Freud down to early disaster. Fliess and Freud believed that in combination, they could cure the range of ailments supposedly caused by masturbation. Freud, as a nerve doctor, would see the patients who had been reduced to shuffling neurasthenia, or raging hysteria, or headaches and stomach pains. He would gently but firmly persuade them to overcome their "masturbation problem".

Fliess, meanwhile, would treat and cure that final and alarming condition he identified as "nasal reflex neurosis".

It's all in the Nose

Unlike Freud, Fliess was a fully-blown crank. He shared the cultural delusion that masturbation was harmful, and further believed he could identify certain abdominal upsets it caused. Thus far he was simply another unfortunate Victorian. But he also believed he could identify particular spots in the nose which related to the abdominal disorders. Treating one nasal spot would cure irregular menstruation. Treating another would end colicky pains. Provided, of course, the lady gave up the dreadful habit of self-abuse! "Women who masturbate are generally dysmenorrheal," Fliess wrote in 1902. "They can only be cured through an operation on the nose if they give up this bad practice."

By 1902, Freud would no longer have entirely subscribed to this ridiculous theory, but ten years earlier he endorsed it wholeheartedly. He even accepted "nasal reflex neurosis" that Fliess postulated as the sadly common outcome of masturbation and its associated irregular periods.

Of course, neurasthenia is such a catch-all term for many different kinds of listlessness and lethargy that Freud might be forgiven for thinking some of them fell into a single class his friend had skilfully identified. But the fact remains, the young Freud and his best friend had become dedicated to curing a wholly imaginary disease. It didn't matter what therapy they devised, it wouldn't do the patient any good.

Fliess, unfortunately, had ideas that did a lot of harm.

Treating the Nasal Reflex Neurosis

As one of the great cranks, Fliess concluded that the best way to cure an imaginary illness was to extirpate its imagined source. Since his unique contribution to knowledge was the crazy observation that parts of the nose caused, aggravated or governed non-existent sexual disorders, it followed that cutting off the nose, or parts thereof, would prove beneficial.

Wilhelm Fliess set about enthusiastically cauterising parts of his patients' nasal passages, or numbing them with cocaine. He persuaded himself that this was demonstrably doing them good, and the effect of his own confidence was that those patients whose condition was remediable by placebo really did feel better.

Fliess was also sure that tinkering with the surface of the nasal passage was not enough – full and proper cure meant the extraction of the appropriate bones. Fliess longed to do this, and prove the excellence of his final and absolute treatment (provided, of course, the patient gave up the wicked habit of playing with her clitoris). He was, however, handicapped by the fact that he had not training whatsoever in surgery. Nor did he know any surgeons who accepted his theories and who would be willing to operate either on his behalf or under his direction.

It was only his good friend Sigmund Freud who shared his mad delusion. It was only Freud who wanted to see a patient enjoy the extraction of a nasal bone and recover perfect nervous health. In the end, it was only Freud who was prepared to deliver an innocent member of the public into the hands of a complete and utter madman who was determined to turn his inexperienced hand to the scalpel rather than forego the delight of testing and outrageous theory.

The Tragedy of Emma Eckstein

Emma Eckstein was fairly typical of the patients coming to the young Sigmund Freud in 1895. A generation earlier she might simply have been accepted as a sickly spinster, but the growing tribe of nerve doctors hoped to do something for young ladies who suffered the discomfort of painful irregular periods and frequent stomach pains.

To no-nonsense bourgeois Victorians, Freud's approach to such symptoms seemed as mad as Fliess's attacking abdominal problems by cauterising the nose. "Give the girl a pill!" might be Herr Biedemeyer's expectation of treatment. Instead of which young Dr Freud let Emma talk and talk about herself, encouraging her to discourse on topics that young unmarried women shouldn't even know about. Freud elicited that Emma masturbated. And of course he told her to stop it. He also leanred that as a child she had been sexually abused by an adult relative. Now Freud was finding this to be a very common problem in the lives of neurotic patients. While Herr Biedemeyer might pooh-pooh the notion that being groped in childhood could give young women upset tummies twenty years later, Freud's percipience in discovering just such traumatic bases underlying many psychosomatic symptoms made him a genius, where his friend Fliess was merely a crank.

Lacking strong intellectual support for his pioneering thoughts during this period, Freud leaned on Fliess, and added to his appropriate observation of emma Eckstein's childhood trauma the inappropriate conclusion that she would benefit from Fliess's operation. He invited Fliess to come to Vienna and remove the nasal bone which the young men hoped would finally cure her.

Épatant le Bourgeois

Since Fliess did not live in Vienna, it fell to Freud to care for the patient after Fliess had removed her left turbinate bone and departed. Freud's care certainly included a deep concern for her. Emma was a patient who seemed peculiarly important to him, so much so that some people have speculated that he came close to falling in love with her. It was certainly Freud's intention that she should be specially favoured in being the first patient to enjoy Fliess's revolutionary surgical cure for neurasthenia.

Far from seeming specially favoured, Emma seemed fated to suffer seriously from post-operative infection that just wouldn't clear up. To Freud's horror the wound in her nose refused to heal, and suppurated until in his presence it expelled a piece of bone the size of a small coin and two bowls of pus.

This was beyond Freud's capabilities. He was not an ENT man but he could see that under the swelling, part of Emma's face seemed to have caved in. He called in the noted Czech plastic surgeon Robert Gersuny who had invented various successful remedial operations, although he was already heading for his own medical disaster by using paraffin wax to smooth out wrinkles. Gersuny advised that the nasal passage was blocked and had apparently been closed up with too narrow an aperture. He recommended breaking the nose and reconstructing the aperture: an operation he might have performed himself had not Emma's condition worsened to the point that another surgeon had to be called as quickly as possible.

The Botched Job

Dr I. Rosanes set about clearing Emma's nose. It was emitting a vile fetid odour and, as soon as he began to operate, Emma bled profusely. Rosanes had hardly started his work when he came across the physical blockage. There was at least a half-metre of gauze-packing left in Emma's nose – she started serious haemorrhaging as soon as the stinking obstruction was removed. Fliess had not only performed a wholly unnecessary operation; not only risked practising surgery for which he was untrained and unqualified; he had botched the job in a classic manner by severing a blood vessel and closing up the wound without remembering to remove the temporary dressing.

Romanes repacked the nose with clean gauze. But Emma continued to haemorrhage for several weeks. Gersuny finally came to the rescue and completed a repair job on Fraulein Eckstein's nose. The patient was left with the disfigurement of having part of her face caved in.

Emma Eckstein became increasingly reclusive staying indoors with her perfectly uncured stomach pains, occasional nosebleeds, and increasing difficulty walking.

Emma Eckstein's Haemorrhage

Freud and Fliess were now in serious danger. Gersuny and Romanes were extremely critical of Fliess's appalling handiwork – as well they might be! They talked about it with colleagues, and there loomed the possibility of a full professional enquiry.

Neither man's career could have survived such a challenge. The operation was absolutely new and highly controversial. Both doctors were guilty of serious malpractice in going ahead without seeking guidance from an experienced surgeon. Freud should never have passed on a patient to a consultant going beyond his consultative powers to physical surgery. Fliess should never have attempted it. Emma Eckstein was not a guinea-pig. She should not have been subjected to any sort of surgery in the interests of a daft theory only given credence by two silly young men in the grip of a folie á deux.

Emma Does Her Bit

The one piece of luck the two malpractitioners enjoyed was the attachment of their victim. Emma trusted Freud implicitly and believed in the close friend and colleague he had brought in to mutilate her. She made no complaint about her surgeon – indeed, even after his forgotten gauze had been pulled out of her nose she insisted that he was not to blame.

This was an uncovenanted mercy for both Freud and Fliess. A formal complaint from the patient would almost certainly have lost them their licences to practice. Both men proceeded to broadcast Emma's favourable opinion of them as widely as they could.

The extreme danger of their position also produced the first hint of a rift between Freud and Fliess, the mutual admiration society. Letters written in 1895 show Freud laying the ground to gradually distance himself from his dear friend, should Emma's treatment blow up in their faces. Freud speaks a little sternly of the botch; makes the favourable observation that there was no botch in Romanes' work; and clearly hoped to let Fliess face the music alone if it became necessary.

Fliess's Defence

Fliess reacted by concocting madder and madder explanations for Emma's haemorrhage, all intended to distract attention from his own incompetent surgery which had severed a blood vessel and done nothing more than pack it with gauze which was then left to rot.

Fliess suggested that nosebleeding was very common in women with dysmenorrhea. He claimed that it was inevitable that Emma should have suffered serious haemorrhage at the time of her operation. It was, he claimed, because her female periodicity of 28 days and her male periodicity of 23 days fell together at that time, and mystic counting back in 28s and 23s led to other dates and days which showed that there had been a significant build-up of the internal imbalances represented by these variant periodicities.

This was clearly utter bunkum. Emma's original complaint was that she had irregular periods and not a regular 28-day cycle. She didn't have a male

23 day period at all, and nor did anybody else. Adding up of 28s and 23s was unscientific numerological twaddle.

The medical profession had rarely seen such a load of silly superstition proposed as diagnosis since astrologers and physicians jointly calculated the dreadful things supposed to befall the realm and the monarch on Good Quuen Bess's "grand climacteric".

However it served satisfactorily to persuade Fliess that the awful things that had happened to Emma Eckstein were not his responsibility.

Freud's Defence

Freud had always prided himself that his medical training made him a scientist, even though the ultimate development of psychoanalysis moved it well away from science's physical measurability. He was certainly never going to endorse a piece of batty numerology as proof of anything whatsoever, but he had observed genuine hysterical delusions occurring in patients. He had also observed symptoms caused by hysteria which could be cured by relieving the mind of anxiety.

Freud put Emma's recurrent haemorrhaging down to hysteria – the tractable Emma willingly agreed that some of her nosebleeds might have been imaginary, and the rest were all caused by her mind and not by Fliess's rotten surgery. Freud was off the hook of having endangered a patient's life by sending her to an incompetent consultant.

The price

For almost the only time in his life, Freud's nerve failed him in standing up to criticism. He urgently needed the support of colleagues who would agree that hysterical delusions commonly occurred. The senior colleagues he most respected – notably the great nerve specialist Breuer – were already quarrelling with his observation that many hysterical patients were sexually abused as children. The doctors simply refused to believe that respectable bourgeois gentlemen often interfered with their daughters or nieces.

Freud managed to buy their support for his claims about Emma Eckstein by abandoning the report that she had been physically abused. This, too, was relegated to the sphere of hysterical imagination. The rapes and assaults which his patients claimed had taken place were now softened in Freudian language to "seductions", and simply dismissed as common fantasy. As a consequence, for nearly 100 years psychologists disregarded most complaints of sexual abuse made by children. In the meantime, Freud's embarrassed followers effectively suppressed the whole story of Wilhelm Fliess and Emma Eckstein, together with Freud's original observations about the traumatic sexual interference which led many children to neurotic adult lives.

When Jeffrey Masson discovered and published the truth among Freud's papers in 1985 he was subjected to a torrent of abuse. Fortunately, it was also realized at the same time that an alarming amount of child abuse really does take place in educated and wealthy circles, as well as among the overcrowded and destitute. So the public was finally allowed to accept Masson's work without further question. Even Freudians had to admit that the master's involvement in one of the great medical mistakes of all time had led to generations of children being falsely accused of harbouring dirty-minded fantasies.

MODERN CRANKS

Medicine has learned a lot from the mistakes of the past. Wild new individual ideas are unlikely to catch on suddenly because a distinguished surgeon or scientist espouses them. The great Nobel Prize winning chemist Linus Pauling was unable to carry the public or the medical profession with him when he became convinced that massive doses of vitamin C were the answer to almost all medical problems.

The modern medical mistake is likely to be a matter of sheer incompetence. The barmy theory is likely to be the preserve of a lone doctor, who runs every risk of getting himself struck off.

Dr Borrell's Urine Injections

Dr Jorge Borrel qualified in Mexico and completed his residency as a urologist in the United States. However, while the urination part of his urological experience remained an important part of his practice, it was as a self-trained allergist that he set up his shingle in Canoga Park, Los Angeles.

Borrell was good at the commercial side of independent medical practice. He was medical director of two private clinics operating under the name of the Allergy Control Medical Group. He ran a private Advanced Testing Laboratory to which he referred patients from the clinics. He had his own weekly radio programme, and he sold audio-cassettes giving medical advice.

California State Authorities first became concerned when they discovered that the Testing Laboratory used cytotoxic leucocyte tests for allergies, rahter than the standard skin tests where a sample of suspected allergen is patched to the patient's skin to see whether it sets up a reaction.

Cytotoxic leucocyte testing mixes the allergen with a sample of the patient's blood and examines the result to see whether a lower white blood count indicates a reaction. The trouble with the method, officials remarked, was that it had "no known scientific value or validity." They added that it routinely produced false results, both negative and positive.

That in itself might not have resulted in the 69-year-old doctor losing his licence to the Board of Medical Quality Assurance in 1990. They were appalled by the century-old "folk remedy" the doc had wished on over 5,000 patients between 1969 and 1990. He had given them injections of their own urine.

"It sounds kind of preposterous or ugly or dirty or whatever," Dr Borrell admitted. "Even though years ago a number of doctors used it here, they've been scared away." The Board was unimpressed by Dr Borrell's attempt to associate himself with local predecessors. As far as they were concerned, his practice showed "an extreme departure from the standard of care in California."

When Borrell explained that urine stimulates the immune system to produce allergy antibodies, the board commented severely on his "shocking and extreme" lack of medical knowledge, and pointed out that urine injections could lead to infection, kidney failure, breathing difficulties and even death. Dr Borrell admitted there had been a few cases of infection "before proper filters were available for urine", but pleaded that none of his patients had died, and all had been told what treatment they were receiving.

Phil Foster, the Medical Board's regional supervisor had some pointed remarks to make about patients, on that one.

But nearly 6,000 fell for it before the state put a stop to Dr Borrell's particular eccentricity.

> "Common sense would tell that if you went to a doctor and he said, 'I'm going to cure you by injecting you with urine,' you'd look at him and say goodbye. That would be the normal person's reaction. It's beyond my imagination how anyone could fall for that kind of quackery."

PHIL FOSTER

Dr Hines and St Paul's Prescription to the Hebrews

> "Now no chastening for the present seemeth to be joyous, but grievous: nevertheless afterward it yieldeth the peaceable fruit of righteousness unto them which are exercised thereby."

Thus speaketh St Paul, in Hebrews, 12.11. Most sane Christians recognise that he is talking about involuntary suffering permitted by God: the age-old theological problem of pain.

However, Dr Kenneth Hines of South Woodford, London decided that St Paul was advocating definite and efficaceous therapy for tension and guilt. He also decided that it would help patients to give up smoking, though heaven alone knows how he persuaded himself that the apostle was so forward-looking as to have foreseen that particular medical problem! It seemed that Dr Hines recommended spanking for tense young women patients. he was especially inclined to prescribe it if their tensions appeared to be caused by sexual practices of which he disapproved. The prescription for petting with a boyfriend was a slap on the wrist. Heavy petting invited

159

a smack on the bottom. And intercourse merited a full spanking on a bare bottom.

Not that Dr Hines invariably undertook the treatment personally. A "Mrs G", whose husband had multiple sclerosis, was told to go to the bed where he was confined, take down her jeans, lie across his body, and let him administer the spanking.

One of Hines's patients said that without his help she would have committed suicide. Five others, giving evidence to the General Medical Council's conduct committee in 1987, declared themselves amazed and angered. A teenage girl said, "I saw him as a devil.... He had an overpowering interest in me. I really thought I was going mad."

Dr Hines was not secretive about his belief in therapeutic spanking, though he was hurt that Christian colleagues found his ideas revolting. He insisted that they were rooted in the concept of forgiveness, and he himself enjoyed no sexual gratification from spanking.

Nurses at St Bartholomew's Hospital were not so sure. They had successfully petitioned for his resignation in 1978 following episodes of unwelcome bottom-smacking and sex talk.

The committee did not express an opinion on the Bart's incidents. However they did express themselves appalled by the inappropriateness of his prescription for stressed females. They suspended the 42-year-old doctor for eight months.

After all, even his advocate before the General Medical Council's conduct committee, Jonathan Caplan, had conceded that Dr Hines had showed "a naivety in this form of counselling and... left himself open to being misunderstood.

Incompetence

In 1976 the Los Angeles Times ran a series of five articles investigating some alarming information coming from medical research sources. It was known that medical malpractice suits were increasing at a prodigious rate. It was assumed that unscrupulous shyster lawyers – the "ambulance-chasers" – were responsible. Since American lawyers were permitted to take cases speculatively, only claiming a fee if they won damages, they could make it worthwhile for any sick person to gamble on winning a tax-free cash settlement from their doctors.

By this time, certain responsible doctors had already carried out their own investigation of colleagues' work. They reached the conclusion that 5% of all doctors in America were unfit to practice.

This meant that 16,000 incompetents were merrily making wrong diagnoses, issuing wrong prescriptions, recommending inappropriate treatment in the USA. Yet the state licensing boards which were supposed to protect the public against malpractitioners struck of a mere 66 each year, on average.

What were the problems of the 15,034 inadequate practitioners? Medical incompetence had various causes. Some bad doctors were alcoholics, or had become addicted to their own drugs. Some went on doing exactly what they had been taught at college, blissfully unaware that medical science had moved on, and the old ways were now either inadequate or completely inappropriate. Some had forgotten most of what they learned in college, and stuck to a little tread mill of cures that were not the universal panaceas they imagined.

Doctors were prescribing antibiotics for illnesses which academic studies showed to be unresponsive to them. Doctors were recommending quite unnecessary operations: especially tonsillectomies and hysterectomies.

Perhaps most disturbingly, patients were dying on operating tables they should never have been on. It was estimated that some 2.3 million unnecessary operations took place in the USA every year. 11,900 people died because of surgery they should never have undergone in the first place. 6 billion doses of antibiotics were prescribed – 22% of them were unnecessary. An estimated 10,000 patients died or came close to death because of antibiotics they should never have been given.

There was every reason for Dr Baden of the California Medical Examiner's Office to declare, "Too often these out-and-out mistakes are said to be just honest differences of opinion. This gives everybody the excuse not to be judgmental. We've got to start becoming a little more judgmental, and develop better means of quality control. Otherwise we're always going to have incompetent doctors in the business."

Doctors' malpractice records were held centrally, but never revealed to the public! Congressman Ron Wyden said, "The public has more information on the performance of a breakfast cereal than the performance of a heart surgeon. The idea that you would take the taxpayers' money and run a data bank... and then keep it secret is absurd."

Even Good Doctors...

The problem of keeping the best doctors in touch with the lates research was highlighted in 1995. Epidemiologist Iain Chalmers of the Cochrane Centre in Oxford revealed that reliance on practices drummed into him at medical school, and sometimes uncorrected in the latest standard textbooks, had led him to give treatments that he believed had killed patients.

As an example, Dr Chalmers described the textbook advice that children with virus infections should never be given antibiotics unless there was an accompanying bacterial condition. As a direct consequence of this advice he had never prescribed antibiotics for children with measles, and several had developed infections and died. A 1990 revision of a standard textbook of medicine, revered by some, still claimed that the value of anticoagulant drugs to prevent blood clotting during surgery "remains to be established."

"Goodness knows how many thousands of people have read that lethal information," said Dr Chalmers.

William Rosenberg, clinical tutor in medicine at Oxford University, pointed to the speed with which new and important discoveries were made in medical science, allowing honest and competent doctors to use new techniques, unaware that they had not been fully tested.

"In the 1980s we were using drugs to stop heart-attack patients suffering irregular heartbeat and those drugs increased their risk of death," Dr Rosenberg said.

Stuart Horner, chairman of the British Medical Ethics Committee pointed out that many negative studies, proving the inefficacy of drugs and treatments, just didn't get published. So doctors were not to know that they were practising worthless or dangerous medicine in good faith.

"At the very least consumers have the right to know which health care providers they should avoid."

RON WYDEN, CHAIRMAN OF THE HOUSE SUB-COMMITTEE ON
REGULATIONS, BUSINESS OPPORTUNIES AND TECHNOLOGY

Wrong Diagnoses

Clearly, irrespective of whether or not a doctor is good or bad, the patient satands some chance of getting the wrong treatment. The mistakes may be made at various stages.

Diagnosis is the first chore falling to the practitioner. The patient comes in and complains of pains, or a high temperature, or vaguely not feeling well. The doctor has to elicit the clearest and most accurate account the patient can give him. If there are physically visible symptoms – swelling, or a rash – the doctor must examine them. He may wish to probe sensitive areas manually, looking for hard lumps or painful responses. He may want the patient to demonstrate his ability to make certain movements.

Then, applying his knowledge and experience, the doctor must try and decide just what the patient is suffering from. The difficulties may be compounded by proper professional recognition that the patient's confidence in his professional competence is important to his recover. If the doctor scratches his head and says, "I haven't the faintest idea what this is..." it doesn't matter whether he goes on to say, "but it doesn't look very important" or "but I think it's serious." The patient will probably doubt his abiltiy to give him the right treatment or send him to the right consultant.

Yet complete ignorance and bewilderment may be an absolutely justified respnse. Thus far, except in certain diseases with quite unmistakeable and unique symptoms, the doctor's craft is more an art than a science.

There are scientific measurements the doctor can make to help him come to a conclusion. He can take the patient's temperature and pulse. he can check his blood pressure. He can send him for X-rays or scans. But the first diagnosis may be absolutely vital – a mistake at this point, be it perfectly understandable or sheerly incompetent, may mean the difference betweens effective treatment and a worsening disease; health and invalidism; at worst, life and death.

Why Trust a Con?

If a patient is a convict, a prison doctor may suspect him of malingering, or think it not worthwhile to give the full and proper axamination leading to a correct diagnosis. Carl Ogle was a crook and he got caught. He was sent to prison in the New York State system, and circulated between four state prisons. The year 1991 would seem to have been a peculiarly bad one for health in the Empire State's penal system: 13 convicts and one guard died from a mutant strain of tuberculosis that resisted the commonly used drugs. The state clearly had no alternative but to test all 86,000 convicts and guards under its care to stop the strain spreading.

By that time Carl Ogle had completed his sentence and visited his lawyer. He told attorney John Bell that he had been ill for four months before the prison doctors consented to treat him. During that time he had complained of pains in his chest and abdomen and numbness in his feet and legs. He had complained every day for four months and in each of the four prisons where he had served his sentence.

The prison doctors did nothing for four months. Why should they? If Carl was tubercular, he wouldn't be cured by their drugs, given the strain that was going round. Finally they conceded that he had Pott's disease – a rare tuberculosis of the spine which responded to treatment. However it was too late. Their unwillingness to act on a "con's" complaint for so long meant that he was permanently injured.

The Court of Claims awarded him $256,000 and severely criticized the doctors, pointing out that whatever their problems with the new strain, it was official policy to give medication to any inmate under 35 testing positive for tubercular bacillus.

Beware Of the Telephone

Diagnosis over the telephone always carries some risk. Without making a personal examination, the physician risks accepting a patient's inaccurate account of his symptoms, or mistaking a serious condition for a minor illness with similar symptoms.

This happened to an unfortunate GP in Barbados in 1982. He was telephoned by the parents of locally much-loved paraplegic pianist, Alwyn Scott, who said that she was suffering from extreme abdominal pains. As it happened, the doctor was over-stretched because an outbreak of gastroenteritis with exactly those symptoms was plaguing the island at that time. he made soothing noises and recommended rest and mild treatment. Two more telephone calls saying that there was no improvement did not discompose him, as he did not expect an instant cure for the tummy-ache. He was devastated when the Scotts, trusting his reassurances no longer, rushed their daughter to hospital, where she died of kidney failure.

At least he was there to field the call. In 1990, The Medical Protection Society reported the case of a woman who telephoned her GP and found herself talking to his answering machine. The outgoing message was unfortunately ambiguous and did not make clear that the doctor was away in Paris for the weekend. The woman's friends made four more calls, expecting him to have returned to hear her case. Two days later she was taken to hospial, where the emergency diagnosis was as little use as the GP's answering machine – she was sent back home, only to return to hospital the following day to die of meningitis. The MPS agreed that the handling of her case was "indefensible", and awarded £35,000 damages to her family. Meningitis is very difficult to diagnose, unless it is known to be occurring in the community, but use of the telephone instead of examination reduces the possibility of an accurate diagnosis.

The Medical Defence Union reported a case of a 29-year-old woman who telephoned her doctor in 1983 with a headache, and was advised to take Panadol. The following day she went to his surgery complaining that her vision was now affected. He diagnosed untreatable migraine. Two days later her headache had improved, but in another four days her husband telephoned the doctor again to say that she had become agitated and uncontrollable. Without visiting her the GP prescribed Largactil over the phone. Later that day the woman died of meningitis. The MDU and the doctor agreed a settlement of £26,000 for her family.

CELEBRITY SPOT

OSCAR WILDE

As the son of a great doctor, Oscar Wilde knew the need for courage and humanity in the medical profession. When he found himself in Reading Gaol he discovered, to his horror, that the diet and regimen meant diarrhoea and insomnia for most prisoners, and the prison doctors were not remotely concerned. During his sentence, Wilde fell and hurt his ear, but the prison doctors failed to treat it. It developed an abscess and never fully recovered. Five years later further infection in the untreated ear precipitated Wilde's final illness and death.

However, it was not of his own undoubted suffering at the hands of the incompetent Dr O. C. Morris that he wrote a public complaint on his release. He was horrified that the prison doctors approved the flogging of a mentally defective prisoner, and through either ignorance or cruelty, refused to diagnose his occasional infractions of the rules as a consequence of his disability.

"This man is undoubtedly becoming insane," Wilde told the Daily Chronicle. "Prison doctors have no knowledge of mental disease of any kind. They are as a class ignorant men. The pathology of the mind is unknown to them. When a man grows insane they treat him as shamming. They have him punished again and again. Naturally the man becomes worse."

Unfortunately for Wilde, he himself had to attempt to recover some self-respect in prison by adopting the preposterous though long-lasting medical mistake that temporarily forced himself to believe that his onw homosexual orientation was itself a disease.

"For they starve the little frightened child till it weeps both night and day. And they scourge the weak and flog the fool and gibe the old and grey. And some grow mad, and all grow bad and none a word may say."

OSCAR WILDE, "THE BALLAD OF READING GAOL"

Decisions Against Doctors

Little Zeena Sa'd was barely two years old when she picked up the teapot and sucked its scalding spout in 1981. She was rushed to the local health centre in Cobham, where Dr Hercules Robinson prescribed a painkiller and an antacid. She would be all right, he said.

She wasn't. Her family called the health centre again, and Dr Alastair Dunlop came round. He didn't think there was cause for alarm, but agreed the child might be better under observation in hospital. He didn't, however, order an ambulance. By the time she reached Epsom District Hospital Zeena's condition had worsened. The consultant paediatrician who treated her was unable to save her from irreversable brain injuries.

Nine years later the High Court decided that Dr Robinson and Dr Dunlop had been negligent. They should have identified the possibility of some serious injury and sent her to hospital forthwith. It may seem a little hard that a doctor should be expected to guess that a baby's scalded mouth could mean brain damage, but that's what the courts decided. Doctors have been warned.

In Virginia, climbing medical malpractice damages threatened the provision of medical services by the 1990s, and the state legislature put a cap of $1 million as the highest award available to the claimant. Mrs Mary Taylor burst through that cap on 10 June 1994. Her husband Harry died of a massive heart attack on Valentine's Day 1991. He was 45 and an operations manager for Mobil. Just one week earlier he had gone to the company's clinic complaining of heartburn.

Dr Clarion E. Johnson clearly thought there was something more than indigestion affection Mr Taylor. For he gave him a stress test and prescribed nitroglycerin – the normal treatment for coronary chest pains or angina. Mr Taylor was told that he was not actually suffering from heart disease, though the result of his tests should have revealed otherwise, according to what was put before the court in 1992. In finding against the company and Dr Johnson the court awarded $4 million, which was promptly cut back in line with the cap by the Appeal Court. The original award was reinstated in 1994 when it was revealed that Dr Johnson's license had not been renewed in 1990. This was no fault of his – he had been told that the renewal was complete. But his information was wrong, and the State Supreme Court decided that the malpractice cap could only be applied to licensed doctors. "We do not believe this was a case of malpractice and we do not believe that any treatment Mr Taylor received in our clinic hastened his death," said a Mobil spokesman.

Now was Mrs Taylor over the moon at becoming a millionairess. "The money is not very important. I'm still a widow," she said.

Doctors at New York's famous St Vincent's Hospital were not gravely perturbed when, in 1979, stockbroker Carl Lockhart came to them with swellings in his underarms and neck. For Lockhart had once been the New York Giant's defensive back, and the hospital reasoned that anyone who had spent his youth taking the pounding handed out in American football was bound to have swellings here and there. They were rudely awakened when he died of untreatable cancer in the lymph nodes three years later. it cost the doctors and the hospital $1.5 million when the widow's damages were finally settled in 1993.

You've Got The Equipment – Use It!

Everybody knows pregnant women must avoid German measles (rubella), lest it harm their unborn child. Mrs Pamela Hicks of Boston was 20 weeks pregnant when she went into Brigham and Women's Hospital with vomiting, nausea and a temperature of 102°. She was given a test for rubella and it proved positive.

However he obstetrician, Dr Evelina Storlazzi, did not pass the information on. Nor did she carry out tests on the foetus to see whether it had been exposed to the virus.

Dr Storlazzi had left Boston and was not available when the case came to court. Had she been present, Mrs Hicks's lawyer said, she would have claimed that she thought the positive result only indicated that Mrs Hicks had previously had German measles or had been immunized against it.

Massachusetts permits abortion up to 24 weeks. Mrs Hicks had just four weeks to arrange an abortion, and she said that had she known an ultrasound test conducted several weeks later would show an abnormally small foetal head, she would have opted for abortion.

Her son was born brain-damaged and was never able to walk or talk. He died within a couple of years. All this was compatible with damage caused by the pre-natal rubella.

Mrs Hicks was awarded $1.3 million damages: a triumph for those who want women to be free to choose whether they abort or not.

Dr Graham Kelly had the misfortune to be the only general practitioner in Cobar, 560 kilometres north of Sydney, New South Wales, on 8 March 1966. There was a road accident in the town that night, and Geoffrey Sherring was brought to Dr Kelly's surgery, obstreperous, drink-smelling, and with a head wound.

Dr Kelly took him to the hospital and stitched the wound without probing or X-raying it. Three days later Sherring was paralysed down one side of his body. Dr Kelly sent him to Sydney where a depressed skull fracture was noticed, under which a blood clot and abscess had formed. The result was permanent paralysis and general disabilities. Caused, the neurosurgeon said, by Dr Kelly's failure to find the depressed fracture.

Dr Kelly claimed that he could not operate the 125 milliamp portable X-ray machine in Cobar Hospital. However, a radiologist and a neurosurgeon both agreed that even an inexperienced doctor, helped by a matron, could easily have X-rayed Sherring's head.

Dr Kelly had to meet the entire $90,000 damages himself, unsupported by the hospital.

How Many Bites at the Cherry?

Three successive doctors failed to diagnose a woman's breast cancer, according to the Medical Protection Society's Annual Report of 1990. She went to her GP to complain of a lump in the breast. She was advised to soothe it with hot fomentations and poultices. She then became pregnant and went for regular examinations at ante-natal clinics. Nobody there spotted that she had cancer. Finally she gave birth, and again was examined medically. Again, her tumour was missed. By the time her trouble was identified she was terminally ill, although she lived long enough to see the settlement of £135,000 awarded against the medics who had failed her so badly.

Three doctors cost a 51-year-old man his leg and part of his eyesight, after he went to his GP to complain of numbness and twitching in the face and discomfort in the lower legs. It was almost the first time in a healthy life he had made a visit to the doctor – who recommended rest.

Over the next 18 months the patient made eight more visits. He complained of blistering, swelling and discoloration in the foot. He lost a toenail, complained of giddiness, loss of weight and chronic thirst. The GP diagnosed gout. On the two further occasions he visited the surgery to find other doctors standing in. He showed them his feet – one diagnosed cellulitis, the other athlete's foot.

When his original GP returned, he suspected osteomyelitis, and sent the patient to hospital. The doctors immediately saw that his leg was gangrenous. It had to be amputated below the knee. The hospital also found him to be suffering from diabetes. They treated him, but it was too late to save him from ophthalmic complications.

The defence assessors appointed for the doctors could not dispute that the symptoms of gangrene and diabetes had been unmistakeable. Consequently, the Medical Defence Union paid out over £60,000.

Even these terrible trios, however, were not as preposterous as the four doctors whose seven consultations killed a 26-year-old woman after she visited her GP one Sunday suffering from a tummy-ache.

She was first seen by a locum, who diagnosed bowel colic for which he prescribed a soothing draught.

Next day the patient was back again. She saw her own doctor and told him her stomach was swelling, and that she had constant thirst and was always having to urinate. Her doctor repeated his locum's prescription.

On the third day a third doctor was manning the fort. The woman told him the symptoms were the same but the pain was increasing so badly she wanted to go to hospital. The new medical genius diagnosed diarrhoea and prescribed diphenoxylate.

Two days later she telephoned the surgery, and whoever was there prescribed the anti-depressant flupenthixol without examining her. However the practice had not abandoned her (unfortunately) – the third doctor gave her a home visit, and learned that she was now feeling hot, suffering pains in the arms and legs, and fainting occasionally.

He diagnosed gastroentiritis. In the small hours she felt so bad that she contacted the practice again. The locum who had first seen her came out to the house and learned that she felt worse. He noticed she was dehydrated, and concluded she had a urinary tract infection.

Her GP came out to see how she was in the morning. She was now vomiting occasionally, and he diagnosed either pyelonephritis or a viral infection. 30 minutes later she collapsed and was rushed to hospital, where she was pronounced dead on arrival. Her blood was found to be chock-full of glucose. Seven consultations had missed the obvious signs to test for diabetes.

"A lamentable lack of clinical acumen" said the Medical Defence Union's assessor, with serious understatement, before he shelled out £34,000 to her relatives.

It isn't always hospitals who correct the errors of GPs, however. A 65-year-old woman who had taken to drink after a bereavement in 1986 suffered a bad fall and was taken to her local accident department. They examined her; found no bones broken; and sent her home. They did not bother to X-ray her.

The following day she felt seriously unwell. Her GP visited and heard about her accident. His examination suggested that she was suffering from a mild infection, for which he prescribed antibiotics.

Within half an hour the poor woman died. A post mortem found that her fall had fractured ribs, broken her breastbone and broken her pelvis!

The profession displayed solidarity and banded together in self-defence over her case. "There was much unwelcome publicity in the local press," was the Medical Defence Union's disapproving comment!

Less comment followed the death, that same year, of a 60-year-old engineer who had visited Africa and returned with fever and cramps. His GP had given him the antimalarial preparation Daraprim for his trip, so a partner in the practice ruled out malaria and gave him ampicillin for a chest infection. Another partner came out in the small hours and gave pentazocine for suspected pleurisy or gall bladder trouble. The original GP visited with pentazocine injections, and dismissed the patient's wife's remarks about dark red urine and possible malaria.

Four days later, after yet more visits and phone calls, the patient went into hospital and died within two hours. Of cerebral malaria.

A Private Joke

Written diagnoses may prove very misleading if doctors do not follow an agreed standard nomenclature. One King's College Hospital surgeon might have puzzled colleagues unfamiliar with his private in-joke if they ever read an internal memo saying, "Please X-ray two piggies roast beef and none."

This mysterious formulation rose from the anatomical problem that there are no agreed scientific names for the individual toes. To overcome this problem the surgeon decided that all toes were "piggies", and they could be numbered according to the nursery rhyme: "market", "home", "roast beef", "none", "wee wee".

PRESCRIPTIONS

The diagnoses may have been wrong, so the treatments may have failed in the last few cases, but at least the patients all received the medicines their doctors intended for them in the right quantities.

Doctors' terrible handwriting has become legendary as dispensing pharmacists complain about trying to decipher some spidery scrawl in an attempt to correctly identify: the medication being prescribed; the measurement per dose; the number of doses per day; and even the patient's name and address.

Who is responsible if a patient suffers a disabling reaction after receiving something his doctor didn't intend from a pharmacist who couldn't make out the doctor's dreadful handwriting? Both doctor and chemist may be, according to an important decision in the Queen's Bench Division in 1988.

In December 1983 when 53-year-old James Prendergast collapsed at home and was rushed to the Hammersmith Hospital. He stayed there for six months, and was discharged suffering permanent brain damage and needing constant care and attention from social workers.

It transpired that Mr Prendergast was an asthmatic who had gone to his doctor with bronchitis. Dr Stuart Miller wrote him a prescription for a safe, sensible and commonplace combination of drugs for a man in his condition: three Ventolin inhalers, 250 Phyllocontin tablets and 21 Amoxil tablets. There was no problem with the first two items, but Mr Peter Kozary, the pharmacist, misread Amoxil (an antibiotic) as "Daonil" (a drug for diabetics which reduces the body's sugar content).

Unfortunately non-diabetics who take Daonil may sometimes suffer a sudden instant reduction of blood sugar levels causing hypoglycemic shock to the brain. This had happened to Mr Prendergast, with the tragic consequence of permanent brain damage.

Mr Kozary defended himself by pointing out that the word "Amoxil" was so badly written that the capital "A" looked like a lower case "d" and the "x" like an "n". So he had to guess what was meant by "dm[?]onil" and decided it must be "daonil".

Mr Justice Auld declared that this was not satisfactory. Mr Kozary was an experienced pharmaceutical chemist. The prescription read Amoxin 250, but Daonil was not dispensed in 250 mg doses. Mr Kozary said he thought Dr Miller had mixed up Daonil with another anti-diabetic drug that was so dispensed. Not a good excuse, said the judge. If the chemist thought there had been some confusion in the doctor's mind, so much the more reason to contact him and have everything made clear. He must have known that Daonil was dangerous to non-diabetics, and he should have noticed that Mr Prendergast was paying for his prescription, whereas a diabetic would almost certainly have been entitled to free drugs. Mr Kozary had, in the judge's view, been negligent.

But so had Dr Miller. It might be subjective impression, but the judge felt that the word Amoxin could be read as "Daonil" as Dr Miller had written it. And Dr Miller had a duty to his patient not to risk giving him the wrong medicine by making things unduly difficult for a busy pharmacist. The court awarded Mr Prendergast £119,000 damages, divided 75% against Mr Kozary and 25% against Dr Miller.

Deafened by Hospital Medication

Antibiotics are the drugs most often prescribed wrongly. Incurable deafness is one of the commonest side-effects. Andrew Kay suffered meningitis in 1975 when he was two years old. A senior house officer in a children's hospital, was instructed to give him 10,000 units of penicillin. Unfortunately, Andrew was given 300,000 by mistake. Andrew went deaf, and his personality changed. He became aggressive and destructive. He lacked affection and schools found that he had become difficult to teach in spite of his high IQ of 122. His father fought his case through the courts at his own expense for nine years, refusing the local health board's "derisory" offer of £6,000 compensation. In 1985 when Andrew was 11 he was awarded £102,000.

The same year, 14-year-old Nicholas Jeary almost finished the long trail of court claims he and three other children in the West Country had been pursuing for 12 years. In 1972 he was two years old when boiling water was tipped over him at his play school. The scalding resulted in scarring burns over 40% of his body and he was sent for treatment to a local hospital.

The burns were treated with neomycin, an antibiotic spray. Nicholas's teeth fell out and he lost his hearing.

Three other children were also deafened by the treatment, and two of them were awarded compensation payments of £140,000 against the health authority in 1982. Three years later Nicholas won a separate claim against the play school, and went on with his suits against the regional health authority, the hospital and the manufacturers of the spray.

But the most serious deafened victim of a hospital's inaccurate prescription was 41-year-old Vincent Gargano, undergoing his final session of chemotherapy for testicular cancer at the University of Chicago Hospital in May, 1995. Testicular cancer is highly responsive to medication, and Gargano was assured he'd be up and about for this daughter's graduation in June.

Until for five successive days an inexperienced doctor gave Gargano four times the correct dose. It destroyed his immune system. He went deaf. Then his kidneys failed. And in June he died.

Five Questions To Ask Your Doctor

- What drug have you prescribed?
- What are its side effects and interaction with other medications?
- How often should it be taken?
- What precautions should I follow while taking it?
- How soon should I let you know if it isn't working?

Can You Trust Your Prescription?

Boston University Medical Center's Collaborative Drug Surveillance Program discovered that American doctors write twice as many prescriptions per patient as Scottish doctors, and were twice as likely to prescribe wrongly, endangering their patients. Since the Scots proved at least as healthy as Americans over all, the study concluded that:

- 50% of all prescriptions written in America are unnecessary
- 1 in 18 is downright dangerous
- 10% of adverse reactions to prescribed medications are serious
- 1.2% are fatal
- 300,000 Americans are hospitalised annually because of faulty prescriptions
- This makes wrong prescribing one of the top 10 causes of hospitalisation.

••

THE DALKON SHIELD

••

By the 1960s medicine had left far behind the Victorian fear of sex, and there were no silly medical pontifications about the healthiness or otherwise of the changes in sexual conduct which occurred in western society.

Edmund Bergler was the last well-known psychiatrist to allege that homosexuality was a disease that could be cured. Influential until the

1950s, he quietly dropped out of favour. Doctors generally got on with their proper business of healing real diseases and not inventing imaginary ones.

But the spread of cheap and effective contraception did concern doctors and medical researchers. They found that prolonged use of the contraceptive pill led to a statistically significant increased risk of thrombosis. Pharmaceutical firms lowered the dosage of oestrogen in their products and researchers gave attention to intra-uterine devices as an aesthetically pleasing alternative.

The fact that a foreign body inserted into the womb inhibits contraception was known centuries ago to the Arabs, who lowered the fertility of working camels by putting small stones into them. In the 1930s the IUD enjoyed a brief burst of popularity in Germany. But in the late 1960s it came into its own.

There were three problems about the designs on the market. Most were difficult and some were impossible to insert in women who had not had children. They had a tendency to be expelled from the womb – sometimes without the owner being aware that she was now at risk of impregnation. And they were three or four times less efficient than the pill.

The Dalkon Shield was designed to overcome these drawbacks.

Dr Davis and Win Lerner

A gynaecologist and an electrical engineer combined forces to try and design the perfect IUD. Hugh Davis of Johns Hopkins University in Baltimore collaborated with inventor Win Lerner to try out different shapes. After 640 patients, most of them poor black women, reported highly favourable results over a period of nine months, the two applied to patent the Dalkon Shield.

It was a 3 cm piece of plastic shaped rather like a kite, and eequipped with three short blunt fins angled down each side. These provided a safe grip like the barb on a fish-hook if the device tried to slip out through the cervix. The whole thing looked rather like a king crab.

An additional feature was the shield's tail – a piece of string 8 cm long, with a knot 3.5 cm from the end. The string enabled the removal of the device. And Davis and Lerner were very proud of the knot. It was a unique feature which would help doctors insert the shield to exactly the right deptch, and locate it easily when they wanted to extract it.

As a flat disc, the shield was easy to insert. With the gripping claws on the sides, it was not liable to be expelled. Over the nine months it was tested, just over one in every hundred women using it conceived. This made it as efficient a contraceptive as the pill.

Davis and Lerner received their patent in 1968 and teamed up with Dr Thad Earl to form the Dalkon Corporation and put it on the market.

A. H. Robins Arrives on the Scene

In the first year of the Corporation's existence 16,000 Dalkon Shields were sold. This wasn't bad going for a tiny new company with no base in the market. But like most self-start small businesses, the Dalkon Corporation was headed for rapid liquidation if it didn't do a great deal better. Davis, Lerner and Earl needed the backing of someone with massive capital and an aggressive marketing team already in place. They exhibited their invention at a medical convention in Earl's home state of Ohio, and they found a buyer.

A. H. Robins was a 120-year-old pharmaceutical company with assets of $186 million, headquarters in Richmond Virginia, sales capacity across America, and subsidiaries in a dozen other countries. A. H. Robins liked the look of the Dalkon Shield, and after negotiating with the three owners agreed to buy the rights for a figure of $750,000 and a 10% royalty on sales.

There was one other implicit condition. Robins sold cough medicines and lip salves and other small medicinal preparations. However, it had never handled a contraceptive before, and it had no gynaecologist on its staff. Dr Davis would be their effective resident advisor and specialist. Quality control and safety would depend almost entirely on him.

The Setback

Even before the deal was signed in June 1970, disappointing technical information had reached Davis. With continued use over a 14 month period, the failure rate of the shield had risen to 2.3%, more than doubling the very competitive figure which had first attracted Robins.

Nevertheless the company's marketing division, apparently unaware of this new information, went ahead with printing 200,000 copies of an article Davis had written about his invention in the early days, which mentioned a 1.1% failure rate. And this was mailed direct to gynaecologists all over America.

The mailshot made no mention of Dr Davis's continuing financial interest in the shield. The inventor and royalty-reaper was being quoted as though he were just Dr Hugh Davis of Johns Hopkins University.

A. H. Robins was indeed marketing the Dalkon Shield aggressively.

Manufacturing Bugs

There was a problem. Because the shield gripped so well, the tail had to be unusually strong. It could require a pull of nearly 12 lb to extract the thing, and if the tail snapped off it would never come out.

Robins developed a special multifilament string with the necessary tensile strength. But the string acted like a lampwick sitting in paraffin oil. It could absorb fluid at one end, and go on absorbing until the fluid had climbed to the other. This was potentially risky. The vagina harbours a quantity of bacteria which do no harm if they stay in place, but nobody could be sure that they would remain harmless if they climbed along the string to the interior of the uterus. Robins ordered the enclosure of the string in a black plastic sheath.

The business of fastening the tails to the shields was the work of Robins' subsidiary Chapstick factory at Lynchburg, Virginia. Chapstick, manufacturing lipsalves, had never had anything like this tricky little job to undertake. They complained to head office that the sheaths were impossibly stiff. Even after soaking in boiling water for several hours they did not become flexible enough for tying the knot. Couldn't the knot be scrapped, asked Chapstick? The response from above was absolutely negative. The knot was already advertised as "an exclusive feature". It must go in the tail.

Chapstick pointed out that 170,000 tails had been crushed during the tying process – this represented an unacceptable rate of loss. "Cut and tie again," ordered the bosses sternly. Then the sales force began to report a problem. Men were complaining that they could feel the string protruding from the cervix during intercourse. Because of its stiff plastic covering it didn't feel like a luxurious addition to the place of pleasure. It felt more like making love to a hairbrush! Chapstick asked whether they couldn't give up the plastic coating altogether.

"Certainly not," replied the bosses. The sheath was absolutely essential to stop bacteria-laden mucus or fluid climbing up into the womb. However, one Chapstick executive knew that this could happen anyway. He had left a coated tail in a beaker of water one day, and watched with fascination as droplets gradually travelled from the tip to the top. He told head office.

An A. H. Robins vice-president sterly rebuked this mutinous grumbling. There were to be absolutely no changes to the design "until directed otherwise."

Chapstick grovelled. They had been the subdivision to notice apparent dangers and failures to come up to specification. Yet they now sent head office an apologetic memo which certainly wouldn't sound good if the company were ever accused of irresponsible trading.

> *"Our only interest in the Dalkon Shield is to produce it at the lowest possible price and, therefore, increase Robins's gross profit level."*
>
> CHAPSTICK MEMO TO ROBINS' HEAD OFFICE

Rocketing Sales

The same fierce managerial greed that rode roughshod over Chapstick's protests was directed at the sales force. They were left in no doubt that the Dalkon Shield had better carve out a big share of the market, and quickly. Never mind that most of them had never handled contraceptives before.

The modern IUD, "safe, dependable, trouble-free," as the literature called it, had got to take off instantaneously from the inadequate sales base of 16,000 in the first year.

One salesman received a telegram instructing him to call the sales manager if he had not met his quota. It was tyrannically threatening – "No excuses or hedging will be tolerated, or look for another job."

As late as 1971 A. H. Robins were still quoting the misleading 1.1% failure rate information. And they were pressing hard for overseas sales, with a representative medical officer in Britain, Dr Stuart Templeton, distributing shields to private specialists and urging the Family Planning Association to examine its potential benefits.

In 1972 the Dalkon Shield became the best-selling IUD in America. Few could have predicted that A. H. Robins would have dropped out of the domestic contraceptive market a year later.

The Complaints

Seven septic spontaneous abortions, one resulting in the mother's death. Several ectopic pregnancies. One deformed live birth. These were the complaints that started to roll in to A. H. Robins' legal department from dissatisfied users.

And complainants with such serious problems were not going to eschew litigation. Robins found itself with ten lawsuits on its hands. The plaintiffs all claimed that the trailing tail of the shield must have carried bacteria into their wombs. Dr Davis acknowledged that such things could happen, but they were very infrequent and providing the plastic sheath was undamaged, they simply would not happen.

The company won seven out of its ten cases. There was no published independent research to prove that the "wicking" really occurred. However, the three suits it lost scared Robins. A near-fatal septic abortion leading to a hysterectomy cost them $6 million. They settled out of court with the Californian woman who bore a deformed child. That set them back $1.4 million. And 2,300 other claims had to be settled out of court. A. H. Robins decided to stop distributing the Dalkon Shield in America.

Rather surprisingly, the Food and Drugs Administration disregarded this in their deliberations on the shield. They had been asked to consider banning it, but their Medical Advisory Panel voted by 12-6 to allow it to remain on the market. Since the FDA was widely respected all over the world, their unexpected decision encouraged other countries to use the Dalkon Shield. The Family Planning Association gave it the go-ahead in England, and clinics in Australia started fitting women with it. They may have abandoned America, but A. H. Robins had no qualms about marketing their device in countries which were not plagued by heavy negligence suits in medical cases.

Ironically, A. H. Robins' approval for worldwide sales of the Dalkon Shield coincided almost exactly as the long-awaited independent reports came in to answer questions about the danger of "wicking" once and for all.

The Proof

"My doctor, a male gynaecologist, told me that cramping, bleeding and infections were better than getting pregnant. I eventually went to a public hospital to have the shield removed."

AUSTRALIAN JOURNALIST SANDRA SHOTLANDER

Professor Robert Rose, a biological engineer at the Massachusetts Institute of Technology, had studied the shield from its early days on the market. In October 1974 his report appeared – the plastic coated multifilament string was defective. In 68% of shields it started eroding within one to six months. By three years 80% of the tails were rotting. By four years the failure rate was 100%. Also, there was no doubt whatsoever that with the sheathed string eroding, "wicking" took place. Bacteria could be introduced into the uterus by the Dalkon Shield.

A. H. Robins acted cautiously. They circulated American and Canadian doctors with a letter suggesting that the shield should be removed in pregnancy or if therapeutic abortion was intended. They put a warning on the shield's packaging that it carried some risk of septic abortion. But the warning was seldom seen by the user. The device was unwrapped and its packaging discarded by doctors, many of whom were men and not much interested in warnings about rare cases.

Indeed, women who wanted their shields removed often found that male gynaecologists were unwilling to attempt the procedure. The little fins on the sides could embed quite deeply in the uterus after several years and it was not an easy matter to get them out.

More Difficulties

Evidence against the Dalkon Shield was piling up relentlessly. Yet paradoxically, research at halfway stages sometimes seemed favourable. Professor Robert Snowden of Exeter University monitored 1,031 women fitted with the shield at eleven different Family Planning Association clinics, and in 1973 he reported to the FPA that it compared favourably with other IUDs. The FPA accordingly approved its use.

Yet when Snowden's observations had been maintained for a full five years, he reported a 7.5% failure rate. And he noted that one in twenty of the pregnancies among shield-users was ectopic – the foetus formed outside the womb, seriously threatening the mother's life.

Before Professor Snowden's research was far advanced or Professor Rose's results were known, Dr Stewart Templeton, Robins's man in the UK, wrote anxiously to head office about the experience of Harley Street doctor James Snyder, the first specialist in England to fit the shield. He reported four or five cases of pelvic sepsis and told Templeton he believed it was caused by the string of the shield acting as a wick along which pathogenic organisms could travel. Templeton promised to ask whether similar cases had been observed in the U.S, and if so what was to be done about them?

Robins's answer was hardly reassuring. "Something that has been a little disturbing recently is the accumulation of some half dozen or so cases of serious septic abortion associated with the Shield," Templeton was told. "One of these was fatal." But Dr Hugh Davis's bland assurances about the sheath's reliability and the rarity of failure were trotted out. It was not until 1974 that Templeton advised the Family Planning Association, in a flurry of cautious near-statement, that there had been "an apparent increase in the number of cases of septic abortion occurring in patients purportedly wearing the Dalkon Shield."

In fact, by the time Templeton wrote that, four deaths had been reported in America.

Waste Not Want Not

In 1975 A. H. Robins threw in the towel. They stopped manufacturing Dalkon Shields for domestic or export purposes and got out of the contraceptive business which had proved so trying. It was rumoured that thousands of shields were included in unsterilised bulk packages sent as aid to third world countries!

Dr Michael Smith, chief medical officer of the Family Planning Association had already written to all its 1,100 clinics advising that the shield should no longer be fitted. But Smith was only empowered to advise.

In England, America and Australia some doctors and clinics with stock of Dalkon Shields on their hands continued to fit them until 1979. The shields only fell into total disuse with publicity over hearings for the class actions started by a group of British women that year, which resulted in victory in the American courts in 1982.

The Reassurances

"On the available information there has been only one miscarriage and two suspected cases of infection"

PATRICK JENKIN MP

Wrong!

"It has been off the market since 1974 and it is unlikely that many women are still using this product."

PATRICK JENKIN MP

Wrong!

Sufficient information has been made available to make doctors aware of potential problems associated with the Dalkon Shield."

DR GERARD VAUGHAN MP

Complacent!

Government Problems

The Dalkon Shield controversy provided an early banana skin for Margaret Thatcher's unhappy Social Services Secretary, Patrick Jenkin. He had the unfortunate habit of repeating anodyne information handed over by his officials and seeming a little stunned when the opposition and the media demonstrated how inaccurate it was.

In February 1980 he calmly advised Parliament that, despite the alleged 17 fatalities in America resulting from use of the shield, English women had suffered no more than one miscarriage and two suspected cases of infection. In any case, it was quite unimportant as the shield had been off the market since 1974 and it was unlikely that many Englishwomen were still using the product.

Uttering prodigious nonsense garnished with the odd thumping great lie was normal governmental practice in the 1980s, culminating in the mass contempt for politicians felt by most people in the following decade.

But Jenkin's misinformation was classic. The truth was:

- 100,000 British women used the shield between 1970 and 1980.
- In 7,000 cases monitored, 59 cases of pelvic infection and 12 ectopic pregnancies had been found.
- Professor Snowden, who supplied the Department of Health and Social Services with official data on the Dalkon Shield, estimated that a probably 10,000 women were still walking around with the little bacterial time bombs inside them.

When the true figures emerged, Renee Short MP demanded that the government call in the remaining 10,000 Dalkon Shields. Health Minister Dr Gerard Vaughan refused to do anything so interventionist. But the characteristic triumphalism of Thatcher government statements was missing from his humble invitation for "any relevant information" to be sent to his department.

Individual Cases

27-year-old Marilyn Cartlich went for a check-up at Hammersmith hospital in August 1974, and doctors advised her they were replacing the Lippes Loop IUD which had served her very satisfactorily since the birth of her second child. She was not told until they had finished that her new device was a Dalkon Shield, regarded as still in its trial period. She was annoyed, but decided against the painful process of having it removed and replaced again.

In November she found herself pregnant. Doctors confidently assured her the shield must have fallen out without her noticing. Mrs Cartlich doubted their word.

Just before Christmas she noticed that she was spotting blood. On Christmas Eve she was in so much pain she could barely stand. On Christmas Day she was rushed to hospital where she miscarried. In the curettage that followed, doctors found the tiny Dalkon Shield clinging to her uterus, high up on the wall.

Margaret Smith was fitted with a Dalkon Shield at a Brighton clinic in 1972. For the next five years she had regular checkups as advised, and everything seemed well. At the end of 1977 she fell ill. In the New Year, she began to suffer from chest pains and breathing difficulties, and her temperature rose to 102°. She was found to have not one, but three ovarian abscesses. She lay unconscious for 12 days. She needed the transfusion of 36 pints of blood.

Sandra Shotlander had a Dalkon Shield fitted in 1975 when she was 33. She immediately noted pain and problems. In 1982 she had a hysterectomy because of uterine fibroids. None of her doctors was willing to confirm that the shield was the cause. Ms Shotlander, noting that 20 other Australian women were preparing to sue A. H. Robins, was deeply suspicious. The Leichardt Women's Community Centre in Sydney reported 120 women as coming to them with problems subsequent to being fitted with Dalkon Shields.

Anne Fellows was one of three British women who sued A. H. Robins in the American courts in 1980. Mrs Fellows, a 30-year-old teacher from south London, suffered an ectopic pregnancy in her fallopian tube, which ruptured and nearly killed her. Surgery followed in an attempt to restore her fertility. It failed.

Mrs Frances Salmon was 27 when she had the shield fitted in 1975. Mrs Salmon already had two children. In 1979 she fell ill. She suffered fever, with diarrhoea, vomiting and abdominal pains. She was taken to hospital on New Year's Eve and told she had an abscess on one of her fallopian tubes and an infection in the other. Both had to be removed, together with her right ovary. Mrs Salmon emerged from hospital after two months knowing that she was now sterile.

The medical profession evaded a direct decision as to whether the shield had caused her suffering, leaving it to the California courts to make up their minds for them.

Fertility Clinic Cases

At the same time as contraception improved, medicine made great converse strides in helping infertile couples bear children. There were remarkable laboratory and surgical procedures, such as in vitro fertilization (or "test tube babies"). There were hormone injections to increase women's potential fertility which led to rather large numbers of multiple births in the early days, so that triplets, quads and even quins ceased, for a few years at least, to be the extreme rarity they are in nature.

Some of the most worrying examples of incompetence or deliberate malpractice came in the simple technique of artificial insemination. The most outrageous of the deliberate malpractitioners was Dr Cecil B. Jacobson, whose fertility clinic in Virginia offered to help women whose infertile husbands could not impregnate them. The clinic offered banked sperm, matched to the patient's physical, mental and social characteristics through an "extensive, carefully regulated donor programme."

In 1992 it transpired that the regulated donor programme was sheer fiction and there was no sperm bank at all. Dr Jacobson personally provided the semen he introduced into his patients, quietly emitting it in the privacy of his office bathroom before consultations. When patients started noticing that their babies markedly resembled the good doctor, his days of continuing practice were numbered. 15 couples came forward at his trial, and several dozens more were believed to have been the dupes of the man whose ironic slogan was "God doesn't give you babies. I do."

The fertility clinic at the University of California at Irvine came under scrutiny in 1995. Women had been encouraged to leave fertilized eggs or embryos in storage at the clinic for implantation at a later stage of their life whey they could more conveniently bear a child. Several complained that they returned to find that their personally deposited eggs or embryos had been given to other childless women who had gone on to bear their children. Three doctors had their records seized by police and tax authorities after the university, acknowledging that 30 women had been affected by improper egg or embryo swaps, closed the clinic.

The most appalling mix-up at a fertility clinic was surely that which affected Mr and Mrs Skolnick of New York. In 1985 they went to a Manhattan fertility clinic where Mr Skolnick donated sperm to be banked before he went for bone cancer treatment which was likely to sterilize him. A few months later Mrs Skolnick went back to be inseminated with her husband's sperm.

She was unaware that anything had gone wrong until she gave birth to a little black girl the following year! Although DNA tests proved that the mistake was the clinic's or sperm bank's, Mrs Skolnick still suffered from false rumours that she had a black lover, and her little girl was teased and taunted at school. After Mr Skolnick's death in 1990, his widow sued the clinic.

Test Cases

Nobody's perfect, but it is always a shock to learn that errors made over a period of years may cast in doubt a clean bill of health received from a hospital. Patients of the Kent and Canterbury Hospital were alarmed to learn in 1996 that errors in pap smear tests meant that all women tested since 1992 were to have their samples re-tested.

Dr Samuel Kiberu aroused still more anxiety the previous year. An independent review of the 43-year-old locum histopathologist's work at the Pilgrim Hospital in Boston, Lincolnshire uncovered a wholly unacceptable 17% rate of error. A colleague at Grantham was alarmed when he found a patient with skin cancer who had been reported by Dr Kiberu as clear of the disease. A review of his work at Boston and Grantham, and at Bassetlaw Hospital in Nottingham was immediately put in hand. 4,000 cases were reconsidered. It transpired that Dr Kiberu had made 601 diagnostic mistakes affecting 554 patients.

Not all the mistakes were serious, and it was not believed that anyone had died as a result of Dr Kiberu's inaccuracies, but 89 patients had to be called in urgently for re-examination, some requiring further tests under anaesthetics.

Dr Kiberu was born in Uganda and qualified at Dar-es-Salaam in the 1970s. Following his arrival in Britain he had worked in Grimsby District Hospital, Victoria Hospital, Hammersmith Hospital, Middlesex Hospital, and Luton and Dunstable Hospital. All these institutions might now have to review their records of cancer patients during the periods Dr Kiberu worked with them.

His case highlighted two persistent medical problems which the Health Minister was invited to address: the need for full and proper checking of locum consultants' qualifications and experience; and the potential inaccuracy of overworked histopathologists, usually working alone and without supervision or assistance as they peer down microscopes at slides of tissue, and have to make quick judgements about their healthiness or otherwise, and offer some opinion as to what form of disease they believe they observe if there is something apparently wrong.

Bad Blood

The AIDS scourge, which emerged without warning at the beginning of the 1980s, led to avoidable and unavoidable mistakes. Petty personal and nationalistic quarrelling between American and French researchers as to which had correctly identified the HIV virus delayed the useful co-operative work need for fuller understanding of the disease. Some authorities were slow to take serious action against an illness old-fashioned moralists perceived as self-inflicted, as long as it mainly struck homosexuals and drug abusers who shared needles.

Arguably the bulk of the worldwide research on the disease has been money ill-spent ever since it was established that it can only be transmitted by an exchange of body fluids, so that it is open to everybody to take proper preventative measures like double condoms or clean needles without even having to forego promiscuous sex or illegal drug injections. There are, after all, other hideous and untreatable epidemic diseases like leptospirosis and Ebola virus. And every penny spent on AIDS and HIV is a penny lost to their victims.

Most public outrage was caused by those victims – many of them children – who were at first unwittingly and later negligently given blood transfusions or plasma that was contaminated with the virus. Britain learned again, the hard way, what Richard Titmuss had said since the 1960s – free and voluntary blood donation is safer and more reliable than buying blood or plasma that has been collected as a commercial enterprise in countries like America.

The blood donor scheme did not result in many cases of AIDS. However, imported plasma did, and victims started legal proceddings against the NHS. France actually jailed four senior health officials when 1,200 hemophiliacs were found to have been given bad blood products contaminated with HIV.

The Australian Case

A very small incident produced an extraordinary panic in Australia when three babies died in September and October 1984 at Mater Hospital, Brisbane. All three showed signs of AIDS, and after a month of investigations, the hospital realised that all had received blood transfusions from the same source: a 27-year-old homosexual who had made 15 blood donations over the previous three years.

Mr Brian Austin, the Queensland health minister, immediately ordered a full investigation, and before it had even started deliberating, the Queensland legislature rushed through an emergency law making it an offence punishable by two years in jail or a $A10,000 fine for practicing homosexuals to donate blood.

However, the panic did not stop there – the Victoria State government stopped a donor sperm programme for artificial insemination which had already been started in four Melbourne hospitals.

The Flinders Medical Centre in Adelaide first insisted that all sperm donors must sign forms declaring that they were not involved in homosexual relationships and then halted its programme. Even though Professor Warren Jones, head of the fertility clinic, observed that the risk of babies contracting the disease from conception was still entirely theoretical and did not seem particularly high.

Australian Prime Minister Bob Hawke was compeeled to act on the spreading anxiety. He called a national conference of state and federal health ministers; doctors and scientists from the leading medical schools; representatives of the Red Cross and the Commonwealth Serum Laboratory and a number of other public health institutions. Out of this meeting came plans to set up a national advisory committee, with representatives from the Australian Medical Association, the Red Cross, haemophiliacs organisations, and the homosexual community. A national AIDS task force to keep health ministers informed was proposed. A $A1 million AIDS eduction programme was initiated, with subsidiary propaganda encouraging more women to become blood donors. Counselling services for AIDS patients were proposed. Finally – the action which would do most to ensure healthy blood from voluntary donation – a $A300,000 national reference centre was established to start monitoring blood screening tests from the end of 1985.

All this high-profile activity because of three babies and one unwittingly sick donor.

Personal Tragedy vs Bloody-Minded Bureaucracy

Martin Gaffney's life started to fall apart in 1981. His Japanese wife Mutsuko carried her pregnancy four weeks beyond normal term, and was delivered of a dead child by Caesarean section. Subsequently she became very ill and received two units of blood.

The following year she gave birth to a healthy daughter, Maureene. Two years later she was pregnant again and in 1985 gave birth to a son, John. In 1986 her doctor told her that she and John had tested positive for AIDS. Mrs Gaffney responded by asking for enough sleeping pills to kill herself. In fact, John died that year and Mutsuko a year later. Martin Gaffney, a Chief Warrant Officer in the US Marines was tested, and he, too proved positive. It seemed impossible to imagine how the family had become infected. The Gaffneys were faithful and monogamous heterosexuals. They did not use drugs or any sort of hypodermic needles. And then Martin remembered the blood transfusion Mutsuko had received in 1981. The donor was traced. He refused to be tested for AIDS and HIV. However, it was observed that he had been discharged from the navy as a suspected homosexual.

With the full support of his senior officers, Martin Gaffney sued the navy for medical negligence. He wanted the money to take Maureene to Okinawa and to set up an educational trust. The Navy's principal expert witness admitted negligence, and the case should have been swiftly concluded. It seems likely that an insurance company would have settled it out of court to save legal costs.

Instead the case became bogged down in the legal process. With arguments and technicalities it was prolonged until 1991, by which time Martin himself was severely ill with lymphonoma from which he could not expect to recover. Judge Rya Zobel awarded him $3.8 million, and another spanner was thrown in the works by a request for time to consider appealing on the Navy's behalf. It seemed that Warrant Officer Gaffney would be forced to accept a lower negotiated figure because of the threat that he would be dead before he got any money if he didn't compromise.

"The bitterest thing," said Martin Gaffney, "is that they have wasted my healthy days and even my life, and this case goes on and on." His commanding officer, knowing how much Martin had wanted to take Maureene to see her granparents in Okinawa while he still had the strength, expressed his disgust with the navy's bureaucracy. The result of their dilatoriness was the suffering of an honourable man who still felt loyalty to his country and his service.

Killer Corpses from Bulgaria

It sounded like a cross between Dracula and Frankenstein. Mad scientists and corpse-scavengers. Two French doctors stood accused in 1991 of killing 14-year-old Ilyassil Benziane by injecting him with a hormone extracted from the pituitary glands of Bulgarian and Hungarian corpses, which were purchased at $6 to $9 each.

Insufficient care had been taken in checking the corpses, it was alleged, and the child had been infected with Creutzfeld-Jacob disease – a fatal brain damage that is thought to be related to Britain's "Mad Cow Disease".

Although France has half of all the world's known Creutzfeld-Jacobs victims, it seemed the French doctors had risked infecting their patients by buying pituitary glands from infectious wards in Bulgaria and Hungary.

And the aim of this "mad scientist" experiement? To cure children's dwarfism and allow them to reach natural growth height without the stunting that results from defective pituitary glands.

In America, three young children died as a result of the same treatment in 1985. Consequently, the cadaver-extracted hormone was promptly withdrawn while researchers set about – successfully – developing a safe synthetic substitute.

Gallic doctors, however, disdained this uncouth and mechanistic Anglo-Saxonism and continued to use Bulgarian corpse hormone until 1990. The results were tragic.

Never Say Die

It made headlines in January 1996 when a vein in Mrs Daphne Banks' leg twitched and she suddenly began to snore. For she was lying in a mortuary while the undertaker waited for the mortician to come along and prepare her body for refrigeration.

Mrs Banks had taken an overdose of pills in a fit of depression on New Year's Eve. Unable to drive because of illness, she felt lonely and trapped on the farm in Cambridgeshire run by her husband of forty years, Claude. When Claude came home from visiting their daughter and found Daphne comatose under the duvet, he called for the ambulance. The ambulance service sent out young Dr David Roberts, and he examined Mrs Banks finding no pulse, no sign of breath, no movement of the eye. He cancelled the ambulance and sent for the hearse. Undertaker Ken Davison, a friend of the family, was just sitting in the mortuary thinking how devastated Claude would be, when he saw the leg twitch and heard the snore.

It made headlines, but it is not an uncommon wrong diagnosis. In another case in Kent in 1989 an 83-year-old man was pronounced dead by his doctor but found alive by his family shortly afterwards. The family demanded an enquiry, though the chief executive of Kent Family Practitioners Union pointed out that such mistakes could easily be made in the absence of monitoring machines.

In 1974 an 84-year-old woman's daughter was present when their GP checked her breathing and pulse and listened to her chest through a stethoscope. The old lady had the pale and waxy appearance of recent death. Her pupils did not respond to light. The daughter agreed that she was dead, but this corpse, too, startled the undertaker by snoring. The old lady spent a few weeks in hospital and eventually emerged as right as rain.

THE SLIPPED SCALPEL

If you have recently been in hospital for any surgical operation you may have wondered whether the staff have grown half-witted.

Over and over again they ask you the same litany of questions: ward reception will ask you. Your appointed caring nurse will ask you. The surgeon and anaesthetist will each ask you if they make pre-operative visits to your bedside in the ward. The orderlies will ask you as they put you on the gurney to be wheeled off to the theatre. The theatre nurse will ask you. And maybe the anaesthetist will ask you all over again just before he puts you to sleep.

- **What is your name?**

- **What is your date of birth?**

- **What was your mother's maiden name?**

- **What's your address and post code?**

- **What are you here for?**

- **Who is your consultant?**

- **Are you taking any medication?**

- **Have you any allergies?**

All this checking! On top of that, by this time they will even have put a little label on your wrist just to remind everyone who you are. Can't they remember anything? Don't they, indeed, know the most elementary things? You've gone in to have a hip replacement. As if the surgeon were a child preparing to make a cut-out toy, a staff nurse asks you all the questions, consults your notes, and proceeds to use a felt-tip pen to draw a circle on your hip around the area to be opened up, with big arrows indicating it. You have a very visible tumour to be removed. The base of it is surrounded with dotted lines. Again, arrows stream in from the compass points, you wonder if you haven't been labelled for the infants' class:

" H - I - P. L - U - M - P. CUT HERE. "

Why? Well, if somewhere along the line an overworked team got your notes in the wrong order and it wasn't all checked, double-checked and clearly and unmistakably marked, you could go to have your left hip replaced and come out with the right one removed. You might go for the removal of a cyst on the neck and wake up to find it still there, and your tummy carefully stitched up. If you were taking a blood-thinning medication, or suffered a strong allergic reaction to antibiotics you might wake up in Intensive Care, or not wake up at all if the surgical team were not warned about your condition in advance.

Accidents Happen

Modern surgery can seem miraculous. Human ingenuity can stitch back hands that have been cut off, reuniting severed nerves and blood vessels. Heart surgery can circumvent clogged and wasted arteries that would have meant certain death a generation ago. Whole hearts can be replaced. Few areas of human endeavour are such a testimony to man's skill, courage and inventiveness.

The surgical scalpel is sharp, keen and deadly accurate. So much the worse if it slips.

Yet with all that, man is still goofy old man – Homo Sapiens and master of the foul-up. Man the tool-maker and man who says, "Oops!" The only animal that can read and write; and the only animal that can write down the wrong information and read the right information wrongly.

Primitive – and Useless?

Trepanning was one of the earliest surgical operations. It was certainly practised by ancient Egyptians and some Amerindian tribes, as well as probably being known to other early societies which left neither records of it nor skulls with tell-tale holes in their burial grounds.

Trepanning is cutting a little hole in the skull. We can tell, from the neatness of some of the holes surviving in old skulls, and the fresh growth of bone around the edges of the openings, that this was done to living people as surgery, and they survived.

Perhaps in a few cases it removed weapons that were lodged in head injuries. But all too often, it seems likely, the painful and alarming surgery was undertaken for no better reason than to "let foul spirits out of the head", or perhaps as a rather drastic approach to relieving a headache.

So while the modern saw observes that, "a hole in the head" is something no one needs, we have nevertheless known for thousands of years that it can be deliberately created and survived!

A Famous Slip

Robert Liston (1794-1847) was one of the great surgeons of the early 19th century. Known as "the first surgeon in Europe" he was immensely strong and athletic, and this was important in the days before anaesthetics, when any serious operation had to be completed as fast as possible to prevent the patient from dying of pain.

Liston was famous for his astonishing ability to amputate a leg at the hip and tie off the main blood vessels in 28 seconds.

Remarkable as this was, we should probably not remember it were it not for the day when the scalpel slipped. And Liston accidentally amputated two of his assistant's fingers and the patient's left testicle.

Surgeon, Beware!

Mankind's earliest written code of laws includes regulations governing surgery. More remarkable, in their way, than the famous Hanging Gardens, the Laws of Hammurabi, King of Babylon and Assyria, were drawn up 18 centuries before the birth of Christ. What's more, they show that doctors of that day used knives made of precious metals; had certain definite responsibilities in relation to treating each other; were expected to charge fees related to patients' ability to pay; were capable of various sorts of surgery, including eye surgery; but most of all, were expected to be successful.

Hammurabi's laws decreed firmly that if a patient died under the surgeon's knife, the surgeon was responsible and he was to lose his right hand.

No documents have survived to show how this Draconian ruling affected recruitment to the profession.

From Barber-Surgeon to Anatomist

Until some rudimentary understanding of the workings of the human body were acquired, surgical skills were necessarily largely concerned with repairing visible and surface faults.

Surgeons bound up wounds, splinted fractures, cut away obvious growths and tumours, amputated potentially gangrenous limbs. In an attempt to alleviate feverish conditions they might tap a bowlful of blood from a vein: a practice which was as superstitious and useless as the primitive habit of trepanning to release foul spirits; yet one which survived into the early 19th century despite the growing numbers of anatomical discoveries.

Since barbers owned good scissors and razors, they frequently combined their vocation with surgery, and the two professions were not clearly distinguished until the end of the eighteenth century. However, by this time, some surgeons were already separating themselves off from the crude bleeders and cutters. Many of them were insisting on a training that familiarized them with the internal organs of the body and the chains of veins, arteries and nerves. And two sophisticated operations were being carried out by specialist surgeons from the early days of the 18th century.

Cataracts and Lithotomies

It is a peculiarity of the eye that its apparent extreme sensitivity is actually a sensitivity of the membranous undersurface of the eyelid. The eyeball itself has no feeling, and will experience no paid if the eyelids be quite firmly retracted from an area where a surgeon works.

This was discovered by surgeons, and after practising on some convicted criminals, William Cheselden, the "father of English surgery" (1688-1752) mastered the removal of cataracts and the replacement of a damaged pupil. In 1727 Cheselden made his other great contribution to surgery: he improved the operation for stone in the bladder which had been devised by the French monk Frere Jacques 100 years earlier. Stone in the bladder, caused by the coarse diet of those days, was so painful a condition that sufferers were willing to risk short-lived agony and possible death at the hands of surgeons who undertook to remove it.

The treatment was frightful. Trussed like a chicken on his back, with his legs drawn up, the patient exposed genitals and perineum to the doctor, who first inserted a probe through the urethra into the bladder and located the stone; then made an incision through the perineum, cut through the bladder wall, and removed the stone from the end of the probe.

Cheselden's rather simple improvement was to enter the bladder laterally instead of from below. Whereas 50% of patients treated by Frere Jacques' method died, Cheselden only lost six of the first 100 patients who underwent his improved operation.

The operation was, you will doubtless have observed, painful even to read about. Cheselden's humane practice was to make himself vomit before he started operating, so that no squeamishness should cause delays and extend the patient's pain. An assistant stood by with a stopwatch in an attempt to ensure that he never took more than three or four minutes operating. A protracted operation of this kind, before the invention of anaesthesia, was bound to cause death.

Until the problem of pain was solved, frenzied speed was essential to good surgery. And it was vital that the surgeon press on with his work, ruthlessly disregarding the patient's cries. Sir Astley Cooper (1768-1841), one of the most prominent British surgeons of his generation, said that a surgeon must have "the eye of an eagle, the heart of a lion and the hands of a lady."

His own leonine heart cracked visibly when a child on whom he was about to perform an operation smiled confidently at him from the table,

198

and knowing the pain he was about to inflict, Sir Astley broke down before his assistants and students.

Snail's Pace Surgery Exposed

Sir Astley Cooper's besetting faults were vanity and nepotism. In 1820 he insisted on appointing his nephew Bransby to a permanent post over the head of his far abler young assistant Thomas Wakley. A poor man, Wakley was unable to continue his surgical career, and in 1823 joined together with William Cobbett to found The Lancet, a journal which reported and criticized the anatomical lectures and surgical operations performed in the hospitals of London.

In a very early number Wakley had his revenge on Bransby Cooper. Attempting a lithotomy on a labouring man, Bransby first failed to locate the stone and had to make repeated attempts to reinsert the probe. He then failed to cut cleanly into the bladder. At every mistake, the bungling surgeon stopped, reconsidered what he was doing, and started again. After twenty minutes the patient was screaming demands that he halt the operation and leave him with his stone in the bladder. After fifty minutes he died on the table.

Over Hasty Surgery Exposed

Dr Robert Knox was shocked by the poor quality of surgery and anatomy in Edinburgh when he started lecturing at the university in 1826, and warned his students against imitating their betters. Robert Liston's celebrated athletic speed received this rebuke:

"Before commencing today's lecture I am compelled by the sacred calls of duty to notice an extraordinary surgical operation which has this morning been performed in a neighbouring building by a gentleman who, I believe, regards himself as the first surgeon in Europe. A country labourer from Tranent came into the infirmary a few days ago with an aneurism (arterial swelling) of considerable extent, connected with one of the main arteries of the neck; and notwithstanding its being obvious to

the merest tyro that it was an aneurism, the most distinguished surgeon in Europe, after an apparently searching examination, pronounced it to be an abscess. Accordingly, this professional celebrity – who among other things plumes himself upon the wonderful strength of his hands and arms, without pretentions to head, and is an amateur member of the ring – plunged his knife into what he foolishly imagined to be an abscess; and with blood gushing forth from the aneurismal sac, the patient was dead in a few seconds.

EARLY PAINKILLERS

The Babylonians and Egyptians tried to ease pain in surgery by offering potions, such as:

● **Opium (lethal if given in excess)**

● **Wine with herbs (patient liable to wake up with a scream at the first incision**

● **Mandrake root (useless)**

These traditional anaesthetics were sufficiently unacceptable that a seventeenth century French law banned the use of any pain-killing drugs during surgery. Some surgeons attempted other methods: for example, applying snow to the area intended for surgery, hoping to freeze it into numbness.

There were others. Ambroise Pare (1510-90) " the father of modern French surgery" applied pressure to the carotid artery to make his patients pass out (extremely dangerous). Baron Dupuytren, "the most callous of all surgeons", insulted women patients in the hope of throwing them into dead faints before he operated. Anton Mesmer's discovery of hypnotism offered some surgeons a way of alleviating their patients' pain. But Mesmer's transparent personal charlatanism made few willing to take his "animal magnetism" seriously.

In fact, when real anaesthetic inhalants were discovered, their potential value in surgery was completely overlooked and the first medical mistake made with them was to treat them simply as recreational drugs.

Humphry Davy and Nitrous Oxide

The great chemist Sir Humphry Davy started his life intending to become a doctor, and after apprenticeship to a Cornish surgeon-apothecary, he went to Wiltshire to work at Thomas Beddoes' "Pneumatic Institute", where experiments were made with gases to treat asthma and other respiratory disorders.

Davy's first important discovery was made with nitrous oxide, a gas discovered twenty years earlier by Joseph Priestley. Davy inhaled it, and immediately noted that it eased painful inflamed gums from which he as suffering. He carried out some experiments with animals, and then reported: "As nitrous oxide in its extensive operation appears capable of destroying physical pain, it may probably be used to advantage during surgical operations in which no great effusion of blood takes place."

Pregnant words, but they were not to take effect for another fifty years.

Davy became a great friend of Wordsworth and Coleridge, and he and they found themselves far more interested in the sensation of general euphoria produced by inhaling nitrous oxide from a bag. For a time, all three thought they had discovered a wonderful breakthrough into higher states of rhapsodic perception altogether suitable to poets – much as Aldous Huxley 150 years later believed that mescalin opened doors to mechanical mysticism. Unfortunately for these romantics, the euphoric effect of nitrous oxide wears off after repeated doses, and they soon lost interest in the wonderful gas. Davy went on to major work on muriatic acid, the isolation of sodium and aluminium, and the invention of the safety lamp. Coleridge fell victim to the seriously addictive laudanum, and Wordsworth, observing this with disapproval, made no further experiments with recreational drugs.

Wells and Laughing Gas

Nitrous oxide passed into the hands of showmen. Since the first effect of inhaling it is excitement accompanied by uncontrollable laughter and giddy lurching movements, it proved amusing to demonstrate these antics in sideshows, allowing unsophisticated yokels to tray the laughing gas for themselves, and amuse their friends by their absurd behaviour.

In 1844, a young Connecticut dentist called Horace Wells went to a laughing gas entertainment which promised to be "genteel" inasmuch as ladies would not be allowed to make a spectacle of themselves by inhaling the substance. Wells noticed that one young man who flailed about all over the stage before sinking into unconsciousness was banging into furniture and scraping his shins painfully without showing the least sign of discomfort.

After the performance Wells asked the young man about his sensations, and the youth confirmed that he felt no pain. Wells immediately perceived that he had made a discovery of inestimable potential value to dentistry, and had himself anaesthetized with laughing gas while a colleague pulled out a perfectly healthy tooth. "I didn't feel so much as the prick of a pin!" Wells exclaimed enthusiastically, characterizing it as "the greatest discovery ever made".

He soon arranged to publicize his discovery in high places, and a lecture demonstration was organized at Harvard University before surgical professors and medical students. A student volunteer had a tooth drawn, but unfortunately the gas was wrongly administered, and he screamed out with pain as it was yanked out. Whereupon the great pain-killing invention was put down as a humbug and Wells was booed off the premises.

At home in Hartford he continued to administer it to his patients. But the use of soporific gases is a ticklish and dangerous business. One of Wells' patients died, and deeply discouraged, he abandoned his practice and left America. In 1848 he killed himself, and nitrous oxide was not restored to the anaesthetist's armoury until other treatments had established painless surgery.

Morton and Ether

It was a former partner of Horace Wells who succeeded in bringing efficient anaesthesia to surgery. William Morton was extremely anxious to make dental extraction painless because his successful invention of a reliable solder securing false teeth to dental plates was going unused. Patients feared extraction and could not wear Morton's bridgework over unpulled stumps without severe discomfort.

After leaving partnership with Wells in 1843, Morton took some refresher courses at Harvard, and learned from students there about "ether frolics": parties where they happily intoxicated themselves with mild doses of ether. Morton saw that, like the yokels at laughing gas shows, the etherized students felt no pain when they fell over furniture. Experiments on animals and goldfish, and ultimately the extraction of one of his own teeth convinced him that he had found a true painkiller. In 1846, after using ether successfully for a couple of tooth extractions, Morton demonstrated its use at Massachusetts General Hospital, successfully anaesthetizing a patient so that surgeon John Warren, how had presided over Wells's humiliating Harvard demonstration, could painlessly remove a tumour from the frightened man's jaw.

Anaesthetics had come to surgery.

ANTISEPSIS AND BLOOD TRANSFUSION

With painless surgery possible, two more vital advances were necessary to allow the tremendous surgical progress of the twentieth century.

Something had to be done about the numbers of patients who died when their surgical wounds became infected. Something also had to be done about the patients who still died of the "shock" of major surgery, even though they did not feel it: a shock which was actually loss of blood.

Cleanliness in surgery was pioneered by the tragic Hungarian obstetrician Ignaz Semmelweiss. His interest in medicine had been aroused by observing pioneering pathological anatomy (the dissection of diseased bodies to examine the effects of disease on the organs). His first appointment was to a position in the Vienna Obstetric Clinic. Here he was appalled by the normal incidence of puerperal fever among recent mothers. At least 10% died of this infection: at times the mortality rate rose as high as 30%. The symptoms were invariably high fever, swollen abdomens, swollen lymph glands and suppuration.

An oddity that struck Semmelweiss was that the incidence was far higher in the wards where medical students were trained than in the wards where midwives were trained. Since bacteria were not understood, and epidemics were believed to be transmitted by "miasmas" in the air, there was no obvious explanation for this. However, the difference was well enough known that expectant mothers would often implore the staff to place them in the trainee midwives' ward and not with the trainee doctors.

In 1847 Semmelweiss suddenly observed a possible cause. His friend Professor Kolletschka died of blood poisoning after accidentally cutting his hand with a scalpel in the dissecting room. His symptoms were exactly the same as those of women with puerperal fever. Semmelweiss realized, with horror, that the lethal septicemia might be transferred on the hands of medical students and demonstrators as they moved without washing from cutting up cadavers to examining women in labour. He insisted on his students and colleagues washing their hands in chlorine water before they entered the maternity ward, and the death rate was cut to 1%. He made more and more observations about the transference of infection from doctor to patient and from patient to patient, leading him to demand clean bedding and clean nightgowns for the women under his care. The results proved themselves – and yet his colleagues positively refused to listen to him. Semmelweiss, desperately aware that in the early days of his own research he must have killed many women because of the time he spent in the dissecting room before examining them with unwashed hands, fervently preached his gospel of hygiene to the deaf.

Women went on dying unnecessarily because pig-headed doctors insisted that Semmelweiss was an obsessive fanatic, and that puerperal fever was caused by "miasmas" in the air, by the women's own fear of it, or by an undefined "epidemic". Semmelweiss was driven distracted by this rejection of his life-saving work, and was committed to an asylum in 1865, where he died of septicemia having tragically cut his own hand in the last dissection he ever undertook.

Shortly before Semmelweiss died, Louis Pasteur proved the role of bacteria promoting fermentation and putrefaction. His work came to the attention of the British doctor Thomas Lister, who was already concerned about the incidence of septicemia and gangrene following surgery, and simply could not imagine why it didn't occur in every single case if oxygen or a permeating atmospheric miasma was the cause. Pasteur's work explained everything to him, and although Lister's anxiety about the quasi-miasmic presence of bacteria everywhere around a patient led to his drenching surgeries and operating rooms in an incessant spray of mild carbolic acid for many years, the principle of antisepsis was at last established on a sound footing.

Blood loss gave competent doctors rather more difficulty. There seemed to be two ideal possibilities: a reliable clotting agent in the vicinity of the wound to hinder haemorrhage, or fresh blood from another source to be injected into the system. The great 18th century anatomist and surgeon John Hunter had experimented repeatedly with implanting human teeth in living cocks' combs until at last he persuaded one to engraft itself properly and take root. He was sure he had found to answer to lost and worn-out teeth: new ones could be simply grafted into the gum.

It would be more than a hundred years before the principles on which the body normally rejects foreign implants were understood, and the ways in which these could be overcome admitted the genuine possibility of transplant surgery. One major step toward this desirable end was the discovery of the human blood types and the ways in which properly selected donors could give replacement blood to be given to those who needed it during and after operations. But the road was not always a smooth one.

Potholes Along The Road To Blood Transfusion

- 1667 Jean Denys, mathematics professor at Montpellier uses lamb's blood in human patients until one dies, and he is ordered to stop.

- 1818 Obstetrician James Blundell attempts human to human blood transfusions, having proved that dog to dog transfusion could be carried out safely, but lamb to dog kills the dog. Blundell's human to human transfusions kill about 50% of his patients, with accelerated heart rate, back pains, vomiting and diarrhoea and the passing of black urine.

- 1884 Surgeon and obstetrician Braxton Hicks experiments with sodium phosphate as an anticoagulant in transfused blood to enable patients to absorb the transfusions more easily. The experiment promptly kills four patients.

- 1900 Dr Karl Landsteiner, Assistant Professor of anatomy and pathology in Vienna, carries out experiments with his own blood and that of five colleagues, proving that there were at least three human blood types which would prove incompatible with each other.

- 1930 The importance of Dr Landsteiner's work is finally recognized with the award of a Nobel Prize.

Two Spinal Accidents

The worst accidents with anaesthetics are likely to be those that come about when the wrong substance is administered. Today there will no longer be just one bottle of ether or chloroform, or one cylinder of nitrous oxide for the anaesthetist to use. Modern anaesthetists are likely to give a cocktail of drugs, both injected and inhaled: tranquillizers to calm patients who may be nervous about approaching the operating theatre; soporifics to render them peacefully unconscious; muscle relaxants to ensure that they don't twitch or tense while the surgeon is at work; painkillers so that they do not come round in agony; and with any or all of these, a measured quantity of oxygen so that anaesthetizing gases don't in fact poison the patient.

Since the drugs affect the nervous system, damage may be frightful, involving paralysis or brain damage. Epidural injection into the outer membrane of the spinal cord is a very effective way of numbing and still-ing the lower abdomen. Mrs Carol Brown was undergoing a difficult labour at a South London Hospital in 1981 when a midwife attending her decided her epidural needed topping up, and by the most appalling error mistook a small container of cleaning fluid for the required injection. Mrs Brown's son Dominic was born perfectly formed and unharmed. But Mrs Brown was left paralyzed, able only to move her right hand and partially move her right arm.

She was awarded record damages of £414,563 but only after the local health authority and its legal department had outraged the public by their strenuous attempts to fight off her claim.

A worse fate befell Miami news photographer Bob East when in 1985 he went into hospital to have a facial cancer removed. The operation was a complicated one which entailed the removal of his right eye and its reten-tion in a tissue preservative called glutaraldehyde for research. During the operation, a nurse was passed a small unmarked bottle, and told it was fluid which had been drawn from East's spine. She marked it as such, and toward the end of the operation the contents were reinjected into his spine.

Alas, the bottle had contained the glutaraldehyde. Senior Surgeon James Ryan Chandler said severely that no unmarked bottle should ever have been brought into the operating theatre. Mr East, who had in his time photographed every American President from Truman to Reagan, was wheeled away to intensive care, irrecoverably brain-dead.

Record Damages

In 1985 Mrs Carol Brown's record damages were topped by the amount awarded to a young woman whose friends and relatives had been struggling to have her claim settled since 1978. Interestingly, both these record per-sonal injury damages were awarded in relation to anaesthesia.

In 1976, when she was 17, the young woman was referred to hospital to have her tonsils out. She was in good health, though a little overweight. And up to two weeks before the operation she had been taking contraceptive pills. She was easily anaesthetized with a mixture of thiopentone, sux-amethonium, nitrous oxide, oxygen and halothane.

The operation went normally, but when it was over the anaesthetist observed that her lips seemed blue and her pulse had weakened. The surgeons immediately gave her manual ventilation and cardiac massage. Her state did not improve.

She was hurried to the Intensive Care Unit where she became hyper-feverish. When she was finally discharged, she was left with severe brain damage. She was physically handicapped, and her behavioural problems were such that she could not be left unattended. Her legal suit started in 1978 produced a formal statement in 1980 that the operation had given her a brain stem thrombosis, and this was in part because she had not been told to come off the contraceptive pill for at least a month prior to her surgery. It was also felt that her cyanosis (blue lips) must have been apparent while the operation was proceeding, and it should have been noticed before the anaesthetist removed the mouth gag at the end of the business.

The further five years taken in reaching a settlement was essentially caused by a difference among the doctors called in for expert testimony as to whether the original report was right to say she had a brain stem lesion. But in the end there was no doubt that her tragic condition had been caused by the operation, and it was agreed that the anaesthetics had played an important part.

The Medical Defence Union had paid over £200,000 into court, antici-pating a settlement. It was the £435,000 the court calculated she would need for future lifelong care which pushed this claim into the record books.

They Felt It All

In the bad old days, the patients who had not been anaesthetized felt every slash of the knife and bite of the saw tooth, and screamed accordingly.

The good surgeon reacted by hastening the process as much as possible. In the period of simple anaesthetics, a patient who started coming round despite the gas would move and possible cry out, warning the anaesthetist to increase the dosage.

In our subtle and multi-functional anaesthetic age it is possible for a patient to feel every agonizing stab and probe; to hear every unreassuring utterance made by a puzzled surgeon; to know the full course of his or her operation with fear and pain; and yet to be bound hand and foot by muscle-relaxing drugs, unable to signal by the blink of an eyelid that the sedatives are not working and painkillers are not sufficient to prevent the shock of feeling oneself lacerated.

In 1985 Dr Michael Wang of Hull University conducted experiments at Royal Hull Hospitals NHS Trust, placing tourniquets on the arms of patients under anaesthesia to prevent paralyzing drugs from reaching their hands, and then finding out whether they could hear questions and respond to them by opening and closing their fingers. He was shocked to find that 50% could: "Half the patients on every operating list showed signs of wakefulness," he told a conference of psychologists at Warwick University. "If you tell them to squeeze their hand they will."

Although it seemed that few of them remembered the experience or felt actual pain, Dr Wang believed that under-anaesthetizing risked psychological damage, and noted that it was especially common in obstetrical cases.

Two years later the General Medical Council's professional conduct committee heard complaints from four mothers who had undergone caesarean operations for childbirth at a hospital in the north-west. All had been aware of at least some part of their operations. Each had been unable to make a sound, or signal that she could feel the incision being made; the child being lifted from her womb; the stitching up concluding the operation. One, however, Mrs Rita Sharples, had managed to open her right eye. Her counsel, Miss Jane Tracy-Foster, criticized the anaesthetist severely for failing to notice this sign that she might well be in distress.

These cases had taken place in 1980-81. Dr Roland Hargrove, a leading anaesthetist from Westminster Hospital, pointed out to the committee that in those years the best anaesthetics still probably allowed a 5% awareness level in childbirth cases, which were particularly difficult as it was vital that enough oxygen be included in the mix to keep the fragile unborn baby alive as well as the mother. But with the new and improved methodology, the level of awareness had now been reduced to 1%.

In 1989, however, Dr John Evans of the Radcliffe Infirmary, Oxford, reported to a conference of senior anaesthetists in London that out of 2.5 million operations every year in Great Britain, about 25,000 patients had some recall of what happened while they were under general anaesthesia. Of that figure, about 100 of those would be sufficiently distressed to start litigation against their anaesthetists. Indeed, law suits against anaesthetists were becoming the most common legal risk that doctors had to face. Furthermore, such experiences could prove traumatic, leaving psychological scars for years.

What the Patients Said

"I can remember the skin of my abdomen being cut. It felt like burning flesh. My mind was screaming out. I could feel everything. I tried to scream, but I could not get it out."

MRS PATRICIA WHARTON, AFTER CAESAREAN SECTION

"I will never forget the pain. I could feel everything they were doing to me but I couldn't twitch an eyelash. It was a nightmare to end all nightmares."

GINNY PRICE, FOLLOWING SURGERY ON ECTOPIC PREGNANCY

"I woke up but I couldn't move a muscle to let the doctors know I was conscious. I felt an almighty pain and passed out."

KEN WHITE, A 61-YEAR-OLD COMPANY DIRECTOR, FOLLOWING SURGERY

Pure Air Anaesthetic

A shocking case was reported to the Medical Defence Union in the early 1980s. A 44-year-old woman went into surgery to have a hysterectomy and the removal of some vaginal cysts. Before the operation commenced she was given morphine, atropine and pancuronium to relax her muscles and put her to sleep. Then she was put on an inhaler feeding her a nitrous oxide and oxygen mix to keep her asleep and unconscious throughout the operation.

When she came round in the recovery room after the muscle relaxants had worn off, the patient complained that she had been fully aware of what was going on throughout the whole proceedings.

The staff doubted the possibility of this until they re-examined the equipment in the operating theatre. This proved her claim to be absolutely true. The tube connecting her inhalation mask to the nitrous oxide and oxygen cylinders had become detached without anybody noticing, and she had undergone major surgery breathing nothing but the air of the operating theatre, although the injected drugs calmed her and prevented her from being able to make any signal or speak about her condition.

An Early Case

George Crele, an American doctor, recorded a fraught occasion in 1908 when he was experimenting with simple sedatives to try and avoid the possible harmful effects of ether and chloroform. In his autobiography he recalled these details:

"About this time I had a revealing but embarrassing experience. I believed that nitrous oxide-oxygen anaesthesia put the patient completely to sleep. While making rounds with my staff and some visiting doctors I asked an extremely intelligent woman who had had an abdominal operation under complete nitrous oxide-oxygen anaesthesia what her memory of the event was.

> "She asked, 'Shall I report everything?' Thereupon she began, 'This is a white female, aged 58,' and continued to give an exact repetition of the notes used by the intern while she was supposedly under full anaesthesia."

211

THE CHELMSFORD
SCANDAL

One of Australia's worst medical disasters was a show that ran and ran for fifteen years in the little private Chelmsford Hospital; a villa in the suburbs, eight miles from the centre of Sydney.

The institution had been set up by the flamboyant Dr James Bailey, who was a student of Dr Sargent of Guy's Hospital in London. Sargent had pioneered the controversial "deep sleep" treatment for serious mental conditions. The principle seemed elementary and unobjectionable. If the brain was overstressed, rest must surely help it to recovery. The barbiturate drugs and their sophisticated successors offered a way of keeping patients asleep for extremely lengthy periods. And it might be hoped that they would awake fully refreshed and mentally stable.

Early experience with barbiturates in England and the Soviet Union in the 1930s quickly revealed that keeping a patient absolutely unconscious for a period of days was actually harmful. It was essential to moderate the doses so that patients could rouse themselves regularly and (for example) walk to the toilet.

By the 1970s, Guy's Hospital was starting to add Electro-Convulsive Therapy to the treatment, ensuring that the patient was fully sedated before jolting the brain with electric shocks: a treatment which, it was hoped, might prove to have all the advantages and none of the drawbacks of the increasingly discredited surgical lobotomy. The late 1960s and early 1970s were, indeed, a time when a number of psychiatrists and brain specialists evinced a belief in their ability to remove personality disorders by chemically or physically altering the state of the brain.

None were more over-confident than James Bailey. He was a charismatic personality with many friends in Australian show business. he gave very persuasive lectures and demonstrations of his methods, and reported a very high rate of success in curing depression and weaning people away from drug addiction. Among his associates with a financial interest in

Chelmsford was a GP who trusted Bailey implicitly and referred many patients to him. The courts, too, came to trust Chelmsford, and sometimes compulsorily referred patients to the institution when psychiatric treatment was made a condition of their sentencing.

Dr Bailey's methods started with the induction of "deep sleep" by massive overdoses of powerful sedatives. He disregarded the need for regular arousal, and was quite willing to allow patients to spend a week or more unconscious, leaving the nursing staff to clean away their excreta when they noticed they were lying in their own faeces. Not surprisingly, his patients tended to lose weight fast. Many developed breathing difficulties, as the intense muscle relaxants made it harder for their lungs to work automatically.

On top of this dangerous chemotherapy, Dr Bailey added constant electro-convulsive therapy. he did not put the patients under renewed general anaesthesia (nitrous oxide and oxygen, for example) as he was satisfied that their state of deep sleep meant they could feel nothing.

Dr Bailey and his colleagues completely disregarded those patients who reported definite and horrifying awareness of the shocks, and were able to describe the dreadful feelings of explosions in their heads which knocked them unconscious. Dr Bailey insisted that they had been unconscious all the time.

Visitors to the hospital were appalled to see patients lying in beds unmoving, with their eyes closed, but the eyeballs visibly straining against the eyelids and darting wildly from side to side: a consequence of the fear and trauma induced by receiving electric shocks to the brain without general anaesthesia.

Worst of all, patients were dying. Dr Bailey's tendency was to certify the deaths as caused by heart attacks, averring that they had already been suffering from dangerous heart conditions before they came under his care. The nursing staff had no reason to doubt him, until an extremely fit and apparently healthy seventeen-year-old girl died of gangrene of the bowel. The nurses were quite unable to accept the official claim that there had been anything wrong with her heart; and, indeed, her condition was one that responsible doctors would have detected before putting her on a regimen of such stringent chemotherapy. Dr Bailey's answer to staff disquiet was to order "another barbecue" to raise morale!

Reports reached an able young District Attorney that patients from Chelmsford who had refused to sign consent forms were being given electric shock treatment while they were too drugged to resist it. This amounted to assault, and he prepared a report which was sent to the Minister of Health. Whose officials recommended no action. For some years no action was taken.

Eventually, as more and more former patients protested that they had been severely traumatized by their treatment; relatives protested that at least 24 patients had died because of it; and some started legal proceedings against the hospital, action had to be taken. An investigation was started and Dr Bailey's licence to practice was suspended. He and his colleagues protested that their prosecution was an abuse of proper procedures by people who did not understand the revolutionary new method. However, qualified anaesthetists looked at Bailey's records and advised that such enormous doses of alarming drugs were obviously extremely dangerous, and should only be given to patients who were in intensive care units.

Finally, Dr Sargent, consulted about his work at Guy's Hospital, expressed complete horror at the travesty of his experimental work carried out at Chelmsford. He said gravely that if he came to Australia to testify it would unquestionably be as a witness for the prosecution.

Devastated by this condemnation from his guru, Dr James Bailey committed suicide. However it was not until 1992 that the case finally closed, after a full enquiry had roundly rebuked all the doctors involved in the "deep sleep" therapy at Chelmsford Hospital for their extraordinary negligence and incompetence. It represented the worst case of medical malpractice in Australia's history.

Memento of Surgery

The Medical Defence Union reported a phlegmatic victim of damaging error in 1989. The patient was a gardener with an ingrowing great toenail. He was not generously equipped with toes, having accidentally cut off his fourth and fifth left toes with a mowing machine five years previously.

The surgeon intended to anaesthetize his toe with a lignocaine ring block, numbing all feeling right around the digit. Unfortunately he failed to check the label on the ampoule with which he filled his syringe, and poured a solid dose of potassium chloride into the toe before setting about to remove the nail. The following day the toe was markedly bloodless. In a little while it mummified and dropped off.

The patient's feet now had too few toes for him to manage a spade or fork. His gardening days were over, and he was inevitably awarded damages as it was impossible for him to work. He did, however, insist on having the mummified toe returned to him as he wanted it for an ornament to wear on his watch-chain.

THE LOBOTOMY STORY

"I wish I were a famous brain surgeon," mused Peter Cook's park-bench philosopher-tramp, E. L. Wisty. In his mind, brain surgeons were at the peak of the professions, commanding huge salaries and all that their hearts could desire. "If I were a famous brain surgeon," he went on, "I would have a big car and I would ask all the lovely ladies to come into my car and take their knickers off. And they would"

The traditional brain surgeon trepanned to ease headaches caused by pressure from tumours, and removed the tumours themselves. The "famous brain surgeons" of the 1960s, however, were more likely to be performing operations to cure personality disorders by excising or destroying a small part of the frontal lobes of the brain.

The fact that the brain could be injured without causing death had been observed in the mid-19th century when, to the amazement of doctors, a labourer survived having a heavy metal bod driven accidentally through his head. After such an accident it was perhaps unsurprising that his personality changed somewhat for the worse however, and he became quietly morose.

In the early 1930s, vivisectionists started experimenting with the brains of chimpanzees. It had long been believed that the frontal lobes of the brain contained intellectual powers. Man's forehead was higher than those of his fellow primates, and although the exterior shape of the skull gives no real indication of the size and shape of the brain inside, popular wisdom and illustrations in children's comics had traditionally seen a high dome as the mark of a "brainy" individual.

The experimenters took trained apes, and excised more and more of their frontal lobes to see whether this caused them to lose their acquired skills. They found that half the frontal lobes could be removed without any impairment. If the entire lobes were removed, the apes lost much of their trained abilities. However, it was also apparent that they suffered far less anxiety and frustration in their cages than had previously been the case.

Something very similar was observed in humans who suffered accidents which injured their frontal lobes. And brain surgeons removing tumours often damaged part of the surrounding brain tissue. (With the instruments available to them at the time, the operation was described as akin to picking up golf balls with telegraph poles!) Patients with damaged frontal lobes appeared to retain their mental faculties, but to enjoy calmer personalities.

All that remained was for someone to capitalize on this discovery for psychiatric purposes.

Egas Moriz

Dr Sobral Cid, one of Portugal's leading psychiatrists, became interested in the new discoveries about the brain, and he encouraged surgeon Egas Moriz to make experimental excisions of parts of his patients' lobes.

Moriz developed a technique of boring three small holes in the skull and extracting small cylinders of brain tissue, much as one might core an apple. This he called "pre-frontal leucotomy". He was highly satisfied with the results, and in 1936 reported on his first 20 cases. 17 of them, he said, had been cured of anxiety. None had been made worse and there had been no fatalities.

"Prefrontal leucotomy is a simple operation, always safe, which may prove to be an effective surgical treatment in certain cases of mental disorder"

EGAS MORIZ

By this time, however, Moriz had lost the support of Sobral Cid. After the first four cases, Cid was worried that Moriz was making exaggerated claims for his success. As a scientist, he was extremely concerned that a treatment was being confidently proposed as reliable when its scientific basis had not been properly established, and it should still be seen as experimental. He refused to send Moriz any more patients.

Unfortunately there was an appreciable element of professional jealousy in Cid's hostility, and his reservations were not given the respect his standing deserved. Moriz's reputation rose steadily, and surgeons in other countries started to attempt his operation.

In 1938 Moriz suffered his first setback. A patient died of haemorrhage during the operation.

Nonetheless, this was one of the normal risks of surgical procedure, and could be accepted as long as the majority of patients still recovered with their anxiety neuroses completely alleviated.

In 1939 two things led Moriz to give up practising surgery himself. A disgruntled patient shot and injured him – which seemed to be an unacceptable risk, even if treating the dementedly agitated. Additionally, increasing gout in the hands led Moriz to mistrust his own skill.

Nonetheless, he remained the pioneering figure in the world of brain surgery.

....

CELEBRITY SPOT

TENNESSEE WILLIAMS

It was a deep sense of personal tragedy that led Tennessee Williams to write "Suddenly Last Summer". In his play the innocent heroine, sensitively distressed by the cruelty of the world, is condemned to brain surgery by her heartless mother. Williams himself had never forgiven his own mother for her behaviour in the treatment of his sister Rose.

In 1935, Rose went away to a Catholic boarding school. When she came home on one occasion she artlessly told how some girls stole altar candles and used them in masturbation games. Her mother was horrified, and in Williams' words, demanded that "This hideous story [be] cut from her brain," adding, "She was so puritanical."

Williams was away from home when his little sister's truthful story of a harmless prank was treated as serious and filthy neurosis. He was shocked when on his return he found that Rose had been forced to undergo a prefrontal leucotomy, and the results had been disastrous. She had become effectively oblivious to the world around her, and was immediately committed to a lunatic asylum where she passed the remainder of her life.

"The petals of her brain simply closed through fear," Williams wrote, "and it's no telling how much they had closed upon in the way of secret wisdom."

....

Walter Freeman

The doctor who seized upon Moriz's operation with the greatest enthusiasm was the American Walter Jackson Freeman. He was a neurologist whose original ambition had been to combine the study of the nervous system with psychiatry and psychoanalysis. His faith in "talk-psychotherapy" was shattered, however, when he gave an extensive verbal examination to a woman who complained relentlessly about pain she suffered. Jackson prepared a long report describing her psychosomatic and hypochondriac disorders. He looked very foolish when a physical examination proved that she was suffering the acute pain of a serious anal fissure.

Rather than blaming himself for his failure to carry out a proper physical examination of the patient, Jackson blamed the Freudian discipline and abandoned it to become a determined specialist in the physical causes of psychological disorders.

Standing Out From The Crowd

Walter Jackson Freeman, the father of frontal lobotomy, was a strikingly flamboyant dandy as a young man. His beautifully cut three-piece suits, broad-brimmed hats and theatrical capes attracted immediate attention. And on his watch ribbon he wore a gold ring which he delighted to explain had been the wedding ring of a sailor who made the notorious mistake of pushing it sentimentally around his penis. The result was that blood could not escape when the penis became erect, and Freeman had to cut the ring off to lower the man's erection. A memento wish such a story attached was quite a daring possession in the American professional classes of the 1930s.

Freeman was not himself trained to carry out brain surgery so he teamed up with surgeon James Winston Watts to carry out Moriz's operation. In 1938 they reported the results on their first 20 patients. They had not been as fortunate as Moriz at the similar point in his career. Seven of their patients were cured. Five had improved, Five had not improved. A year before Moriz suffered his first fatality, one had died.

Freeman was far from dismayed. He was extremely conscientious about following up patients after their surgery, and was convinced that he was effecting radical cures of depressive and manic conditions. The characterization of a lobe-damaged patient, derived from the days when such damage only occurred accidentally, described a character who became slow, deliberate, single-minded in completing tasks, hard-working, stubborn and free from anxiety. Altogether rather a boring bigot who might fit well into the American Protestant work ethic from which Freeman and Watts sprang, though rather different in kind from the exciting and excited enthusiast Freeman had become.

Questions and Doubts

From the early days there were doctors and psychologists who doubted the value of cutting into the brain merely on the empirical grounds that this seemed to reduce anxiety (along with zest for life) in a significant proportion of patients. Dr Lewis J. Pollock wrote a blistering article for Archives of Neuro-Surgery in 1937. "This is not an operation, but a mutilation." he thundered.

Three years later Stanley Cobb continued the attack when he asked in "A Review of Neuro-Psychiatry", "Is the surgeon justified in depriving a patient of the most important part of his intellect in order to relieve him of emotional troubles?" Cobb was not proposing an outright ban on such surgery, but he argued that the operation should only ever be recommended for patients over the age of 60 who had suffered from prolonged and agitated depression. As several worried doctors remarked, depression is an illness which cures itself without treatment in many cases. It seemed hard to justify dangerous and unpredictable surgery for such a condition.

Freeman and Watts were unrepentant. Watts was now excising a good deal more brain tissue that Moriz had taken, and describing the operation as "frontal lobotomy". Freeman snapped that "A surgeon may see what he cuts but he doesn't know what he sees!" (Which, oddly enough, was almost exactly his critics' reservation about his and Watts's own activities!) Throughout the controversy Freeman remained a conscientious scientist, observing and reporting his patients' reactions and behaviour after lobotomy.

Undoubtedly the most alarming were those who simply lay like wax dummies in trance-like catatonic states. It was faith rather than observation or good sense which decided these people had been "cured" of some anxiety before they settled down to vegetative lives in asylums. An interesting reflex Freeman the neurologist observed in other patients was the "China Doll syndrome".

In these cases, patients' eyes automatically closed as they moved into a recumbent position, and opened again as they raised themselves, just like little girls' "sleeping" dolls.

••

CELEBRITY SPOT

ROSEMARY KENNEDY

The most famous victim of lobotomy in America was John F. Kennedy's sister Rosemary. She was born retarded: a matter of deep shame to her odious father, who urged his whole clan to compete strenuously with each other, and unitedly against the world.

220

Despite the need for Rosemary to attend special schools, Joseph P. insisted that she be treated as perfectly normal, and had her presented at court with his other children when he was ambassador to England. Then the desperate throw of brain surgery was attempted to try and stop Rosemary wandering out alone at night.

The surgery was a failure. Rosemary simply withdrew from the world without mastering its complexities any better. She had to be placed in a home, and her father insisted that for years the family pretend she was teaching retarded children as a charitable vocation. When it leaked out that Miss Kennedy was a resident, not a staff member, Joseph substituted the lie that the daughter he refused ever to see or discuss had been injured by meningitis in infancy.

Freeman and Watts Split Up

In 1937 the Italian surgeon Amaro Fiamberti pioneered a technique for passing a sharp needle through the orbital bone of the skull behind the eye to make injections into the frontal lobe.

In 1945 Freeman, who was anxious to carry out his own surgery, decided to see whether this approach could be used for lobotomy. He was not satisfied with the strength of available surgical instruments, so at his first attempt he improvised by using the ice pick from his kitchen. This proved perfect, and Freeman had new leucotomes designed, based on the simple ice pick.

He found the operation so easy that he took to practising it in his own office, without benefit of sterilized robes, drapes and masks, or a supporting team of anaesthetists and nurses. It took him a mere ten minutes, and the casual style and accompanying notoriety suited his flamboyant love of public attention. Watts was horrified by the unprofessionalism of practising brain surgery in an unequipped office, and declined to work with him any more.

Freeman, however, insisted that his transorbital surgery was so safe and easy, and did so little damage, that it could be practised by untrained psychiatrists as well as surgeons. And he ceased to recommend patients for lobotomies carried out in hospitals by specialist brain surgeons. He demonstrated his own peculiar technique of brain surgery to students and colleagues, making a strong if not altogether favourable impression by the casual way in which he would stick an "ice pick" in through the corner of the eye socket, and give it a cavalier twiddle, quite careless of which part of the lobe he was attacking. Sometimes he did this with both hands at once, twirling away like a pair of helicopter blades.

In 1948, Edwin Zabriski, Emeritus Professor of Clinical Surgery at Columbia University was so appalled by the spectacle of Freeman stirring around a patient's brains with a pair of ice picks stuck through the eye-bones that, experienced surgeon though he was, he fainted.

The Nobel Prize

By the end of the 1940s, enough questions were being asked about the controversial operation that it might swiftly have passed out of practice by anyone but Freeman and a few acolytes. However, in 1949 the Nobel Prize Committee decided to award the prize for medicine to Moriz in recognition of his contribution to brain surgery. In the popular mind, that settled the question. If the most prestigious scientific prize in the world was awarded to the man who had invented prefrontal leucotomy a decade and a half earlier, those who had advanced it to frontal lobotomy and transorbital surgery must represent even further progress. In America, with medicine an expensive commodity in a commercial market, there was now increased demand and surgeons sprang up to supply it.

The New York Times praised Moriz for demythologizing the brain. "It is just a big organ with very difficult and complicated functions to perform," the paper editorialized, "and no more sacred than the liver." True enough, no doubt, but this begged the question whether Moriz and Freeman and Watts really understood its complicated functions and could justify what they were doing to the organ.

Freeman and Watts might no longer practice together. But they had no objection to the reissue of their joint work "Psychosurgery", which had first appeared in 1942 giving an optimistic and essentially distorted picture of their successes. The 1950 edition was a triumph. Readers' Digest was among the many popular journals which published articles drawn from it and endorsed its enthusiastic conclusions. The number of lobotomies and leucotomies soared. Between 1935, when the operation first appeared, and the award of the Nobel Prize in 1949, about 10,000 had been carried out. Over the next two years there were a further 12,000.

Opposition

Yet while the more the popular press praised the operation and laid the groundwork for E. L. Wisty's vision of the "famous brain surgeon", the more responsible voices in the profession were being raised against the practice. Nolan Lewis, Director of the New York State Psychiatric Institute put forward telling objections in 1949:

"Is the quieting of the patient a cure? Perhaps all it accomplishes is to make things more convenient for the people who have to nurse them because the patients become rather childlike.... They act like they have been hit over the head and are as dull as blazes.... It disturbs me to see the number of zombies these operations turn out. I would guess that lobotomies going on all over the world have caused more mental invalids than they have cured.... I think it should be stopped before we dement a large section of the population." There was evidence to support the suggestion that, as so often with the treatment of mental illness, social convenience was taking a higher priority than the patients' welfare. There were more men than women in mental hospitals. Yet lobotomies were carried out on more than twice as many women as men. Doctors who favoured the treatment were inclined to point out that after lobotomy, women often went willingly back to housework and household accounts which they had previously resented. Advanced thinkers were bound to suspect that such doctors rather hoped that frontal lobotomy might be used to put Ibsen's Nora back in her Doll's House and quell the modern women's movement.

In 1951, a study of over 100 cases was published, and the authors, Moore and Winkelman, concluded that "lobotomy causes most and perhaps all patients to suffer some personality defect."

The same year Dr Chevtchenko of Moscow carried out autopsies on lobotomized brains. he discovered that the damage was far more extensive than enthusiastic surgeons were reporting, and so informed the authorities.

Stalin's Soviet Union perpetrated many scientific sins of its own. But it had no intention of importing new and unnecessary ones from the arch-enemy, America. Lobotomy and leucotomy were forthwith banned in Russia.

Freeman Fights Back

Freeman was not one to take criticism lying down. Nor was he a tactful conformist, willing to temper his arguments to the prevailing opinions.

Far from challenging the view that he was creating placid zombies out of alert and sensitive citizens, he mounted a defence of his "cures" that would have Stalin rushing to reinstate brain-mangling in the USSR had it ever been drawn to his attention.

> *"Society can accommodate itself to the most humble labourer, but justifiably distrusts the thinker.... Lobotomized patients make rather good citizens."*

WALTER JACKSON FREEMAN

There can have been few other men with claims to intellectual distinction who regarded McCarthyite America's notorious distrust of the thinker as justifiable! Freeman went further. He recommended that all mental patients who had been more than two years under institutional care should be lobotomized. They evidently needed it, or they would have been cured within that time. His autocratic attitude to patient care is a reminder that leucotomy originated at a time when the Fascist and Communist dictatorships reflected a mental climate in which the right of the superior individual to dominate and suppress the inadequate was often seen as necessary for the advancement of progress and human happiness. Euthanasia and selective breeding were both advocated by men who thought of themselves as humane and democratic. Bernard Shaw believed in Nietzchean "Supermen" and Carlylean "heroes" no less than Hitler. Bolsheviks and bishops claimed to speak for the "masses" or "their flocks", even when ballot boxes said otherwise.

Out of the same moment in history had emerged the ability of the skilful to stir up the brains of the depressed "for their own good" and the greater efficiency of mental health care. Walter Jackson Freeman was a true intellectual child of the 1930s.

Happily for American mental patients there were not many leucotomists so fanatically dedicated to their art as Freeman. The surgical profession as a whole rose up and strongly denounced the idea of compulsory operations for anyone, let alone enforced brain operations for the mentally disturbed.

Worst Case Scenarios

Despite the horrific physical spectacle which made Professor Zabriskie faint, lobotomies were not usually life-threatening. There were, however, occasional fatalities when the calming effect proved too total. With all tension removed it was possible for the very rare victim to die of his own inertia.

A few simply stopped breathing, lacking the muscular tension to continue working their lungs. In a tiny number of cases there was a cessation of peristalsis: the steady, involuntary and usually unnoticed muscular constriction and downward rippling of the gullet and bowels to carry food through the digestive system. This meant they could no longer swallow, and choked to death on their food.

Fortunately for Freeman, new drugs came to his rescue. The amphetamine group of "uppers" restored some of that nervous energy which vanished with the frontal lobes. Freeman would prescribe up to 50 mg a day to his patients, conscientiously noting that this had the additional advantage of checking the increase in weight which had proved one of the undesirable side-effects of lobotomy.

Freeman's Last Stand

Ironically, the new drugs which seemed to have saved Freeman's surgery from the charge of being lethal were to write its epitaph. For alongside the stimulating amphetamines (the "uppers"), chemists developed the tranquillizing chlorapromazine family (the "downers"). If new tranquillizers like valium and largactil and mogadon could produce just as sedating an effect as twiddling an ice-pick through an eye-bone, most doctors knew which they would recommend.

Some of those who thought surgery more effective than chemistry were nevertheless convinced that it was the shock to the brain rather than the destruction of tissue which made the difference. They championed electro-convulsive therapy rather than the ice pick.

However, Freeman's battles at the end of his career were not to be with the chemotherapists or electro-therapists so much as with a deeply scepti-cal Freudian. Dr Allen "Kris" Kringle was director of the El Camino Hospital Psychiatric Service in New Mexico, where Freeman had settled at the end of his working life. Dr Kringle was quite convinced that psycho-surgery was dangerous and ineffective; now was his sympathy for Freeman increased by the brain surgeon's well-known belief that Freudian psycho-analysis was unscientific quackery. Dr Kringle was in the winning position for these intellectual battles. Not only was he the Director appointed over Freeman's head, but he had a sense of humour. Freeman tried to respond in kind, but he really couldn't match Kringle's impish little rhymes knock-ing his notions in the house magazine:

> *"A fellow named Freeman said, 'I've a sharp little knife that I drive; If you want to be dead I'll bore holes in your head And then you won't know you're alive."*

The Verdict Of The Arts

Ken Kesey's novel "One Flew Over the Cuckoo's Nest" came out in 1962. Based on Keye's experiences as a volunteer in government drug testing experiments carried out at a Veterans' Administration Hospital, it painted a shocking picture of authoritarian staff ruling sick men with a rod of iron. And always holding out E.C.T. or lobotomy as a final threat for undisci-plined behaviour was an obviously outrageous abuse of therapy.

When the film version ended with zany Jack Nicholson wiped out on a gurney with the visible sign under his chin showing that he had been lobotomized, the public was invited to agree that this was evil punishment, not medicine.

Ten years later Anthony Burgess took an equally cynical view of the operation as a means by which a brutal establishment could hold down thuggish rebellious youth. Since anyone capable of inflicting the operation must be as violent as those who were supposed to be cured by it, Burgess indicated in his title that lobotomy was (in the words of the old Cockney saying) "as useless as a Clockwork Orange".

WRONG! WRONG! WRONG!

Nobody could suggest that the patients we have discussed were anything but very unlucky in their surgeons or their treatment. But at least they got treatment that was intended both for their conditions and for themselves.

Others have been less lucky.

Sometimes the briefest reports in newspapers tell of mistakes which seem positively incredible. A man in Vienna went to hospital with a broken leg in 1982. He came out with a heart pacemaker which had been accidentally and unnecessarily inserted! In 1995 a woman went into hospital for an operation on her ankle and came round to discover than an oral surgeon had given his professional services to extract a perfectly healthy tooth!

A worse fate befell the client New York medical malpractice lawyer Charles Kramer disguised under the name "Mrs Gaines" in the 1960s. Her daughter Angela was born with a dislocated left hip; not an uncommon problem for newborn girls. Orthopaedic surgeons put Angela in a body cast, changing it over the year as she grew. However it seemed to make little improvement. It was decided that surgery would be necessary, removing some bone from under the processes attaching muscles to her upper thighbone, and then putting her in a new cast.

Mrs Gaines returned after the operation was over, and fainted. The cast was on Angela's right leg. Her perfectly healthy thigh had been opened up; the bone scraped, and a plate with four screws inserted.

"The thing to put in perspective with these kinds of mistakes — is that every day there are nine million interactions between patients and surgeons, and 99% of those are successful."

KIRK JOHNSON, AMA

The Tragic Case Of Willie King

51-year-old Willie King was a diabetic whose legs were severely diseased by circulation problems. On 20 February 1995 he went into the University Community Hospital in Tampa, Florida, to have his right leg removed below the knee. "You're sure you know which one you're going to cut?" he joked with the staff, and they assured him they did.

Dr Rolando Sanchez was the surgeon deputed to carry out the amputation. He was not in the theatre while Willie was anaesthetized and prepared for the operation. When he walked in, Willie was already unconscious and draped, his leg sterilized and presented for surgery. Dr Sanchez checked the staff nurse's list of the day's operations on the blackboard to make sure he had the right operation and the right leg in mind. It all tallied, as indeed it should have, since it was correct by the printed operating room schedule and the hospital's computer records. Doctor Sanchez proceeded to start cutting through the shin.

As he was halfway through the incision he realized that one of the nurses was shaking and crying. Asking her sharply what was the matter, he learned that she was looking at Willie's records, and realized they were amputating the wrong leg. The left leg.

Dr Sanchez said later, "I tried to recover from the sinking feeling I had." He looked at the leg before him. It was certainly diseased, but it was most likely that amputation was not yet essential, even though it would probably one day become so. There could be no going back. This was not a healthy leg which could be frozen for reattachment by neurosurgeons and plastic surgeons. With a heavy heart, Dr Sanchez completed the operation knowing that someone would then have to remove the right leg and leave Willie a double amputee.

The Repercussions

Dr Sanchez knew he also faced the possibility of losing his licence. Willie chose not to have the other leg removed at University Community Hospital – and who can blame him?

Indeed, he started suit against the hospital and Dr Sanchez immediately, and settled with them for $1.2 million. His right leg was amputated at Tampa General Hospital when he had recovered from the surgery on the left leg. He didn't know, he said, whether Dr Sanchez ought to be disciplined or not; he was certain he didn't blame him entirely for the loss of his leg, and he remarked, "There's a problem there somewhere that needs to be corrected, and I don't know what it is and I don't know how to go about it."

How right Willie was showed up two months later when another patient died. 77-year-old Leo Alfonso was on a ventilator, and an orderly was directed by a respiratory therapist to disconnect it as he no longer needed it.

Only he did. The patient who was ready to come off ventilation was somebody else. The hospital noted that proper procedure should have required the therapist to make visual identification of the patient; check his name against the wall chart; and check his identity bracelet. The therapist was suspended while the failure in procedure was investigated.

In July Dr Sanchez's license was summarily suspended when patient Mildred Shuler charged him with having removed her toe illegally and without her consent when he was supposed to be merely removing dead tissue from under her foot.

At his hearing in September, however, Dr Sanchez gave a very good account of himself. Ms Shuler's toe, he pointed out, had suddenly "popped" while he was working on it. Diseased bone had snapped and come through the skin, and the toe was left hanging by a tendon. Had he left it as it was and waited for Ms Shuler to recover from her anaesthesia and give permission for further surgery, she would have been left with diseased bone protruding from her foot, with all the risk of infection that entailed.

As for poor Willie King and the loss of the wrong leg, there was not a doctor in the state who thought he might not have made the same mistake under the same circumstances. Both Mr King's legs suffered severe circulatory disease, so Dr Sanchez was not guilty of recklessly removing an obviously healthy limb. The patient was the right patient. Every instruction Dr Sanchez received had been to remove the right leg. The error went back to the hospital computer and the records department was at fault, not the surgeon.

The Official Reaction

"Accidents like these shake the public's basic level of confidence. It should make people out there extremely nervous. The amputations are almost laughable because it seems so unbelievable."

ARTHUR LEWIS, CENTER FOR MEDICAL CONSUMERS

"It's almost unbelievable that this particular institution has had two incidents like this in such a short time.... They better quickly look at all their procedures and protocol. I'm shocked."

EMILIO ECHEVARRIA, FLORIDA BOARD OF MEDICINE

A British Case

This story has a happy ending, thank goodness. For it concerns two little boys. Nowadays, charming hospital staff will ask even a fading old grandfather like myself whether I prefer to be called "Martin" or "Mr Fido".

However, doctors and nurses have always affectionately addressed children by their forenames, which led to confusion in December 1980 when two little boys called John were both in Bromsgrove General Hospital in

Worcestershire, awaiting surgery. Seven-year-old John Burley was deaf and needed ear surgery. When he recovered from general anaesthesia he was still deaf, but there was a large dressing on his tummy. The surgeon had found a minor umbilical hernia and corrected it.

But why was he messing around inside John's abdomen when he should have been operating on his ear? Because little John Wardle was waiting for his hernia operation, and waited for no less than nine hours, to the absolute fury of his parents.

This mix up was merely the climax of five years' accumulated troubles at Bromsgrove. The worst had occurred when newborn baby Emma Darby was due to receive a routine injection of vitamin K1, and was accidentally given the powerful drug Ergometin intended for her 22-year-old mother Julie. Emma became seriously ill and had to be hurried to the intensive care unit: then sent on to Birmingham Children's Hospital for dialysis and blood cleansing, and three days on a ventilator.

Mr Johnson-Thomas, secretary of the Bromsgrove and Redditch Community Health Council, went on television and made no bones about wanting an immediate public enquiry. Though there were calls for his resignation, he was supported by the General Medical Council.

An enquiry was held after a few months, and it made certain clear recommendations. It was agreed that the lack of communication between staff had arisen from the pressure of working in an old and overcrowded hospital. To avoid such disasters in the future, the committee recommended, all patients should be labelled with name tags, and the area in which an operation was to take place should be clearly identified with a felt-tip marker, preferably while the patient was still conscious and able to comment.

A final enquiry showed that a newly appointed Senior Nursing Officer had given a text-book example of administrative reform. Like Mr Johnson-Thomas he didn't exasperate the public with politic evasions. He admitted at once that there had been a management failure. He made some administrative staff changes and made all nursing staff directly responsible to himself.

For little John Burley everything ended happily ever after. He was over the moon in January when the correct operation restored him to perfect hearing. Also, his tummy hadn't been opened up for nothing: there actually had been the small undetected hernia to correct.

"A surgeon is a savage with a knife in his hand."

WILLIAM HUNTER (1718-83) PIONEER OBSTETRICIAN

More Mistakes

Those crude felt-tip markings really are necessary, as a 31-year-old mine official found when he injured his left knee. Physiotherapy didn't make any difference, so he was sent on for surgery. He was given an identity band which referred the surgeon to his notes, but no check was made, and back in the ward he realized that his right knee had been opened up instead.

A more complicated confusion happened in the years before the felt-tip marking practice became standard. It does lead one to wonder, though, just how the patient would have been marked for either of the two operations that were confused with each other. A surgeon who had been on holiday returned to start operating on a list of patients who had been seen by his locum and not himself. The patient had signed the usual consent form before being taken to the theatre, and this had been gummed over his case notes, exposing only the basic instruction "division of the fraenum". A fraenum – (the word is from the Latin for bridle) – is a small soft ligament gently holding a flexible or movable organ or part of an organ in place: the stringy bit under your tongue which stops you from bending it too far back and swallowing it is an obvious one.

The anaesthetist interviewed the patient before he went into the operating theatre, and concluded from his diffident remarks that it was indeed the fraenum of the tongue which was giving him problems. He so informed the surgeon, who promptly severed it and freed the young man's tongue.

Which satisfied nobody when the young man recovered. His complaint had been a tight fraenum of the penis: the "G-string" binding the foreskin to the shaft just below the glans. It caused him difficulty in intercourse, and he had not problem at all with his tongue.

In that same year a soldier's wife who had been listed for dilation and curettage to help her irregular menstruation was sent to a surgeon who had never seen her before. So he had no idea that the notes accompanying her referred to another patient. Following the directions on the notes he sterilized the unfortunate woman by tying off her tubes. Two years previously another surgeon had asked for "Patient no.2" on his list to be sent up to the theatre, for the removal of a small fibroid from her breast. He received the right notes but (though he did not realize it) the wrong patient. She was still able to communicate when she reached the theatre, but woozy from her anaesthetic and did not answer his questions.

The surgeon was puzzled to feel no trace of a fibroid, but thought his external diagnosis must have been wrong, and he must have felt a cyst which had now burst. So he opened the breast, scarring the unfortunate woman, who had come in to have her appendix removed.

TWO CANCER CONFUSIONS

I am not sure why cancer causes such fear and horror. Even a small and relatively harmlessly placed melanoma or sarcoma diagnosed early enough for its easy removal without further damage tends to be announced as though the patient was under sentence of lingering and agonizing death.

A short walk through a burns ward treating serious and potentially lethal cases should swiftly show that there may be worse ways of dying; and we're all going to die sooner or later.

"They treated him badly," said the judge.

It seems sadder to die from one of the occasionally inevitable failures of surgery – embolism or haemorrhage – especially if the surgery was in itself unnecessary. This happened to the unfortunate Patrick McCann in 1979. He was given major surgery for cancer and died of it. Only he didn't have cancer. He was perfectly healthy when he went into the theatre. His diagnosis had been wrongly based on tests given another patient. A consultant pathologist assured the inquest that there could not possible be any improvement in the system.

A patient who really cannot be blamed for the anger and distress he suffered after a hospital gave him cancer was Peter Sumners, a 51-year-old baker from Haywards Heath. he had suffered from kidney troubles since he was in his twenties, and in June 1986, a hospital in Sussex gave him a transplant. Then they realized that the donor − a deceased woman − had suffered from cancer and they had actually put a potentially diseased organ into Mr Sumners' body.

The best medical opinion of the time was that the kidney should be left in his body. Mr Sumners was not told of the dreadful mistake at first, and when he was told that he had cancer he naturally feared for his life and felt furious that the malignancy had actually been transplanted into him in hospital and he had not been warned. Fortunately the disease went into remission and Mr Sumners was given another transplant in 1990. After which it became as certain as one can ever be in such cases that he was completely cured.

The hospital, while noting that methods had changed substantially over the last ten years, and agreeing that Mr Sumners would nowadays be kept completely informed and consulted from the moment the mistake was discovered, expressed relief and satisfaction that he was doing well after the successful second transplant.

However, Mr Justice Collins, finding against the hospital in the suit Mr Sumners brought in 1996, felt that he deserved compensation for the anger he suffered on learning how he had been treated: "They could not really have made greater blunders in the way they treated him once they realized they had put in a potentially cancerous kidney, even if they meant well," he said. "They clearly treated him very badly, there is no doubt about that."

The Indian Patient

The western world's insatiable appetite for health care has led to a sort of economic pillaging the former colonial countries for staff who have been well trained in western medicine. Nurses from the West Indies and doctors from India are now an essential and highly visible part of the National Health Service, and many are deservedly at the very top of their professions.

Some immigrant Indian doctors have also arrived with excellent medical qualifications but poor language skills which have handicapped their doctoring. Clearly, if ever a medical malpractice suit is brought against an Indian, his name will make his country of origin apparent to everyone who reads about it. This has led to some unjustified racist suspicion of Indian doctors in England and America. So it is remarkable to read of a case where the patient's Indian nationality, and not the doctor's, caused the problem.

Mrs Rajeswari Ayyapan is the mother of Sridevi, a popular Tamil-language film star from Southern India. Mrs Ayyapan was diagnosed as suffering from a malignant tumour on the left lobe of her brain. She went to the Memorial Sloane-Kettering Cancer Center in New York, and was operated on by their chief neurosurgeon, Dr Ehud Arbit, on 26 May, 1995. As it happened, Dr Arbit was expecting to carry out a similar operation on another patient from India on the same day, and when he addressed Mrs Ayyapan by the other patient's name he was not contradicted. So, taking Mrs Ayyapan for the other patient, he operated on the healthy right lobe of her brain. He was suspended from duties a month later, as this was the second time he had gone into the wrong side of a patient's head.

The previous case had taken place in December 1994. That time, Dr Arbit said, he knew just who the patient was and just what he intended to do. The patient complained that with a tumour on her left lobe, Dr Arbit had entered the right side of her head and failed to find the tumour, which necessitated an unplanned return to the operating room. Sloane-Kettering decided that this "violated the hospital's standard of care." Dr Arbit protested that he had acted perfectly professionally. He had entered through the right lobe as that was the safer approach for a small lesion, just to the left of the brain's midline. He said that two things had combined to cause his failure to locate the tumour: the patient was very obese, and the hospital's standard imaging procedures had not been useful.

Although Sloane-Kettering's physician-in-chief felt that Dr Arbit's dismissal was painful, he decided in September after several hearings and appeals that it was essential. Dr Arbit, who had worked at Sloane-Kettering since 1985 and been chief neuro-surgeon since 1993 protested that he was being made into a scapegoat for an unfortunate situation which had no bearing on his professional competence, and declared his intention to appeal further to the physicians' grievance panel.

The Swiftness of the Eye Deceives the Hand

The proper diagnosis of cancer is by a histo-pathologist making a microscopic examination of tissues extracted from the suspect area (biopsy). Any doctor may, however, suspect that a growth is malignant from external examination by touch or the naked eye. When a surgeon is at work inside a patient he may act swiftly if he realizes he is looking at a malignancy. But perhaps he should not be too swift.

An unlucky woman was admitted to New York Municipal Hospital to have her gall bladder removed. While carrying out the operation, her surgeon noticed a tumour on her kidney, and decided to remove it immediately. He extracted the entire kidney, and the woman died shortly afterwards. Nobody had noticed that she had already lost one kidney. As is standard practice, a section was taken from the tumour and sent to the histo-pathologist. Who found it was benign. The surgeon's instant decision had killed his patient for no reason at all.

A Florida surgeon removing tissue for biopsies was even more definite in his instant diagnosis. His woman patient had cysts in both breasts, but the surgeon was relieved to see as he exposed them that neither was cancerous. He therefore ordered the nurse to put both specimens in one jar and send them to the resident pathologist to have his conclusion verified. He assured her that they did not need to be separately labelled jars as both came from the same patient and both were benign.

The pathologist prepared slides, and found that one cyst was benign; the other was malignant. In dissecting the samples to make his examination, however, he had so mutilated them that it was no longer possible for anyone to determine which came from which breast. The luckless surgeon felt compelled to amputate both breasts, and his hasty decision cost him and the hospital $100,000 when the patient sued.

Perhaps the British surgeon who failed to find a salivary gland was merely incompetent. His patient, a young man who suffered persistent swelling of the gland, went to have it removed. Before doing so the surgeon cautiously extracted a piece of tissue and sent it to the histology lab. The surprising report came back that the biopsy revealed "no obvious salivary gland tissue."

A little daunted, the surgeon proceeded to operate. He found what he took to be a stone in the duct and removed it. But the patient's swelling and pain was unabated. A second surgeon repeated the operation. He found the infected gland and removed it. He concluded that his colleague had extracted part of an enlarged lymph node.

Don't Look: EXTRACT!

A young woman in New Zealand suffering from severe pains was referred to hospital for laparoscopic examination: inspection of her organs on a monitor after a "keyhole" incision in her abdominal wall admitted a miniaturized camera.

Her consultant surgeon always left the preparation of his operating lists in the hands of his junior staff. A young houseman interviewed the woman and made brief notes, which he did not check properly when he admitted her for surgery. So he put her down for an operation instead of an examination.

The registrar at the theatre had never seen the woman before, and accepted the houseman's directive without checking the patient's full case notes. The consultant, who had received the patient unconscious on the operating table, opened her up to have keyhole access to the abdomen, and proceeded to sterilize her. All three were severely reprimanded and made to pay for the inquiry which followed.

More Keyhole Problems

Laporoscopy, or keyhole surgery, promised to be the wonder technique of the 1990s. The advantage was minimal flesh injury and scarring, compared with open surgery. A much shorter recovery time. A much lower risk of infection.

The disadvantage, as Kelly Hook discovered, was that no proper training in the technique had been established. Surgeons had to teach themselves, and in their first 50 cases were likely to make an inordinate number of errors.

Kelly's gall bladder removal was supposed to keep her in hospital just three days, and leave her with three small puncture scars in the abdomen. In reality she suffered five days of excruciating pain when the keyhole operation went wrong, and had to stay for major open surgery leaving a large scar after all. Professor Irving Benjamin of King's College Hospital told a conference in 1993 that one in a hundred laporoscopic gall bladder operations ended with the bile duct torn or cut. Taking operations over all, one in two-hundred keyhole patients had post-operative problems compared with one in twelve-hundred conventional patients.

Kelly's sensations after her original operation were, in her words, "Like being burnt alive. They found two-and-a-half litres of bile in my stomach cavity because my bile duct had punctured. I could have died."

Professor Alfred Cuschieri of Dundee remarked that 10% of surgeons would never master the technique of watching the actual operation on a monitor. A proportion of surgeons would always find it impossible to manipulate the instruments properly from a two-dimensional image rather than three-dimensional reality.

A common danger of laporoscopy was puncturing the bowel: it happened to a 49-year-old woman undergoing simple diagnostic examination in a Midlands private hospital who was never told that the technique was experimental; it killed Ruth Silverman in 1992 when she was being given a laporoscopic hysterectomy in a private hospital in London.

A British surgeon was threatened with legal action in 1995 by two patients he had given keyhole surgery three years earlier. One, who was moved into intensive care after her keyhole operation for prolapse went wrong, suffered extraordinary complications including a collapsed lung, and remained prone to infections. The other patient, undergoing a hysterectomy, suffered damage to her kidney when a staple was misplaced in her urether.

···

UNNECESSARY SURGERY

···

These figures shocked America in 1977: a full analysis of surgical practice in 1975 showed that 18 million operations had been carried out, and one in every 72 patients had died following surgery. That in itself might seem to be acceptable risk, but two additional figures cast doubt on the acceptability. The acknowledged dangers of anaesthesia seemed to have been well heeded, since only one in five thousand deaths was due to anaesthetics. Nor were patients recklessly putting themselves in danger against the advice of their insurance companies' medical examiners: "elective surgery" – risky operations patients insisted on receiving although their insurers declined to pay for them – only cost one life in every two hundred.

"7.5% of doctors are responsible for 65% of malpractice suits."

TEXAS STUDY CITED BY PUBLIC CITIZEN CONSUMER GROUP IN 1995

The worry was the number of common operations being carried out, almost routinely, and quite unnecessarily; rarely questioned by insurance companies, and sometimes bringing post-operative death.

Far and away the worst example was tonsillectomy. 724,000 sets of tonsils were yanked out in 1975. 150 patients died as a result. But careful examination of the records showed that 70% of those operations should not have been recommended. 105 people had died unnecessarily.

Even more patients died of prostatectomies: 2,700 out of 223,000 operations carried out. This, however, is likely to be because prostate trouble affects old men who would be less likely to bear surgery easily than the young folks whose tonsils were whisked away. Nonetheless, 29% of those extracted prostate glands might just as well have stayed where they were, according to the careful re-examination. 783 old men had died prematurely for nothing.

The biggest unnecessary killer of women was hysterectomy. Of the 787,000 women who lost their wombs in 1975, 1,700 died. But 22% of them had been wrongly or unnecessarily referred for hysterectomy. 374 women had died needlessly.

Gall bladder removals were the other common operation causing unnecessary deaths – more, indeed, than any other category. 472,000 operations had been carried out; 6,700 patients had died; 938 of them should not have done so. 14% were wrongly referred.

It may be difficult for doctors to decide whether conservative (minimal) treatment is the right thing in every case. There is also no doubt that fads for operations can lead to over-willing excisions: children's tonsils, adenoids and foreskins are often especially at risk.

But the scandal America faced was that a considerable percentage of the unnecessary and dangerous surgery it witnessed was a direct result of doctors enriching themselves. In a private commercial medical system, more operations mean more fees.

Tonsil Scandals

An investigative committee was shocked by the case of Mrs Marie Valenzuela in 1969. She took her youngest daughter Linda with a high fever to see a doctor in California who told her Linda needed her tonsils out. He also suggested that she bring her other three children for examination. Mrs Valenzuela did so, and he advised her that they all needed to have their tonsils removing. Her niece happened to be with her on this visit, and she mentioned that the niece suffered occasional nosebleeds. Her tonsils, too, were immediately condemned.

The surgery went well for all the children except Linda, though one of them suffered brief respiratory difficulty during the operation. Linda suffered serious complications. Six days after leaving hospital she began to bleed from the neck and very nearly died. She had to be taken back to hospital and given three further operations, which left her with only half the normal blood circulating to her brain. She contracted pneumonia and had to be given a tracheotomy. Subsequently she contracted hepatitis and anaemia. The diminished blood supply to her brain left a real threat that she would suffer brain damage.

Pathological tests determined that every one of the five children had given up perfectly healthy tonsils to the surgeon.

The motive for such reckless and useless surgery was exposed by William Haines, investigative reporter for the Chicago Tribune, when he took a job as a janitor at the 100-bed private profit-making Von Solbrig Hospital on the South West side of Chicago. He had to work as a janitor to obtain information, because doctors refused to answer press questions, and the hospital insisted that all records were confidential.

Haines was amazed at the large number of tonsillectomies performed on young black children from poor families on Medicaid (American free public health care). Whole families would have their tonsils out: Five brothers on 15th May, three of them being circumcized at the same time; one also having a cyst removed and one having an umbilical hernia repaired. The doctor who did all this work completed it in six hours, and billed Medicaid for $2,647.32.

Haines interviewed the mother of the five boys to find out what symptoms of chronic tonsillitis had led to this mass excision. He learned that they had occasional colds and sore throats in the winter, like everyone else; but none of the symptoms indicating tonsillectomy. No recurrent fevers. No intermittent deafness. No drainage from the ears.

A Dr E. J. Mirmelli with a clinic in the poor black South Side district was found to be instrumental in referring most such cases. He performed may of the operations himself, in two weeks carrying out 14 tonsillectomies. One mother who took her three boys to Dr Mirmelli to be circumcized was abruptly told that they would have to have their tonsils out too. In the space of a year, it seemed, Dr Mirmelli had relieved Medicaid of $124,000.

The Chicago Board of Health was outraged, and ordered Von Solbrig Hospital closed pending further hearings. The Illinois State Board of Medicine went after Dr Charles Von Solbrig to remove his medical license. They charged him with running an unsafe hospital. Dr Von Solbrig was unfazed. He'd made the pot of money that justified his investment in the profit-making hospital. He turned in his license voluntarily, closed the hospital permanently, and retired.

Surgeons Who Hurt Each Other

In 1988 the British Medical Journal reported on injuries inflicted on their colleagues while operating. Classic cases were:

- The surgeon who chopped off the tip of a colleague's index finger during a stomach operation
- The surgeon who ran a pin intended for his patient's leg into her other leg, too, and sewed his assistant's hand in between
- The surgeon who turned around to explain what he was doing, and stabbed a fellow surgeon in the stomach with his scalpel

••

THE NORK SCANDAL

••

Dr John G. Nork of Sacramento was the worst of the medical malpractitioners exposed and greedy and incompetent by investigators in the 1970s. Giving judgement against him and Mercy Hospital, where Dr Nork admitted performing at least 37 unnecessary back operations, Judge Abbott Goldberg said he had operated:

"With evil purpose...simply to line his pockets"

Nork was sued by 32-year-old grocery clerk Albert Gonzalez, whose physical and mental life he had ruined. When Gonzalez went to Nork with backache, Nork, as the judge summarized, "performed a perfunctory examination..., and made no substantial effort to treat the patient conservatively, discouraged consultation, hurried him into unnecessary surgery, which he bungled and achieved a bad result which he concealed.... In a nutshell: Dr

Nork not only harmed Gonzalez's back but he also ruined his personality. And he is liable for the bodily harm resulting from the emotional disturbance caused by his misconduct."

Gonzalez was in pitiable condition when he appeared before the court in 1973. His surgery at Nork's hands in 1967, adjudged completely unnecessary on Nork's own admission, had left him paralyzed from the waist down. He was in constant pain and suffered severe depression which led him to make several attempts at suicide. He became impotent and his wife left him. He became an alcoholic. Despite an understandable mistrust of doctors, his pain compelled him to consult them again and they found he had cancer of the testicles. These were removed, but too late. The cancer had metastasized to an inoperable state, and Gonzalez was given three years to live.

In a trial that lasted five months and heard 85 witnesses, Nork's case was not so much a defence as a confession. In 1963 when he was 35 years old, he felt harried by creditors and became dependent on uppers and downers. A constant state of alternately resting under chemical sedation and working under chemical stimulation did nothing for his competence. Nor did it solve the problem of his debts. So Dr Nork started taking on patients for unnecessary surgery to grab the fees. Since his stressed and drugged condition meant that he botched many of the operations he undertook, and his patients had to return for further surgery, it was estimated that he was personally responsible for more than 50 unnecessary or bungled operations. Of 38 patients who appeared to testify against him, Nork only claimed that one had truly needed back surgery.

He had twice been sued for negligence, and as he admitted, had perjured himself on both occasions. It wasn't his fault, he whined. His insurance company and their attorneys had forced him to lie. Even so those cases had been lost with damages of $495,000 and $595,000 awarded against him.

After a trial which Judge Goldberg called "a five-month horror", in which patient after patient testified against Dr Nork, and the judge's written summary of the case ran to 195 pages, the court awarded Gonzalez $1.7 million compensatory damages for his injury, and a further $2 million punitive damages. Mercy Hospital shared the punishment with Nork for its failure to monitor his work.

Perhaps most horrifying of all, after all this time, three trials and Nork's confession, the California State Board of Medical Examiners were still only "investigating" the matter. Technically Nork might yet have been licensed to malpractise again.

Necessary Surgery?

While Great Britain has not suffered from America's plague of medical malpractice suits, in one field litigation by dissatisfied patients leaped to startling level in the 1980s. Legal actions against obstetricians trebled between 1983 and 1989, and there has been no evidence to suggest that this tendency is slowing down in the 1990s. In 1993, it was reported to the National Childbirth Trust that 90,000 women were given Caesarean sections every year; this was three times the number in 1963, and at 13% of all births meant that between four and five thousand of them had been unnecessary.

The most significant reason was fear of litigation. By 1991, 85% of Britain's obstetricians had been hauled into court at least once. And the number of litigant parents who alleged that necessary Caesareans had been improperly delayed outnumbered those who protested that Caesareans had been unnecessarily performed by a ratio of 40 to 1. A survey in Liverpool revealed that 82% of obstetricians responded to this pressure by giving Caesareans they did not think were medically necessary, simply to avoid the hassle of being sued.

Fraud

Duane Stroman's study of unnecessary surgery in America uncovered one surgeon whose consultation with his patient was adjudged to be sheer fraud. A pregnant woman who had suffered several miscarriages was referred to him with stomach pains that might have been appendicitis. She absolutely refused to have surgical treatment unless appendicitis was confirmed, and the surgeon could assure her that the operation would not affect her pregnancy. The surgeon gave both such assurances and removed her appendix. After which the patient miscarried.

In court expert witnesses testified that the pathology report gave no indication to support the diagnosis of appendicitis. And they observed that there was an obvious and extremely high risk of damage to the foetus in undergoing appendectomy.

Since the surgeon stood to profit by the fee from the operation, the court was not willing to accept his deliberate misstatement about the risk of complications as some form of condescending concern for the patient. He was convicted of fraud as surely as any swindling car salesman.

Judgement on the Nork Case

"The drama played out here was not a fantasy contrived to satisfy a casual fancy for morbid amusement; it was real, permanent and tragic.

_____

"Here have come the poor, the maimed and the halt to testify against their once beloved physician for the wrongs he committed against them with evil purpose.

_____

"The defendant, Dr Nork, for nine years made a practice of performing unnecessary surgery, and performing it badly, simply to line his pockets."

SUPERIOR COURT JUDGE B. ABBOTT GOLDBERG

400,000 OPERATIONS – HOW MANY ARE NEEDED?

In 1995, research at Birmingham University's Health Services Management Centre concluded that five of the commonest surgical procedures in Britain, totalling about 400,000 NHS operations every year, were often unnecessary; even "of dubious value". Research fellow John Yates listed:

● Tonsillectomies: two thirds of those carried out are unnecessary, even if the position has improved since the 1950s when a third of all children had their tonsils extracted.

● Dilation and curettage: "Therapeutically useless and diagnostically inaccurate"

According to the British Medical Journal.

● Hysterectomies: comparison between different regions shows such extreme variation in the numbers performed that some gynaecologists must be carrying them out unnecessarily.

● Glue ear surgery: of dubious value, and purchased far too often by health authority managers.

● Wisdom tooth extraction: of dubious value and purchased far too often by health authority managers.

The Greedy Dentist

A British dentist was struck of for professional misconduct, but reinstated after undergoing retraining. He found himself in the High Court six years later, sued by over 70 patients who charged him with trespass and aggravated damage. Children aged eight were said to have had teeth unnecessarily extracted. Some children allegedly had perfectly good teeth crowned. Patients complained that their bridgework was a poor fit; that their gums were rotting. One girl claimed to have visited him 25 times and undergone 99 pieces of dental work which actually did so much damage that it would cost £43,000 to put right.

Australian Surgical Extravagance

The Australian Pediatric Society reported in 1982 that 95% of tonsillectomies were unnecessary, and that up to a dozen children died every year because of this pointless surgery. Tonsillectomy was performed in New South Wales at five times the rate in Sweden, and substantially more often than in Britain. Unnecessary circumcision, however, was falling – only 40% of male infants were now circumcized, compared with 50% in 1970. Hysterectomies, on the other hand, seemed as fashionable as tonsillectomies.

Dangerous and Unnecessary X-Rays

Before it was realized that Roentgen rays were delivering potentially carcinogenic doses of radiation, there was a tendency to use X-rays in ways that later came to be seen as reckless. The "pedoscope" disappeared from shoe-shops in the 1950s: the obvious advantage of looking into the X-ray machine and seeing that children's growing feet were not being pinched or cramped was outweighed by the danger of giving a child a shot of radiation every time it received a new pair of shoes.

Prior to the invention of non-injurious magnetic scanning there was still a tendency for doctors and dentists to use X-rays in circumstances that were not deemed essential. The US Public Health Services discovered that 129 million Americans were X-rayed in 1970; many of them more than once, so that 210 million X-ray examinations took place. And since each usually entailed more than one photograph, there were actually 650 million exposures to radiation.

This represented a rising curve. In 1965, 50% of the population was X-rayed at one time or another by a doctor. In 1970 this had risen to 56%. Dentists X-rayed 27 people in every hundred in 1965. They X-rayed 34 per hundred persons in 1970.

The serious outcome of all these X-rays were an estimated 13,500 cases of grave disability, and 7,500 deaths from cancer. Dr Karl Morgan of the Georgia Institute of Technology reckoned that ten times more radiation exposure than necessary was occurring because of X-rays. He and the US Bureau of Radiological Health reported that more than half of all X-rays exposed people to unnecessary danger because the beam was too large. They noted the following causes:

- Untrained personnel who did not know how to take effective photographs with the minimum X-rays.

- Outdated equipment that gave an unnecessarily high dose of radiation.

- Unserviced equipment that was no longer delivering the low dose for which it was designed.

- Failure to use a beam restrictor or collimator which would narrow the X-rays to the precise area being photographed.
- Failure to use lead aprons to protect other parts of the patients' bodies.

- Failure to find out whether X-rays of the patient already existed which obviated the need for new ones.

- The familiar short pointed cone on the end of old-fashioned X-ray machines tended to scatter rays. An improved open-ended cylinder about eight inches long gave a far more controlled beam. Dr Morgan and the Health Research Group made certain clear recommendations, some of which were generally taken up.

They Proposed:
- Women should never be X-rayed in pregnancy if it was possibly avoidable.

- Lead shields or aprons should always protect the reproductive organs of X-ray patients, including children, unless it was essential that the reproductive area itself be photographed.

- Certificates should always be posted beside X-ray machines giving the date of their last inspection and servicing. Patients should examine these, and refuse to be photographed by any equipment which had not been inspected within the last year.

● Women of childbearing age should only be X-rayed during the first ten days after the start of each menstrual period.

● Patients should always ask whether the X-ray was really necessary and what benefit could be expected from it. They should ask whether any previous X-rays existed that could be used instead. They should also ask whether the doctor or dentist was taking every possible precaution to ensure that the minimum radiation dosage was being delivered.

Naturally, the awe with which most patients regard doctors ensured that the last advice was only followed by the most determined old grouches and nags.

OBSTETRICAL DISASTERS

It took eight years for Karen Scott to win her battle with the US Government and claim the vital compensation her disabled son Jonathan needed. Karen's husband David was an army police officer stationed at Elmendorf air force base in Alaska when Jonathan was born in 1982.

Karen had a difficult pregnancy, and a military doctor decided wrongly that surgery was indicated. He performed an unnecessary operation and bungled it, leaving an infection that damaged the foetus. Jonathan was born prematurely with cerebral palsy that crippled him and left him little control of his bodily functions.

The combination of misdiagnosis and a degree of incompetence was not disputed, and a $3.5 million settlement was agreed in 1986. The Reagan administration, however, was determined to stop paying out huge claims against the government from taxpayers' money, and passed a bill that vetoed all settlements above one million dollars.

Undeterred, karen struggled on an in 1990, threatened with a new law suit, the government caved in and paid Jonathan eight million dollars. Their stinginess four years earlier had cost them dearly, as Jonathan's condition had worsened in the interim. Karen and David had split up, and Karen, living on welfare in a mobile home, could not afford the daily therapy which would have kept his hips in their sockets and their joints loose.

With her just award granted at last, she was able to move into a proper house with custom-built features for Jonathan, and start getting her son the treatment he needed, and expensive equipment like a computer to enable him to lead a proper life.

The $8 million record settlement was broken two years later when Mr and Mrs James Cooley sued an obstetrics and gynaecology practice, together with four named doctors, on behalf of their brain damaged daughter Caitlin. She, too, had cerebral palsy, but in her case it entailed blindness as well as leaving her unable ever to walk, talk or feed herself.

The cause of Caitlin's disability was shocking. She had been conceived as a twin, and her sister had died in the womb. The gynaecologists failed to detect the second foetus, and the obstetrician who delivered Caitlin was astonished when her birth was followed in a couple of minutes by the birth of her still-born twin. The undetected death in utero had caused toxic fluids and chemicals to spread to Caitlin, damaging her brain.

The jury awarded the Cooleys $9 million: a decision which horrified the gynaecologists. They had won their case before a medical arbitration panel in 1989, claiming that Mrs Cooley, who had suffered a miscarriage previously, refused their offer of a sonogram which would have detected the dead baby. Even if she had been scanned, they observed, there was no treatment that could have saved the baby's life.

Medical arbitrators with the medical profession's interests in mind might agree with the argument. The jury clearly did not. Whether or not they believed Mrs Cooley's counterclaim that she certainly had not refused a sonogram but (as the practice's records tacitly suggested) she had never been offered one, they pretty certainly took a layman's view that it was extraordinarily incompetent for a gynaecologist to fail to detect twins. And whether the death of the infant in the womb could have been prevented was irrelevant. At issue was the failure to take measures to save Caitlin from infection by her dead sibling.

Musician James Cooley and his wife Cecelia, a nurse, had juggled their work schedules to care for Caitlin. And the damages, they noted with relief, would enable them to buy the special equipment she required.

These massive settlements were dwarfed by the extravagant damages awarded by New York juries in natal malpractice cases. Sylvia Rodriguez was awarded $42 million when she charged the Lincoln Hospital with malpractice at the birth of her daughter Jasmine Matos.

Jasmine was born late, not prematurely. In the view of Ms Rodriguez's lawyer she was so late that competent obstetricians would have realized that labour must be induced. When labour started naturally, a test showed that the foetus was being deprived of oxygen: a problem which threatened subsequent brain damage and should have indicated a need for Caesarean section. Instead the obstetricians decided to deliver the baby with forceps – they yanked little Jasmine out with such violence that they caused bleeding in the brain and almost killed her.

In 1982, when Jasmine was four years old, her mother realized she was not walking properly, and having her examined discovered that she was brain damaged. By the time she finally brought the hospital to court in 1995, the girl with a body of a 17-year-old had the mind of a 10-year-old. She was in 9th grade at high school, and struggling to keep up. Her IQ was assessed as 66. She had no boyfriends, no social life, and would never drive a car. She stayed around the house, keeping close to her mother.

Unusually, Mrs Rodriguez's suit did not blame the obstetricians themselves. They were all inexperienced housemen: in effect, students undergoing their probationary period of practical experience in the hospital. The decision to perform the delivery by forceps was taken by a fourth-year resident and carried out by a second-year trainee. The hospital was at fault for not having ensured that a fully qualified and experienced consultant was on hand to supervise these young men.

What the Cooley's Said:

"It was a vindication for Caitlin. She was not cared for in the way she should have been."

CECELIA COOLEY

"It's been a long tough road. We are confident we can take care of Caitlin with all the love she deserves without devastating the family."

JAMES COOLEY

Damages

Biggest damages ever awarded against a public hospital? $73 million against Bronx Central.

The case? Another botched delivery.

A Surgical Tragedy

Much the saddest case recorded by New York malpractice attorney Charles Kramer was that of the 50-year-old lady he gave the pseudonym Arlene Windsor.

Mrs Windsor was a happy woman in excellent health when she slipped and fell on a dance floor, breaking her hip. An orthopaedic surgeon decided that her thighbone was too damaged to heal properly, and a replacement for its ball-joint was necessary.

He ordered an Austin-Moore prosthesis: a metallic round head on a stem which had to be driven into the neck of the femur to replace its own original ball-joint and fit into the pelvic socket. To ensure that the stem was properly aligned inside the femur, it was essential that the surgeon

252

work with an X-ray monitor to give him a view of what was happening inside the bone.

Unfortunately the technician ordered to work with Mrs Windsor's surgeon was inexperienced, and found himself quite unable to take the very difficult side view required. The surgeon had to stop the operation in the middle and telephone the X-ray department, asking them to send him a competent operator. He waited a long time, but no one came. The surgeon telephoned X-ray again, demanding to speak to the head of the department. He was put through to a technician who told him the departmental head was not available – he was too busy. In fact all the machine operators were too busy. The only person available in the X-ray department at all was the technician himself, and he couldn't leave the place as he was on his own fielding telephone calls and explaining that nobody would be coming for emergencies.

The frustrated surgeon returned to his operation after an hour's delay, knowing that he would be working blind and simply would not know whether he fitted the stem correctly or not. Through no fault of his own, he failed badly. He left the point of the stem sticking into the sciatic nerve – one of the most sensitive and painful nerves in the body, as any sufferer from sciatica will testify. Mrs Windsor endured intense pain.

Within two months she was back in hospital for corrective surgery. The hospital acquired a special diamond-tipped electric saw with which to remove the tip of the stem. An intern with a retractor stood by to hold the wound open while the surgeon sawed through the metal. However, the intern was nervous and let the retractor slip out of his hands. Trying to catch it he jogged the surgeon, and the diamond pointed saw severed Mrs Windsor's sciatic nerve.

When she came round she was in agony. Her foot dropped, and she required a brace and a special shoe to stand. She returned to the hospital to have complications treated. She was given a heavy narcotic prescription to dull the pain, and became severely depressed. After a year it became impossible for her to put any weight on her leg at all.

Charles Kramer did not get the opportunity to secure damages from the hospital for Mrs Windsor. Before the case ever came before a law court

Arlene Windsor put a plastic bag over her head and put an end to her misery.

Making a Bad Leg Worse

A 22-year-old athlete training for the marathon injured his right knee, and the joint locked. Following an orthopaedic examination it was suggested that he had torn the meniscus: a fibroid cartilage inside the joint. He was booked for surgery to have the meniscus removed.

While the operation was in progress excessive bleeding was observed. The surgeon concluded he had damaged the popliteal vein in the hollow at the back of the knee, and he tied it off to staunch the flow. The bleeding continued after the operation. After his discharge from hospital the young man came back complaining that his calf tended to seize up and refuse to move. This proved to be claudication: the extreme temporary lameness caused by lack of blood to the legs. A vascular surgeon reopened the leg to see what the trouble might be. He found a clot in the artery where the surgical damage had actually taken place, not the vein which the orthopaedist had tourniqueted. It transpired that the orthopaedist, guessing rather than knowing what had happened, had ligated the wrong vessel and left the young man's leg to be starved of blood.

It's Flat Feet, Your Majesty

Several members of the royal family have suffered health problems as a result of heavy smoking.

When King George VI suddenly found that he had difficulty in walking up hill, his doctors sadly diagnosed the problem as being flat feet.

They Were Wrong

Excessive indulgence in nicotine had narrowed King George's arteries, cutting off the flow of blood to his legs and causing claudication.

A Surgical Comedy

Like most slapstick comedy, the farce which cost the Medical Protection Society £5,000 in a damages settlement in 1976 was hilarious for everybody except the victim.

A woman was wheeled into the operating theatre of a British hospital on a canvas stretcher resting on a gurney. Inside the theatre, orderlies lifted the stretcher with her on it to place her carefully on the operating table. Then they slid out the poles of the stretcher and left her to undergo her operation with the canvas still under her body. Under that canvas stretcher was another one, also without its poles, left in place after a previous operation.

When the surgeon had finished his work the orderlies returned, and replaced the poles in the stretcher loops dangling at either side of the table. What they had failed to notice was that one of them had put his pole into the upper canvas on which had brought the patient: the other had slid his pole into the lower canvas which was already waiting for her.

With their sight gag carefully set up, the two went to the head and foot of the table, and briskly picked up the poles. Laurel and Hardy couldn't have done it better. The top stretcher smartly shovelled the patient over to its poleless side: she bounced over the single pole of the other stretcher and cannoned onto the floor. There the comedy ended. The blow disfigured her face and left her with double vision.

LEGS AND FEET – THE LOST LEG

In 1985 Laura Molino, a registered nurse, tore a ligament in her knee. It was a minor injury requiring a simple repair job, and she checked into Buffalo General, the largest teaching hospital in upstate New York, where 35-year-old orthopaedic surgeon Donald J. Nenno II was assigned to her case.

When Mrs Molino came round in the recovery room she knew at once that something had gone badly wrong. Her calf was swollen, and she was suffering a searing pain.

The nurses attending her were unsympathetic. "Doctors and nurses always make the worst patients," they chided. Yet evidently recognizing that she was suffering something out of the ordinary, they gave her morphine. "It didn't begin to dull the pain," Mrs Molino recalled. "I couldn't even bear to have a sheet touch my leg."

The following day Dr Nenno took her back into surgery to lance her leg in which thee was an evident build up of fluid. A vast quantity of blood gushed out, but there was no alleviation of the pain. Mrs Molino's foot gradually turned numb, and her toes turned black.

A day later her adult daughter came to visit her, and raised Cain on seeing her mother's condition. She descended on the nurses' station and threatened to tear the ward apart if something wasn't done immediately. The nurses sent for a vascular surgeon. He took one look at Mrs Molino and rushed her into emergency surgery. He had one simple message for her daughter.

"I'm going to try to save your mother's life, but I'm not sure that I can save her leg."

The problem was quickly identified. A main artery in the leg had been severed while Dr Nenno had been operating on the cartilage. The vascular surgeon tried to repair it and save the leg, but within a week it was clear that he had failed. Gangrene had infected Mrs Molino's foot and ankle. The leg had to be amputated below the knee.

Mrs Molino was forced to give up her job as a nurse and use a wheelchair. She became depressed and had to undergo psychiatric treatment.

In 1986 she sued nenno and the hospital, and in 1991, when the case was about to come to court, the hospital settled for an undisclosed figure, believed to be in the region of $2 million.

The case came to public attention again in 1992, when the New York Health Department suddenly filed charges against Dr Nenno, accusing him of gross negligence and inadequate record keeping in Mrs Molino's case and two others, all back in 1985. They said he had operated wrongly on the right hip of a man whose left hip required attention, failing at the time to make a proper physical examination, check the patient's records, or take any notice of the anaesthiologist who told him he was starting on the wrong hip. They also charged that in the case of a man with an infected hip replacement, Nenno delayed for eight days before making the necessary surgical removal of infected tissue.

The authorities of Buffalo General Hospital indignantly denied that Dr Nenno was incompetent, insisting that they had considered Mrs Molino's case very carefully, and their appropriate action had included monitoring Dr Nenno's work over a period of time, before concluding that he was a member of staff in good standing and a highly competent surgeon.

It seems likely that the state's very belated interest in Dr Nenno's failures is likely to have been a scapegoating token response to consumer protests that patients were unable to find out anything about doctors' past records and any history of incompetence.

Cut Your Nails – Cut Off Your Legs!

69-year-old Mrs Grace Moore simply went for a routine toenail-cutting in 1980: a service her local health authority made available to the elderly who could not reach their own toes. For Mrs Moore it proved a horrible experience.

"The chiropodist cut into my flesh when she was cutting my toe nails," Mrs Moore complained, "and then put a spray on me. I was poisoned within minutes." Goodness knows what was in the spray, but a short time after it had been applied Mrs Moore was taken to hospital and found to have gangrene.

To begin with, two of her toes had to be amputated from her left foot, then the left leg had to be amputated. During the time she stayed in hospital she also contracted an infection in the right leg, and that had to come off as well.

The local health authority offered her a paltry £5,000 as an out-of-court settlement, but Mrs Moore was not satisfied. Her reason for pursuing the case further in 1985 was, she explained, because, "My life is ruined. All I want to do is buy a bungalow adapted for my needs."

"I can't even run after my grandchildren. Losing a leg is like losing a loved one."

LAURA MOLINO

Keep Those Bunions!

Perhaps the consultants who wrecked Jane Soanes' feet were lucky. Instead of suing them to Kingdom Come, Ms Soanes used her professional ability to describe her disastrous treatment to her readers in The Times.

Nature cursed Ms Soanes with flat feet and bunions, the one on the right foot especially tending to soreness. Friends recommended that she undergo the operation for bunion removal. The consultant warned Ms Soanes that she would be in plaster for a month and it would be painful, but all should be well in six months after a course of physiotherapy. Ms Soanes had her great toe joint replaced with a plastic implant, and three other toes broken and re-set to improve the arch.

They improved nothing. The toes curled under and wouldn't touch the floor, and the great toe stuck out to the left. It steadily began to hurt more and more.

A second operation to shorten the great toe also failed. The consultant expressed himself unwilling to "mess around with it any more." After her 18-month experience, Ms Soanes' heartfelt advice to her readers was to suffer patiently and not to accept surgical cures for bunions.

GET A SECOND OPINION

$14.5 million seems a lot of money for a doctor's insurer to pay out simply because he didn't invite a patient to check his opinion against that of a colleague.

However, that was indeed the first form of negligence alleged against neurosurgeon Dr Leslie Schaffer when a Cook County, Illinois jury found against him and Mercy Hospital on the plea of former nurse's aide Lillie Ruth Roberts.

Mrs Roberts, who was employed at the Skokie Valley Hospital, and at home cared for her 94-year-old mother, started suffering severe backaches in 1984. A nerve was being pinched, and the pain grew sufficiently intense to force her to give up her job and hire help to look after her mother.

In 1987 Dr Schaffer operated on her spine, but did not take away enough bone to prevent the swollen nerve from being compressed against it. In effect, the separation had alleviated the symptom, leaving the basic condition to develop and grow gradually worse.

The pressure ultimately deadened the nerve completely, and poor Mrs Roberts found herself unable to control her bowels and bladder. She also found herself unable to walk more than a block without experiencing intense pain. She was taken into the University of Chicago Hospital for a second operation in 1989. Although this relieved her pain it did not restore her control over her bodily functions. As a result she was largely confined to her home and needed rehabilitation care and counselling the help of an attendant to run simple errands.

The jury heard that Dr Schaffer did not suggest that Mrs Roberts take a second opinion, from which she might have learned that more conservative treatment like exercising, losing weight or taking medication might have been beneficial. And they made the heavy award against him.

> *"I would tell people to let {surgery} be the last thing possible, because if I had known what I know now, I wouldn't have done it. I'd tell them just to leave it alone."*

Mrs Lillie Roberts

What's An Arm Worth?

Little Anthony Mitchell was awarded £35,000 against Liverpool Area Health Authority in 1988, and his father was furious. The award was inadequate, Mr Mitchell complained, and the Health Authority was at fault in having dragged its feet for four years before admitting its liability.

Anthony, born in 1984, was a premature baby and required artificial care. A tube was strapped to his arm with a bandage, but the bandage was fastened too tightly. Circulation was cut off, and the baby's forearm withered. And it had to be amputated.

Slip-Ups

According to Mr Justice Michael Davies, 35-year-old driving instructor Sean Hickey was "unquestionably a troubled and unhappy man," after he underwent circumcision at a South London hospital. Perhaps the 35-year-old was unhappy and troubled before it, too, since he believed the operation would improve his sex life. In fact it impeded it, and even corrective surgery two months later still left him suffering soreness and pain. The local health authority admitted partial negligence, and Mr Hickey was awarded £5,700 damages.

Ritual Fails

A more alarming circumcision disaster was the religious ritual arranged for a 5-year-old Muslim boy in North London. The joyful party celebrating the primitive rite in 1981 turned to "almost hysterical despair" when Dr Haroon Ali Muhammad awkwardly chopped off half the child's penis. Luckily for the little lad there was sophisticated neuro-surgery available, and his dislocated member was sewn back on.

In the High Court three years later, the boy was awarded £10,196 in compensation for his pain and suffering, and each of his parents were awarded £3,000 for "nervous shock".

Tell or Pay

There was nothing wrong with the vasectomy that the surgeon performed on railway guard Donald Thake in 1975. It just reversed itself, as these things will. Mr and Mrs Thake hadn't been warned of this possibility, and were distinctly shocked when Mrs Thake became pregnant with their sixth child, Samantha.

The failed vasectomy cost the surgeon's insurers £9,677 for the Thakes' expenses in bringing up another child, and £1,500 for Mrs Thake's pain and suffering before and during birth.

Get Permission, Doctor!

Vanessa King, a 43-year-old mother of four, was poised to start a test case after her 1993 hysterectomy at a Home Counties hospital. It was known that there was a cyst on her right ovary which would have to be removed if its condition had deteriorated. Obviously if her womb and one ovary had been removed, the remaining ovary would never serve its primary function again, even if Mrs King had wanted a fifth child. Nevertheless, said Mrs King, she had specifically written on her consent form that her left ovary was not to be removed.

Her surgeon, for reasons that could not be stated while the case was pending, decided to remove both ovaries. In doing so he became the first doctor in Britain to receive a summons for assault and battery on the ground that he had improperly extended his gynaecological operation beyond the patient's wishes.

Equally worrying to the Hysterectomy Legal Fighting Fund were the numbers of women who went into hospital for hysterectomies and were never informed that while operating the surgeons discovered they were pregnant. So that in practice a decision to abort was made by the surgeon without the mother's being consulted. Three cases from King's Mill Hospital, Nottingham were cited:

● Barbara Whiten believed she was infertile when she went for a hysterectomy to ease her pain from the inflamed lining of her womb. Only after the hysterectomy had been completed did she learn that there was an 11-week foetus in her womb.

● Amanda Flewitt wanted a third child when she went in for a routine inspection entailing dilation and curettage. The hospital took a pregnancy test beforehand, but never told her the results. After the D and C she miscarried, the hospital having apparently failed to detect the pregnancy.

● Jane Henson was positively told she was not pregnant, only learning after her hysterectomy that she had been.

The message for the doctors? Tell patients everything, and tell them the truth.

DETRITUS

It always makes for good newspaper headlines when surgeons accidentally leave something behind in a patient's body after an operation. Swabs are particularly easy to overlook.

Saturation with blood camouflages them perfectly, and the peristaltic movement of the bowl may gently ease them into a concealing abdominal cavity. Nor will they show up on X-rays. After a number of cases had been reported in the 1940s, the practice of carefully numbering and accounting for all swabs used became standard in operating theatres.

Given that more than two million operations are performed every year in the UK, really very little detritus is left behind. Which means that any case that comes to light is sure to make headlines, as Treliske Hospital in Truro discovered when it left a 2Œ-inch needle in the back of a baby girl in 1995, failing to detect it when it showed up clearly on X-rays, because staff assumed it to be the outline of a pointer left on the film to indicate the area of interest.

It is possible for quite a large instrument to remain in the body without doing any harm: the classic case was a Spencer-Wells forceps which remained undetected inside a patient for 20 years. It was only discovered when it showed up on a routine X-ray. But it is not unusual for detritus to cause discomfort and, possibly, death.

Injurious Swabs

After giving birth to twins by Caesarean section in 1946, Mrs Lillian Arthur of New York suffered severe abdominal discomfort for two years. She and her husband spent $30,000 in doctors' bills over the next two years before a hospital decided that it must try exploratory surgery. When they opened up Mrs Arthur's tummy they found the cause. A surgical towel, still clearly marked with the name of the hospital that had delivered Mrs Arthur's twins.

In 1947, Mrs Evelyn Tugwell died twelve days after an operation in the Royal Adelaide Hospital to remove a large tumour. A post mortem established that she died of peritonitis, acquired through infection of the cavity where the operation had been performed. It also established that the operation had left a 12-inch square surgical pack inside the body, and it was possible that this had encouraged the spread of the infection.

The surgeon who had removed the tumour thought it possible that a pack of swabs supposed to contain six had actually contained seven, two of them sticking together and being mistaken for one until they separated inside the body.

He also pointed out that Mrs Tugwell's body had been massive, so that surgery was carried out under a distinct disadvantage. She weighed 19 stone, and the tumour he had to remove lay a clear foot below the surface of her abdomen.

The Lost Spatula

On 15 January, 1946, Ada Griffiths went into Newmarket Private Hospital on the outskirts of Brisbane, where surgeons J. Lloyd Simmonds and Hugh Anderson Performed an abdominal operation. She was discharged, but continued to suffer severe stomach pains. An X-ray in March revealed a foreign body in the abdomen, and she went into Brisbane General Hospital on March 28th to have it removed. Dr Thelander discovered a 9 ½-inch spatula inside her.

It proved to be the property of Dr Simmonds. It must, he thought, have slipped into the abdomen "in a twinkling" as the operating table was lowered. He had not, in fact, missed it from his case until six or seven weeks later, so he did not associate it with Ada Griffiths. In any case, he pointed out, bigger foreign bodies could be left inside patients without doing any harm.

The defensive reference to other people's experience was small consolation for Ada Griffiths. She died the day after the spatula was recovered.

A Might-Be True Story

A story gleefully repeated among surgeons relates how a patient who suffered several operations at different hospitals was found to have an instrument left in her body. As the various institutions quarrelled with one another as to who was responsible, one surgeon settled the matter by writing to another, "If you are going to leave forceps in the abdomen it is just as well not to have your initials engraved upon them."

The Case of Sara Colgan

At 82 years of age, Sara Mildred Colgan was a brave old lady who enjoyed playing the piano, and co-operated willingly with the doctors who helped her in the struggle against rectal cancer. She lived at Indiana, Pennsylvania, and on 16 November 1992, the Indiana Regional Cancer Center implanted five tiny catheters into her tumour, and then fed into them hair-sized irradiated wires to destroy the cancer cells. The radiation treatment was intended to be brief and intense. After exposing the tumour to the wires, the catheters were removed, and the old lady was discharged to return to the nursing home caring for her.

But Dr James Bauer's team had ignored warning lights from a monitoring machine when they discharged Ms Colgan. One of the wires had broken inside the catheter, and she went back with the lethal probe still inside her, where it caused fatal damage to her internal organs.

On 20 November it fell out, and a nurse not knowing what it was, simply swept it away and threw it out with other medical waste for incineration. The following day Sara Colgan died.

She was in her grave before the nursing home incinerator's radiation monitors reported danger in one batch of rubbish, and the truth came to light. The National Regulatory Commission promptly suspended the license of Oncology Services Corp. which had provided the radiation machinery. Since Sara Colgan had brought her sliver of nuclear detritus home with her, no less than 94 people: nurses, doctors, attendants, ambulancemen and friends, had been exposed to dangerous radiation. None of them suffered from radiation sickness, but all had increased their risk of contracting cancer.

A story gleefully repeated among surgeons relates how a patient who suffered several operations at different hospitals was found to have an instrument left in her body. As the various institutions quarrelled with one another as to who was responsible, one surgeon settled the matter by writing to another, "If you are going to leave forceps in the abdomen it is just as well not to have your initials engraved upon them."

In 1946, a Melbourne hospital advised a patient that after revising their waiting list they were ready to give him the operation they had listed him for – two and a half years earlier! Too late. The Geelong man had had it done elsewhere after waiting three months.

Pin and All

In 1986 a 67-year-old woman underwent very difficult surgery to her abdomen and perineum. A defect in her pelvis had to be drained while the operation was carried out, and this was done through a strip of corrugated rubber held in place by a safety pin.

The operation was completely successful and the patient left the hospital. However her wound healed slowly and painfully, with a constant discharge. Four months after she had gone home, her GP was still checking the progress of the suppurating wound, when he suddenly noticed the rubber drain starting to protrude. He had it removed at once.

A week later she went back to hospital for a further check-up, and there the staff discovered and removed the safety pin, still in her body.

Pains in the Urethra

A middle-aged Englishwoman complaining of excessive menstrual flow and abdominal pains was found to be suffering from an ovarian cyst and to require hysterectomy and the removal of her left fallopian tube. The operation was long and difficult, but successful. After it was over, as is not uncommon, the patient had great difficulty in urinating. So the nursing staff inserted a self-retaining catheter to drain urine out from her bladder into a bottle. Two days later, the nurses entered on her record, "The catheter fell out last night." As she could now urinate freely, it was not replaced. After two months she presented herself at the out patients department, complaining that her urination was now painful and excessively frequent, and she was occasionally passing blood. However it was another hospital that, later in the year, discovered and removed a piece of rubber from the burst catheter which had been retained in her urethra.

A 13-year-old boy complained of painful urination and abdominal pains. Under a general anaesthetic, his bladder was internally examined with a cystoscope, size 3F, passed through a catheter, sized 4F, in his urethra. It revealed no problem, and the boy was discharged. Two weeks later he was back. His urination had become extremely painful ever since he left the hospital, and that morning he had been frightened to discover a small solid blue object start emerging from the end of his penis along with the stream.

It was a 10 cm length of the catheter which had been sliced off by the cystoscope, since the wrong sizes had been put together. Like the woman with the piece of catheter left in her urethra, he had suffered no permanent harm, but the Medical Defence Union paid them both modest damages for their distress.

Dental Detritus

Dental surgeons are as likely as the sawbones to leave pieces of equipment inside their patients. It is always possible for patients to swallow small instruments, false teeth, or pieces of material while the dentist is not looking. A surprising collection of dentistry paraphernalia has been recovered from patients' stomachs. Reamers. rubber dam clamps, burrs and post crowns have all turned up, sometimes unsuspected by the dentist. One argument for always having a dental assistant present while a dentist is working is that the patient may involuntarily sneeze or yawn while his back is turned, and unwittingly ingurgitate some small and easily overlooked piece of his equipment.

Worse suffering may be caused if the dentist accidentally leaves something in a patient's gum after carrying out complicated treatment. In 1980, a five-year-old girl went to her dentist for root canal work on her upper right canine tooth. The dentist reamed the canal and inserted a dressing. Despite this, the gum swelled, and a week later the tooth had to be extracted.

Six years went by, and another dentist took a routine X-ray and noticed a foreign body lying in the gum. The girl was referred to hospital where an oral surgeon opened up her mouth, and found 20 mm from the tip of a silver root probe lying in a groove of the bone. Fortunately the metal had only discoloured the bone, without apparently causing any injury.

When the original dentists were taxed with negligence, both he who had reamed the canal and he who had extracted the tooth insisted that they would never have used a silver-pointed instrument for the work. It seemed there was an insoluble mystery as to the provenance of the broken probe. The Medical Defence Union decided against opening up a can of worms. It settled with the girl's parent for £1,200 without admitting the liability of either of the dentists involved.

In the same year that the silver point was found in the girl's jaw, a dental assistant in Germany doing very extensive preparatory work on a woman who was to have her upper incisors crowned broke his reamer in the root canal. He knew about this, but gutta percha points had been set to fill the canals and provide a support for the crowns before any action was taken. Then the patient's mouth was X-rayed, and she was told the tip of the reamer lay in her jaw, where it was not expected to do any damage.

The crowns had to be fitted twice, as the wrong colour was used the first time. On the second occasion, the dentist noticed that a holding post had slipped out of place and perforated the root wall. However he was confident that this would right itself as the new crowns were cemented in place.

His judgement was disastrously wrong on both counts. The patient's gum became inflamed. Unlike the young girl who had adapted so easily to the silver point of the reamer, this woman suffered bone loss. There was no doubt that this was because the piece of detritus had been left in her jaw, and because no immediate effort had been made to remove the misplaced post and heal the perforation. The cost to the Medical Defence Union was £3,000.

General Advice

Tell your dentist if you swallow when he's got equipment in your mouth, and he isn't looking.

....
HOSPITAL PROBLEMS
....

If the surgeon doesn't kill you, the hospital may: that seems to be a rising tide of opinion in the western world.

Dr Vernon Coleman conducts an ongoing campaign through his European Medical Journal to suggest that intrusive doctoring and inept hospital care aggravate more ills than they cure, and cites startling statistics to show that when industrial action closes hospitals to all but emergency cases or, as in Israel, doctors' strikes almost withdraw medical care from the public for a period, the mortality rate falls significantly.

Junior hospital doctors have rightly complained for decades of the outrageously long hours and understaffing that make them fearful of their own competence in dealing with emergencies in the small hours of the morning, or after preposterously protracted periods without sleep.

The public should be appalled that cases of junior hospital doctors actually dying of fatigue have occurred: we have even seen that in one malpractice suit the successful plaintiffs deliberately chose not to name the overworked interns with excessive responsibilities thrust upon them.

Frozen in Hospital
In October 1982, it was reported that Gertrude Laxton contracted hypothermia while a patient at Tooting Bec Psychiatric Hospital. The Regional Health Authority did not deny that the hospital's heating system was entirely inadequate. It was old-fashioned, they observed, and they simply could not afford the £250,000 needed to repair it and bring it up to proper performance.

Minister of Health Kenneth Clarke robustly attacked his critics with a blunt statement: "The rash of recent reports about cuts in the NHS, freezes on new hospital buildings and radical solutions proposed by some regional health authorities are a collection of nonsense based on misunderstanding."

This was forthright and no doubt politically well judged, but it didn't do much for Gertrude Laxton.

Coy Cleaners

St Bartholomew's Hospital, the oldest teaching hospital in Britain, was not sure how the explain the regularity and thoroughness with which its lavatories were cleaned in 1989. The body of a patient who suffered a heart attack while on the lavatory was not discovered for six days!

"Operation Clean Up"

In 1993 the Royal College of Nursing decided that a national campaign was needed to improve hygiene in hospitals and cut the number of infections patients were acquiring from their hospitalization. Patients and nurses were complaining of copious visible dirt. Dust floated down from light-fittings onto the sterile-gloved hands of nurses. Showers stank. Lavatories had blood over their floors, and overflowing containers of used sanitary towels.

Hospital waste was held for hours in overheated wards to brew up bacteria. Legionnaire's disease was known to have been contracted in some hospitals by patients who assuredly would not have caught it had they remained at home.

The nurses felt they were struggling in a middle ground to cope with excesses above them and below them. The number of domestic cleaning staff had almost halved since 1979, and many of the newcomers were slovenly and incompetent. As they came from private "tendered out" contracts, NHS nurses had no jurisdiction over them.

What's more, some of the new generation of consultants seemed akin to the boneheaded infection carriers who drove pioneers like Ignaz Semmelweiss and Joseph Lister to distraction in the 19th century – they were either too busy or too grand to wash their hands between patients.

Don't Stop The Op – I'm Only On The Telephone

Orthopaedic surgeon Fereydoune Shirazi of Van Nuys, California, was hauled up before the state medical authorities in 1994. He was called to explain why he had left an electric-powered cutting tool running in a patient's spine while he disappeared from the theatre to make a telephone call and go to the bathroom.

The tool, called a nucleotome, was activated by a foot pedal. Dr Shirazi put a sandbag on the pedal which kept the blades rotating in the man's spine, and proceeded to leave the machine to work itself while he was away for 11 minutes.

Dr Shirazi told the medical board that he had forgotten to turn off the nucleotome, adding that it didn't matter because in a few minutes an anaesthesiologist who was standing by saw that it was running unattended, and turned it off. Not that Dr Shirazi thought it would have done any damage in any case – the machine was designed to cut diseased tissue, and he believed it could not cut healthy tissue. Admittedly nobody was injured, but a spokesman for the medical board remarked that "the potential was there" for some very serious harm to the 30-year-old patient.

The incident took place at Westlake Medical Center in Westlake Village, where Dr Shirazi had transferred after having lost the right to practice at Simi Valley Hospital, where he had found himself unable to manage three successive keyhole operations on patients' knees to the satisfaction of Dr William Frank, the head of surgery. Dr Shirazi had been unable to place the monitor in such a position that he could see it while manipulating his instruments, and was effectively operating blind in response to spoken directives from others in the theatre.

In Dr Shirazi's opinion, however, all his problems were the result of a personality clash with Dr Frank, whose report to the state medical board had started the investigation of his competence.

••

CELEBRITY SPOT

ANDY WARHOL

In 1991 the painter's estate sued New York Hospital, Warhol's personal physician Dr Denton S. Cox, his surgeon Dr Bjorn Thorbjarnarson, and his private duty nurse Ms Min Cho.

Warhol's premature death occurred after surgery on his gall bladder. Although the operation was entirely successful, his death, the estate claimed, was due to faulty aftercare. Warhol was left virtually unattended after surgery, they declared. The result was that his body became overloaded with fluids, and he died.

Lawyers for Warhol's doctors rebutted these claims, but the hospital chose to settle out of court.

••

It may seem extraordinary that early physicians with their prescriptions for bleeding and blistering; their personal potions and placebos; their optimistic prayers and incantations; their half-baked half-awareness of Galen and Paracelsus, should have dared to label any individual practitioner a quack. But they did.

The definition of quackery is the practice of medicine, presumed to be incompetent because it is undertaken by someone who is not a member of the profession, or who makes use of practices disapproved by the profession.

All professions, as George Bernard Shaw remarked in his "Preface to The Doctor's Dilemma", are "conspiracies against the laity."

Alongside the medical profession he listed the military, the legal, the sacerdotal, the pedagogic, the royal and aristocratic, the literary and artistic and the industrial, commercial and financial worlds as comprising such conspiracies.

In this sense, a profession is not one of those callings best exemplified by "the oldest profession": an occupation in which the practitioner willingly devotes his or her physical or mental personality to the benefit of another for an agreed period and an allotted fee. It is a group of practitioners who band together and approve each other's practice to the exclusion of the laity.

The exclusiveness is the mark of this type of profession: not the voluntary temporary self-abnegating personal service epitomized in prostitution, which has never succeeded in becoming an exclusive and licensed profession, able to penalize intruders!

As such, a doctor might be accused of quackery: but only for those specific actions that were not approved by their profession. In other respects a doctor may be a qualified and recognized specialist.

A genuine doctor may offer you utterly useless treatment. He may give you a quite unnecessary prescription selected almost at random from the vast and growing pharmacopoeia pressed on him by the drug companies, wholly and solely because you have come to believe that you have not been properly treated if you get the proper recommendation of rest and a lot of water to drink which will perfectly cure almost all of the feverish colds lavishly described as 'flu. But the doctor who does this is not a quack. This treatment is the approved practice of the medical profession.

In the days when doctors believed in bleeding and blistering, a competent healer – a village midwife or bone-setter, for example – who was not recognized by the approved Company of Physicians was a quack, and liable to persecution or prosecution if the approved doctors were sufficiently powerful or the law sufficiently clear. Had the doctors been organized into a profession under the Roman Empire, Jesus Christ might have been hauled before Pilate as a quack, no matter how many of the lame leaped and the blind testified they could see, where all other physic had failed them.

A BRIEF HISTORY OF QUACKERY

Quacks predate imposters, because the role of doctor was not seen as particularly desirable until relatively late in the 19th century. Apart from royal physicians, the medicos did not rate highly among the educated classes.

No self-respecting 18th century judge or archdeacon would have been likely to invite his doctor to dinner. A petty aristocrat would rate physicians with tradesmen and surgeons alongside artisans. Even those great scientists who were genuinely advancing medicine and winning glory for the future – the Hunter brothers, for example – notoriously engaged in anti-social practices like cutting up dead bodies and buying them from grave-robbers. Classically educated Victorian society that wrote off all school science as "stinks" did not at first accord eminent status to doctors and surgeons.

The quack might genuinely have believed that he had a new way of healing. Or he might cynically have known that he could make a lot of money from people desperate about their own or their relatives' sickness. However, he always managed to work quite seriously in the health business, one way or another.

An imposter might be someone who felt cheated of the education that should have made him a doctor, or he might just want the respect he saw accorded to doctors. The greatest imposter of the 18th century was George Psalamanasar. To this day no one knows who he really was. He achieved fame by passing himself off as a Formosan, although he had never been to Formosa and his romantic accounts of his "homeland" were utterly preposterous. It never crossed Psalamanasar's mind to pass himself off as a Formosan doctor with new healing powers. There was far more to be gained by pretending to be a gentleman traveller.

The First English Quack

We don't know what he did, but we do know what was done to him. A 14th century account mentions a "counterfeit physician" who was punished by being made to ride backwards on a horse, holding its tail in his hand as a bridle. Chamber-pots were strung around his neck and a whetstone was suspended from his chest. He was led through the streets of London while the mob jeered and him and banged on basins. Then he was banished.

Power to the Priesthood

Henry VIII, always keen to bring society under central control, passed a statute forbidding anyone to practice medicine in the City of London without permission of the Bishop or the Dean of St Paul's. In cases where they were uncertain about granting a licence, either might call on a panel of medicos for advice. Outside London the authority was passed to the other bishops.

The principle was quite clear. Establishment approval came first; experienced medical opinion came second, and even then only if the establishment was unable to make up its own mind.

In any case, the medical profession would have been those approved by the establishment. Any healer outside its ranks was a law-breaking quack.

ROYAL PROTECTION

There was one decisive way round the exclusive control of the bishops and the Royal Colleges of physicians and surgeons. The quack could win the protection of the monarch in person.

Dr John Dee (1527-1608) was notorious as a necromancer, alchemist and astrologer. A sorcerer who risked ecclesiastical persecution. He was a follower of recondite pursuits for which there was little public demand. Dee was not a rich man. To make a living he peddled herbal potions. So not only was he a quack he was also a dabbler in black magic.

He managed to survive because Queen Elizabeth herself patronized him. The Virgin Queen, like Adolf Hitler and Mrs Ronald Reagan, nursed the delusion that astrological predictions would help her arrive at sensible political decisions. (Happily for England, she was better able to do that on her own account than were her successors in consulting the stars for their fortunes.) Elizabeth did not mind if her astrologer conjured up demons in his spare time. If the church dared not prosecute him for his diabolism, the physicians feared to attack him for his quackery.

It was only in the last years of his life, with the more aggressively intel-lectual James I on the throne, that Dee had to skulk through London, selling his remedies very covertly.

His son Arthur (1579-1651) was more fortunate, and graduated from the ranks of the quacks to become physician to the Tsar of Russia and sub-sequently to Charles I.

Queen Anne – always capable of silliness when her personal interest was aroused – became the only English monarch ever to knight a quack. William Read (d. 1715), a "botching cobbler" and tailor, improved his livelihood by travelling through the provinces hawking remedies, and claiming to "couch" cataracts (curing them by displacing the lens in the eye).

He came to the queen's notice when he started treating soldiers and sailors free of charge, offering to cure blindness in the navy. In 1705, Anne knighted him and designated him her personal oculist.

Read was illiterate. He hired a hack to write verse advertisements for him, and distributed broadsheets with this masterpiece:

> *"Whilst Britain's sovereign scales such work has weighed, And Anne herself her shining favours paid, That sacred hand does your fair chaplet twist, Great Read, her own entitled oculist."*

The poor cobbler died a rich man.

Joshua Ward (1685-1761) was nicknamed "Spot" because of a birthmark, and stigmatized by Dr Johnson as the dullest man he knew. In 1717 he made an attempt to enter parliament by fraud, and was exposed as a Jacobite sympathizer. He fled to St Germain where he made a name for himself among the exiled Stuart supporters by the sale of his "drop and pill" remedy.

In 1733 he was pardoned and returned to England. Here he had the good fortune to meet George II when the king was suffering from a dislocated thumb. Trusting his luck, Ward gave it a violent wrench back into place, and the grateful monarch offered immediate rewards. Ward was granted an apartment in the almonry at Whitehall. He was granted permission to drive his coach through St James's Park. And he was granted royal protection against the College of Physicians!

This was important. When Ward became fashionable, patronized by aristocrats like Lord Chesterfield, the physicians examined his drop and pill. It proved to be an extremely dangerous compound of the poison antimony. That didn't stop Ward from selling it. Nor did the epigram:

> *"before you take his drop or pill, take leave of friends and make your will."*

He did make one contribution to English scientists, however. He introduced them to the method of obtaining sulphuric acid by burning sulphur with saltpetre. He died rich and controversial – a subject of satire in the newspapers and idolization in some fashionable circles.

The Father of Quack Advertising

Thomas Case, born in Lyme Regis around 1660, came to London when he was 15 years old. A bookish boy, he had published his first treatise before he reached the age of 23. He settled in Lambeth in 1682 and became a friend of John Partridge, the astrologer ridiculed and effectively destroyed in 1708 by Jonathan Swift. Case made his name as an astrologer and a writer on astronomy, anatomy and medicine.

In the age of the Royal Society he proved himself foolish and quackish by publishing a book attempting to refute the empirical scientific principles of Francis Bacon. In the 1690s he went to live in Blackfriars where he hung up his sign of the "Golden Ball", and rather charmingly inscribed below it:

"Within this place Lives Doctor Case."

He took pride in his darkened room and collection of mysterious appliances used to see visions of the departed and conjure up oracles of the future. He also practised as what he called a "spagyrick physician", advertising his services on broadsides and leaflets, and selling expensive wonder-working nostrums like his "Mundus Sanitatis – The World's Wonder for Inward Wounds. Price 2s.6d."

Around his pill-boxes he pasted another little rhyme:

"Here's fourteen pills for thirteen pence; Enough in any man's own conscience."

The Licensed Quack

Thomas Saffold went through the orthodox route and was licensed to practice by the Bishop of London. His verse advertising with mild knocking copy warned other physicians, however, that he was not a reputable doctor. Already the exclusive profession was making non-competitiveness an important aspect of professional conduct:

"It's Saffold's pills, much better than the rest, Deservedly have got the name of Best. The half-box, eighteen pills for eighteen pence. Though 'tis too cheap in any man's own sense."

Saffold was denounced as "an empiric", and the profession was delighted when his own pills killed him in 1691!

NOSTRUMS AND PATENT MEDICINES

Selling patent pills and potions with secret formulae or folk-remedy ingredients is the oldest trick of the quack's trade. Diagnosis is unnecessary. The would-be patient has only to describe his symptoms and be assured that the medicine will infallibly cure them. Or advertising may list the ailments which will yield to the wonder-working salve. The patient can buy the stuff and treat himself.

From the Middle Ages, the itinerant quack nostrum pedlar was a familiar figure, providing popular entertainment with his patter, tall stories, and even songs and dances. The Italians gave him a name – "monta in banco", or mount on a bench. This became the English "mountebank", and the word rapidly grew synonymous with a charlatan or a simple clown. The quack entertainer of Tudor times set up a little portable platform under an awning and gathered a crowd at fairs or markets to enjoy his performance before buying his pills.

The trade had a long and wonderful succession well into the twentieth century. The snake-oil salesmen of America became internationally famous. One of the authors watched a self-styled "Gypsy Lee": a brazen-voiced, barrel-chested character with enormously powerful presence, who travelled England's west country markets in the 1950s, and put on a marvellous show with pots of virulent green ointment which he claimed was "hedgehog fat, the ancient gypsy remedy", and liberally daubed over his skin to "prove" that it would cure hives or acne or blisters, and lapped up with his tongue to demonstrate its excellence for the digestion and its power to expel tapeworms!

Sadly the race has almost died. They did provide amusement although they did nothing for the health. They were, for the most part, small tradesmen, as unlikely to leave a mark on history as a Petticoat Lane stallholder or a carnival barker.

To make a mark on the history of medical error, it was necessary for a quack to propound a new theory or enlist the patronage of a great person.

Joanna Stephens

Surely Joanna Stephens must be accounted the greatest nostrum fraud of all times? No other hawker of medical rubbish managed to succeed in blackmailing parliament into paying for the revelation of an unappetizing and completely worthless secret. No mere mountebank could claim to have shortened the life of so great a statesman as Sir Robert Walpole.

In 1738 Mistress Stephens announced that she had an infallible remedy for stone in the bladder. And she was opening a subscription list to raise £3,000 to persuade her to part with the secret.

There was nothing demeaning about financing an enterprise by inviting subscribers to donate their money in return for being listed as patrons in the 18th century. Alexander Pope made his fortune by opening a subscription list for his translation of Homer. Dr Johnson financed work on his dictionary by soliciting subscriptions from patrons, and never forgave Lord Chesterfield for dangling hope and not coming up with the cash.

Joanna started well with subscriptions from the Dukes of Richmond, Leeds and Rutland, who were followed by other aristocratic patrons, the bishops of Oxford and Gloucester, and Prime Minister Godolphin. But they only managed to raise £1,360, and without the remaining cash Joanna was keeping the remedy to herself.

Fear of the surgeons' agonizing and dangerous lithotomy was widespread. Parliament was persuaded to take an interest, and voted Joanna the rest of the money. Whereupon her remedy was published in the London Gazette.

Joanna's remedy was a powder of calcined shells of eggs and snails; a decoction of herbs boiled in water with a ball of soap, swine's cresses burnt to blackness, and honey. And pills made of calcined snails, wild carrot seeds, burdock seeds, ash keys, hips and haws, all burnt to blackness, with Alicant soap and honey.

Over the last three years of his life Sir Robert Walpole took so much of Joanna's medicine that he was estimated to have swallowed 180 lbs of soap! Three large stones were found in his bladder after his death.

John Hill

A genuine professional apothecary and a keen amateur botanist at the beginning of his career, John Hill (born around 1716) set up practice in James Street, Covent Garden, and attracted the attention of the 3rd Earl of Bute.

In 1746 he took to journalism, conducting the British Magazine for four years, and rashly attacked a number of far better writers who could defend themselves.

Henry Fielding rebuked him severely in his Covent Garden Journal, and Christopher Smart satirized him in The Hilliad. Hill wrote a farce, "The Rout", which was booed off the stage.

He also attacked the Royal Society for refusing to admit him, and exhibited his lack of scientific understanding. But he inveigled the award of the degree M.D. out of St Andrews University, and the Earl of Bute's patronage won him appointment as Superintendent of the Royal Gardens at Kew.

In 1759 Hill started the long drawn out publication of 26 volumes on "The Vegetable Kingdom" – a respectable attempt at taxonomic categorization. At first this proved a great success. The King of Sweden bestowed the order of knighthood of Vasa on him, and Hill started to call himself "Sir John".

However, in the long run, the publication drained away Hill's money, and he was reduced to selling quack herbal potions. His voluminous writings covered all manner of semi-scientific topics, a naval history, a couple of plays and a novel. But he would be remembered best for the epigram with which Garrick revenged himself on him:

"For physic and farces, his equal there scarce is, His farces are physic, his physic a farce is."

Although Hill was generally discredited in 1775, killed by the gout which his own "Elixir Bardana" was guaranteed to cure, his physic did not entirely die with him. He was the first to make a fetish of herbal and vegetable-based medicine: a fad which would prove very long-lived.

HOMEOPATHY

Despite the survival of such distinguished and valuable institutions as the Royal Homeopathic Hospital on the one hand, and a statue on Scott Circle in Washington D.C. commemorating homeopathy's founder Dr Samuel Christian Hahnemann on the other, homeopathy had its beginnings in mere crankiness, and by its very success contributed to the public's willingness to tolerate other more dangerous quackeries. In particular, the availability of "homeopathic remedies", sometimes disapproved of by orthodox doctors, but taken by the rich and famous, gave ease and comfort to all sorts and conditions of persons who preferred buying something cranky or faddy or "alternative" to going through the dull routine of accepting an ordinary medico's advice.

Hahnemann was born in Meissen, Germany in 1755, and at the beginning of his career carried out normal scientific studies on Peruvian bark, from which quinine is extracted. In 1796 he enunciated the principle which was to make him famous: Similia similibus curentur – like cures like. However, this was not the product of tested, measurable, repeatable experiment. It was Hahnemann's own personal wheeze. Substances which caused certain symptoms if taken in moderate to large doses would, he believed, actually cure those same symptoms if taken in minuscule doses.

In fact, of course, it is normally the case that something which is bad for you in moderate doses is not particularly good for you in small doses, either. Hahnemann might seem superficially to have suffered some vague confusion with the principle of vaccination.

hahnemann did not believe that his homeopathic doses would cause the rapid production of antibodies to fight off the potentially toxic substance. For, as he explained in his influential book "The Organon" (1810), he also believed that the smaller the quantity taken, the more effective was the homeopathic medicine. Hahnemann recommended "tinctures". The "medicinal" substance – which might be virtually any substance – was to be dissolved in a large quantity of distilled water. Then a teaspoonful of that distillation was to be diluted again. The process was repeated. And repeated. And repeated. Finally the presence of the original substance in the distilled water would be undetectable by any scientific instruments.

He actually recommended a solution to one decillionth of a grain – a millionth of a millionth of a millionth of a millionth to ten of these millionth re-dilutions! If you dropped a cup of instant coffee powder into the sea, and allowed it a few years to wash thoroughly around all the oceans of the world, and then took a cup of seawater, you might find a homeopathic dose of your original coffee powder in it.

By the time Hahnemann was through with his endless rediluting, it could sometimes be shown that not an atom of his original substance remained. He was simply offering distilled water as a remedy. This was of little concern to Hahnemann – he had reached the conclusion that the spiritual quality it left was even more curative that the substance's physical presence!

With that final piece of barminess, many of his disciples left him, insisting that there must at least be some minuscule molecular trace of the substance in the remedy. Whether homeopaths insisted that a molecule or two must remain in the medicine or not, all agreed that the pharmacopoeia must be extended by "proving" substances. This meant feeding the raw substance to people until definite symptoms of some kind could be observed. Noting them down. And enthusiastically super-dissolving the stuff with the assurance that it would now cure the symptoms. The curative part, of course, was never tested experimentally with controls.

It didn't matter very much that they were all propounding scientific nonsense for much of the 19th century. Orthodox doctors, as we have already seen, had very little but purgatives to offer by way of remedies. During this period a doctor's most curative contribution was likely to be his reassuring presence – his bedside manner. In this way, a reassuring homeopathic doctor might do as much good as a normal doctor, and his remedies would certainly not do any harm, unlike other notorious patent medicines of the period.

Disraeli introduced Queen Victoria to homeopathy, and during the 1880s there was a boom in the cult. Some doctors prescribed homeopathic medicines as it was apparent that they never made patients worse, unlike the irritant laxatives in most doctors' medicine chests.

The cult spread across the Atlantic and numerous homeopathic medical schools were set up in America. Some of them were even attached to the medical departments of normal universities. It became possible for the trainee medical student to learn perfectly orthodox and scientific anatomy; to be taught as far as possible the latest and most reliable methods of diagnosis; to understand just when and why he might have to recommed a patient for surgery; and only use homeopathy to supplement or replace the standard pharmacopathy.

Thus homeopathic doctors might have jogged along happily as a minor branch of medicine resisting traditional "allopathy" (as the homeopaths started naming orthodox pharmacy). Unfortunately, their apparent rejection of chemicals and biochemistry made them appealing allies for the growing armies of "naturopaths" who feared and resisted the growing tyranny of science.

Homeopaths at the turn of the century were all too likely to ally themselves with those who dismissed "the germ theory", foolishly deriding the observations of Pasteur in the same way as people who want to go on believing the book of Genesis foolishly dismiss the observations of Darwin and Wallace as "only a theory".

In practice, two things happened. The overwhelming majority of homeopathic practitioners became orthodox medicos who might occasionally use tinctures as other doctors used placebos. But a vocal minority insisted that they knew truths hidden from the learned, went on "proving" more and more substances, and risked drifting into sheer quackery.

One such homeopathic quack actually became identified with murder for two generations.

DR CRIPPEN

Dr Hawley Harvey Crippen who killed his wife "Belle Elmore", buried her under the kitchen floor, and fled to America with his lover Ethel le Neve, was a dangerous quack.

He was born in Coldwater, Michigan in 1862, and attended the University of Michigan's School of Homeopathic Medicine in 1882, leaving a year later to pursue a course of study at the Royal Bethlehem Hospital ("Bedlam") in London, and completing his medical studies with an M.D. awarded in 1884 by the Homeopathic Hospital College in Cleveland, Ohio. His twenties coincided with the heyday of homeopathy. He practised as a respectable homeopathic doctor for ten years.

By the 1890s America was suffering a depression and many patients were doctoring themselves with nauseating patent pills. Crippen, living in New York with his extravagant second wife Cora "Belle Elmore", was constrained to give up his failing practice and work as office manager for "Professor" Munyon's Homeopathic Remedies. The homeopathic quality of the remedies was about as genuine as Munyon's professorship, but unlike many other patent medicines, they were neither poisonous nor addictive.

Munyon was a brilliant salesman. He had a charismatic personality and a big, booming voice to match his big expansive frame. He advertised in religious journals and made a feature of his conservative evangelical Christianity. He also became one of the leading patent medicine manufacturers in America. Crippen thrived as a businessman-doctor and became the firm's principal medical consultant. Finally Munyon promoted him to the lucrative management of the new London branch in 1897.

Two years later Munyon learned that Crippen was moonlighting as Belle's manager in her abortive attempt to build a music-hall career. Munyon fired the little doctor. Crippen was on the verge of ruin. The craze for homeopathic medicine was over. A new homeopathic doctor starting up a new practice was not likely to succeed. So he went to work for another patent medicine concern, the Sovereign Remedy Company. It was undercapitalized and folded eight months later. Crippen invented his own patent nerve tonic, "Amorette", and used all his sales skills to market it.

After the manner of the quack, he placed advertisements in papers aimed at the least educated sections of the populace: Tit-Bits and Comic Cuts. But Amorette never took off.

In 1902, the Drouet Institute for the Deaf advertised for a consultant physician. Crippen applied for the post, and was given the job. His experience was appropriate – the scientific sounding "Institute" with handsome offices, first in Regent's Park Road and then in Marble Arch, was the front for a disgraceful and dangerous swindle. Drouet needed a quack seller of quack medicines, not a genuine consultant.

The Drouet Disaster

"Dr Drouet" was not the man of science he pretended, but a drunken rogue from a bad district of Paris. He peddled drops, snuffs and gargles, and specialized in little plasters to be stuck behind the ears which were supposed to "penetrate" an improve the hearing. Far from being homeopathically harmless, Drouet's plasters contained a powerful dangerous irritant. Crippen, as his London manager, was exposed as fraudulent in a specialist journal for the deaf. Its editor made an appointment, without identifying himself, He observed that the little doctor was foppishly dressed, but not over-clean. This impression was reinforced when Crippen took an unsterilized speculum from a box of instruments and examined first one ear and then the other without cleansing it, finally dropping it back among the instruments to await the next patient without the slightest suggestion of a sterile bath.

The investigative journalist, was stone deaf beyond the expectation of a cure. So he wrote off Crippen as a quack when, after this cursory examination, the consultant said, "I cannot promise anything, but if you will try the treatment I will do my utmost for you."

It was rare for patients to make their way into the office and actually see Crippen – most answered advertisements and were required to fill out a questionnaire describing their symptoms. Crippen would then make "diagnoses" which were reported to the patients in form letters, together with advice to take one or more of Drouet's medicines.

A servant girl who paid a year's wages to the Drouet Institute was told she had "middle ear disease". In fact she had lost the nerve apparatus of both ears to congenital syphilis. A 30-year-old man who had suffered discharges since childhood was not helped by the drops, plasters and snuff prescribed. His ear was full of polyps which needed removal.

The Institute was ruined in 1903 when a Staffordshire locksmith died from an abscess the Institute was treating. The examining doctor found that middle-ear disease had infected the right lobe of his brain, and his skull was so diseased a knitting needle could have been poked through it. The Drouet plasters he had been prescribed could only have made the inflammation worse.

The Aural Remedy Company

Crippen did not suffer from this collapse. He bought up the bankrupt stock and established himself as the Aural Remedy Company from a postal drop in Kingsway. He went on diagnosing from questionnaires, and despatching useless and dangerous pills and patches. He sent his patients a spurious specialist journal the Ontological Gazette. he was financed in this ramp by a professional con-man called Eddie Marr. Under the names of "Professor Keith-Harvey", or "W. S. Hamilton, obesity expert", Marr was already peddling patent medicines. He also sold fraudulent stocks and shares. When Crippen was exposed as a murderer, Marr rushed round to the convenience address in Kingsway and scraped his name off the "Aural Remedies" plate lest the association should lead the police back to him.

The last of Crippen's illegal medical activities was tooth-drawing. With a fellow-American called Gilbert Rylance, he set up in New Oxford Street as "Yale tooth Specialists", promising the American painless dentistry which had become famous. Rylance did crown work and made dentures. Crippen performed extractions, for which he was not licensed. All in all, Crippen's professional life was at least as damaging to humanity as his notorious marital life.

ELECTRICAL CURES

The successful abuse of electricity for spurious medical purposes sprang quite naturally from a false syllogism:

MEDICINE SHOULD BE SCIENTIFIC. ELECTRICITY IS A DISCOVERY OF SCIENCE. ELECTRICAL MEDICINE, THEREFORE, IS TRULY SCIENTIFIC MEDICINE.

When Benjamin Franklin started his experiments demonstrating the existence of electricity, they attracted the attention of all the optimists who hope that an invisible scientific force may explain the phenomena they wish to verify without putting their verification to experimental tests. Like gases and magnetism before it, and radio and radiation in later years, electricity was offered by the unscientific as a universal explanation for the inexplicable, and by some quacks as a panacea for all manner of ills.

James Graham

James and William Graham, the sons of a successful Edinburgh saddler, both went to Edinburgh University and studied medicine under Alexander Monro, first of the dynasty of professors of anatomy and surgery. Both commenced, and then abandoned, the practice of medicine: William to take holy orders; James, after marriage in Pontefract and a successful period working as an oculist and aurist in Philadelphia, to practice quackery. His huge success was partly ascribed to his good looks and winning manners. But it must also have owed much to his imagination and showmanship.

James Franklin has been referred to as the most interesting quack of all time. While working in Bristol in 1774 he began offering his patients milk baths and "electrical and friction treatments". What this entailed is not absolutely certain, but it included seating patients on a "magnetic throne", where they were probably administered mild electric shocks. His enemies also hinted that he made uses of electricity too disgusting to describe, which suggests that he might well have discovered the principle of the electric vibrator and marketed the discreet use of some clitoral- or penile-exciting machine.

He was certainly interested in Franklin's work, and Franklin appears to have thought at first that Graham was a fellow-spirit. Although he subsequently decided that he did not deserve encouraging.

In 1779 Graham treated the Duchess of Devonshire in Aix, and charmed her. With her patronage the way was open for him to return and conquer London. 1780-82 was his heyday. He opened his Templum Aesculapio Sacrum (Sacred Temple for Aesculapius, the Greek god of health) in an Adam mansion in Adelphi Terrace. There was a gold star over the door. It cost two guineas merely to set foot inside the place and look at all its wonders. There were lectures expounding Graham's theories. There were new and ever more expensive treatments. The milk baths were varied with earth baths in which patients sat buried to their necks, looking, an observer remarked, like so many cabbages. The electrical treatments continued.

The piece-de-resistance was the "Grand Celestial bed, whose magic influences are now celebrated from pole to pole and from the rising to the setting of the sun." It was supported by 40 pillars of brilliant glass "of the most exquisite workmanship", and they supposedly contributed to the electrical effects of the 12ft by 9ft couch. This, it was claimed, had cost Graham £10,000. It also supposedly cured infertility for couples who worshipped Aphrodite as well as Aesculapius under its covers, and probably, with all the attendant hoo-ha, was expected to make short work of impotence and frigidity at the same time! The usual fee was £50 for a short visit to the bed. Aristocratic couples could pay up to £500 to spend a night in it. It also had a discreet door on to the street for those who did not want to be seen using it, as well as the magnificent entrance from the Templum's interior.

The most lastingly famous aspect of the Templum leads one to wonder whether the bed may not have served as a very expensive accommodation house for illicit couples. Graham's masterpiece was to illustrate his lectures with beautiful young women, appropriately posed and suitably undressed as "Goddesses of health". The excuse was that the exposure of their charms demonstrated the deirable effects of the various treatments on figure and complexion. Like Playboy bunnies, these deminudes were strictly "look but don't touch". And they were supposed to be anonymous. Nevertheless, 16-year-old Emma Lyons, who would become world famous as Nelson's Lady Hamilton, made her first public London appearance as one of the plastique poseuses in Graham's elegant burlesque show.

The business moved to Pall Mall in 1781, but crashed resoundingly a year later when Graham's property was seized for debt. He eked out a living over the next eight years by giving lectures in places as various as the Isle of Wight and Edinburgh. By the end of the decade he had become a religiomaniac, and in 1791 he was removed to a lunatic asylum, where he died three years later.

A sad end, but the phase of flamboyant quackery had been wonderful while it lasted. He pioneered features that would make fortunes for his successors: regulated baths, be they in water or other fluids; immersion or bathing in earth or mud; the use of electricity as an unexplained therapy.

Showmanship, too, would become a necessary feature of the great quack. Graham is the true great-great-great-grandfather of the Wizard of Oz; the rococo pioneer of the "Medical Show" which offered a free variety entertainment before the Master of Ceremonies made his pitch to sell patent medicines.

Above all, though, Graham demonstrated the phoney-medical use of sex: the half-dressed young women used both as a lure to bring men in to see the demonstrations, and as a promise that other women would become equally alluring after treatment; the electric vibro-massage which may have been applied to the sexual organs; the use of an actual amazing bed for real copulation as the final holy of holies. Graham might equally have made his fortune in California in the 1960s.

ELECTRICAL DEVELOPMENTS

His "discovery" seems to have come from the coincidental cessation of pain when he had just stroked a piece of metal over an aching arm. The invention's success owed everything to the placebo effect, as Oliver Wendell Holmes remarked when describing a woman who had a fake Perkins tractor made of wood pulled across her arm, and exclaimed, "Bless me! Why who would have thought it that them little things could pull the pain from one."

The tractors sold for five guineas each. George Washington bought one and apparently believed in it. So did Chief Justice Oliver Ellsworth. Twelve doctors in Copenhagen produced a book defending "Perkinsism". And Elisha's son Benjamin, more opportunist than his father, prodcued a book full of testimonials; pushed the invention quite relentlessly; and retired to New York a wealthy man.

By and large, other unscrupulous manufacturers ignored an "electrical" effect they could neither understand nor demonstrate. However, when Thomas Edison perfected the electric light, and showed that electrical devices could be used in the home as well as the laboratory, the manufacturing quacks were swift to prove their own inventiveness. The 1890s saw a tremendous boom in electrical corsets, belts and rings offering all manner of spurious cures for men women and children.

Addison's Galvanic Belt

The advertisements (see below) revealed what this wonderful product of the Electrical Appliance Co. was supposed to do: Graham's appeal to sexual anxieties ("lost womanhood and manhood") and aspirations ("underdevelopment") were not discarded, and Acton's neurotic sexual fears were added in the coy reference to "night losses".

The belt was a crude but gaudy object of vivid yellow and red cotton strips, containing pieces of copper and zinc, and generating no electricity whatsoever.

The company knew that it would sell well through the medical showmen and modern-day mountebanks, and another advertisement which was not intended for the general public addressed itself directly to them in The Billboard, a specialist journal for "medicine showmen, agents, palmists and hustlers".

> "*If you are weak you need electricity. For lost womanhood and manhood there is nothing like electricity, it is the greatest power on earth. It puts life and force into everything it touches: gives relief to rheumatism, backache, kidney, liver and bladder troubles, early decay, night losses, lack of nerve vigor, nervous debility, constipation, dyspnoea [laboured breathing], underdevelopment and lost vitality. Price $2.50."*

> "*You are losing nice easy money if you fail to work our high grade electric belts, appliances, body batteries. Also a nice side-line for performers making 1–6 day stands. 500–1000% profit. The Electrical Appliance Company Incorporated, 1891."*

THE ADDISON BELT SOLD TO THE TRADE AT $1.10 PER DOZEN, TO BE SOLD ON AT $2.50 EACH.

The promotors of the device described above offered an alleged explanation of its efficacy. Disease, they claimed, was the result of acid in the blood. The action of sweat from the finger on the ring produced electricity which neutralized the internal acids. (Quacks are fond of "neutralizing" undesirable substances in the body).

The Electro-Chemical Ring Co. sold 45,600 of these worthless devices in a year, before the government convicted them of "obtaining money through the US mails by means of false or fraudulent pretences."

The Inventions of Hercule Sanche

J. Rufus Wallingford's various pieces of equipment were anti-electrical rather than electrical. As "Hercule Sanche", this rogue claimed to have discovered "the Laws of Spntaneous Cure of Disease". Disease, it would seem, was caused by digested food creating an electrical imbalance!

"The electropoise" (see below) was the first of "Doctor" Sanche's inventions. It was an empty piece of ordinary metal gas piping, sealed at both ends, with a flexible cone and a small disc attached to one end. An elastic band and a buckle enabled the user to secure it to his wrist or ankle. "The negative elements so abundant in the atmosphere"? Simple oxygen or H_2O.

"The electropoise supplies the needed amount of the electric force to the system and by its thermal action places the body in condition to absorb H_2O through the lungs and pores.... It introduces this potent curative agent, oxygen, into the remotest and recondite parts." The result? There was no disease it could not cure!

The electropoise, selling at $10.00, was such a commercial success that Dr Sanche improved it by putting a stick of carbon in the pipe, and selling it at $35 as they "Oxydonor Victory". This not only cured all diseases and fevers, it banished yellow fever "in a few hours".

Wallingford invented a "Fraternity of Duxanimae" – (the word seems to mean "Leader of the Mind") – for his customers. They were invited to make "Donations to the cause of Duxanimae in Diaduction, in trust with Dr Hercule Sanche, its discoverer." An accompanying form licensed the good doctor to use the donations "to the best advantage, according to his own best judgement and discretion, upon his honor, which we trust implicitly herewith." This, no doubt he hoped, would spare him from fraud charges. Wallingford porduced useless Sanche devices for many years. He was quite a remarkable swindler.

"The gases from decaying food are positive in their electrical quality and cause disease. With the electropose we cause the negative elements so abundant in the atmosphere to be attracted into the body in sufficient quantity to consume the accumulation of combustible matter stored up by the imperfect action of the vital organs."

HERCULE SANCHE

ALBERT ABRAMS "THE DEAN OF CHARLATIANISM"

One of the most remarkable quacks of all times, Dr Albert Abrams of San Francisco, started as a perfectly respectable physician with qualifications from Heidelberg and Berlin. From 1885 to 1909 he worked blamelessly in California and wrote a dozen reputable textbooks.

Then he started to go off the rails. Dr Abrams discovered diagnosis by what he called "rapid percussion" – the tapping of the spine or the abdomen. His theory was that nerve fibres in the spine vibrated at a rate that differed from disease to disease. And Dr Abrams claimed that he could determine the disease by hearing the sound the vibration produced following his tap.

His diagnosis was improved when he invented the electrical "dynamiser". A box with a tangle of electrical wires inside was connected to a battery or power point. Another wire ran to the forehead of a healthy assistant. The patient being diagnosed merely contributed a drop of blood, which went into the box. Then, with the assistant stripped to the waist and facing to the west, Dr Abrams would "percuss" the assistant's abdomen, and "accurately" diagnose the patient's ailment. The patient need not be present, or even in the same country for the diagnosis to work.

Growing more and more eccentric, Dr Abrams went on to decide that he was also able to detect an absent patient's age, sex and religious persuasion – Catholic, Protestant, Jewish, Seventh Day Adventist, Methodist or Theosophist.

It then became apparent to him that handwriting samples worked as well as blood samples. Consequently, Dr Abrams started diagnosing the dead. Dr Johnson, Edgar Allen Poe, Oscar Wilde and Samuel Pepys had all suffered from syphilis, he declared. American admirers who swallowed the blatant slander on Johnson without a qualm baulked when he reached the same conclusion about Henry Wadsworth Longfellow!

The Mystery of Abrams' Boxes

In 1920 Dr Abrams produced a new machine: the "oscilloclast". this could be used for healing as well as diagnosing: it directed the proper "radio waves" toward bacteria, and killed them as effectively as old-fashioned drugs. Abrams followed the smart commercial principle of never selling oscilloclasts, only leasing them out for a figure of $250 with another $200 for a training course in their use. Each box would therefore earn Dr Abrams the useful sum of $1,500 each month. Although the lessees were sworn not to look inside Abrams' magic boxes, a committe of scientists managed to get hold of one shortly before the doctor's death in 1923. They reported its contents. They found an ohm-meter, a rheostat, a condenser and some other electrical bits and pieces, wired together without any apparent purpose whatsoever.

Following this discovery, a sceptical Michigan doctor sent Abrams a sample of blood from a Plymouth Rock cock, claiming that it came from a human patient. Abrams tested it, and reported back that the patient was suffering from malaria, cancer, diabetes, and two venereal diseases.

Drown Radio Therapy

Dr Ruth B. Drown of Los Angeles, a former employee of Southern California Edison, started making electric and electronic diagnostic and healing gadgets in 1929, which purported to deal with many patients at once in different places. She kept patients' blood samples filed on blotting paper and broadcast "healing" to them by short-wave therapy. Hollywood actor Tyrone Power received "healing" beamed out from her in California when he was in a car accident in Italy.

A University of Chicago Biological Sciences Division examination of Dr Drown at work in 1950 offered her ten blood samples to test. Her failure was so complete with the first three that she declined to attempt the other seven!

Nelson's Magic Spikes

Marketed by the Vrilium Products Co., these were small brass nail-like cylinders about two inches long supposed to contain "vrilium", a science fiction "cosmic energy" invented in a Bulwer Lytton novel; described by Madame Blavatsky as used in the lost continent of Atlantis; and purportedly "discovered" by Dr Abbott E. Kay in the 1920s. Robert Nelson and his son marketed the spikes, to be worn under lapels, to ward off bacteria for twenty feet. They sold at $307 each, and were found in 1950 to contain cheap rat poison emitting no rays at all. "I believe we have an unrecognized form or radioactivity," bleated Robert Nelson Jr. before he went to prison.

More Gadgets

THE INDUCTOSCOPE

An arthritis cure. A series of metal rings were placed over the affected parts, with wires to attach to a power point. Medically worthless and gave potentially dangerous shocks. Banned by the FDA.

THE SOLARAMA BOARD, EARTH BOARD, OR VITALATOR

This was placed under the mattress to emit "free electrons to rejuvenate the body". Worthless.

ELECTRO-MASSAGE
A wide range of treatments for the relief of arthritis, such as vibrating chairs, cushions and pads. These may be damaging to certain forms of arthritis.

ELLIS MICRO-DYNAMETER
Supposed diagnostic machine of impressive appearance. Sold for $875. Actually a simple galvanometer which will register an impressive swing on the dials for dead bodies just as well as live. Useless for any diagnostic or (as some practitioners offered) therapeutic treatment. Usual charge about $10 a "treatment". Over 1,200 destroyed by US marshals.

RELAXICISOR
Produced electric shocks through pads that would supposedly slim the body and tone the muscles. Banned in 1970, when shown it could cause miscarriages and aggravate (inter alia) epilepsy, hernia and varicose veins.

CELEBRITY SPOT

Upton Sinclair
Author Upton Sinclair exemplifies the radical thinker whose critical attitude to the injustices of society spills over into a willingness to mistrust orthodoxy in scientific areas he does not understand. The gull of mediums and clairvoyants all his life, Sinclair also gave ringing endorsement to Dr Abrams, saying, "he has made the most revolutionary discovery of this or any other age." He passionately devended Abrams' honesty and sincerity, and claimed that many supposedly revolutionary new ideas were actually to be found in Abrams' earlier writing.

NATUROPATHY

Two apparently contradictory tendencies combine in the loosely defined medical cult of naturopathy.

"Determined to cure with herbal pills. All the ailing of all their ills."

The spirit of scientific enquiry led 18th and 19th century practitioners to experiment with new treatments. Priesnitz and Kneipp extended the old practice of drinking and bathing in "healing waters" at spas by trying various types of immersion in water. Adolph just looked to mother earth and recommended barefoot walking, sleeping on the ground, and using compresses of clay. Louis Kuhne recommended steam baths, sunlight, and a vegetarian diet. Heinrich Lahmann eschewed salt and drinking water with meals.

These men and their followers, persuaded by coincidence and the placebo effect, believed that they had found cures that were better than the drugs of orthodox medicine.

However, a counter-scientific tendency also encouraged a move towards "natural" health care. The rise of science was accompanied by the rise of technology and industrialism. The mushrooming of hideous factories and urban slums shocked sensitive people.

Their opposition to technology could be associated with churchmen's warnings that the new science was leading to godlessness. And the desire to live in an idyllic and romanticized primitive way, unburdened by science and engineering, became a pervasive part of western imaginative life.

So the various naturopaths – hydrotherapists who tried water cures; vegetarians who blamed meat for all ills; diet faddists and the like – were all ultimately in agreement that pharmacists' drugs and the surgeon's knife were to be avoided.

The fallacy lies in the belief that, for example, "natural" willow bark is "better for you" than the prepared aspirin which has refined exactly the same pain-killing element and may even have been coated to prevent the aggressive action on the stomach which is its major drawback.

Faced with the growing success of scientific medicine that followed the great discoveries of Louis Pasteur, naturopaths jumped hopefully aboard the dotty theory of Antoine Beauchamp that it was not germs that produced disease: it was disease that produced germs. Consequently, wasting time killing germs would simply leave the disease flourishing!

Quack the Ripper

A flamboyant naturopathic quack was "Dr" Francis Tumblety (1833-1903). As a boy in Rochester, New York, he peddled pornography on canal-boats, and worked for "Doc Lispenard" whose drugstore was said to carry on a "disreputable" medical business. Presumably it sold abortifacients and contraceptives. When he was about 17 he left town and went to Detroit, where he seems to have made his fortune rapidly, passing himself off as a doctor. By the late 1850s he was in Canada, alternately calling himself an "electric physician of international reputation", and a doctor. His "theory" was that for every single ailment there was a precise substance in nature that would cure it. Sometimes he hinted that this was Amerindian lore, but mostly he contented himself with producing testimonials from leading citizens of the places he had visited, many of which he was suspected of forging himself.

Tumblety was a tall, handsome man who dressed in a sort of theatrical quasi-military style, and went about accompanied by a pair of greyhounds or riding a white horse. he was driven out of St John, New Brunswick, when a patient called Portmore died, and those who had started to suspect Tumblety of vulgar charlatanism forced an autopsy. The investigation revealed that Portmore's death was entirely owing to the doctor's "atrocious treatment", and a coroner's jury found him guilty of manslaughter.

By this time, though, Tumblety had already taken his beautiful curls and moustache to Boston where he offered to cure acne and built up a thriving trade among the ladies. He wrote a poem which well expressed the naturopath's creed:

"We use such balms as have no strife With Nature or the laws of Life; With blood our hands we never stain, Nor poison men to ease their pain."

An Assassin?

Tumblety would never again let himself get into trouble by so treating a patient as to be accused of causing his death. But he did suffer two encounters with the law. At the end of the American Civil War he was arrested, and accused: first of having unlawfully passed himself off as an army surgeon; and next, more seriously, of either being a notorious Confederate doctor who had tried to spread yellow fever in the Union, or of having been implicated in the plot to assassinate Lincoln. Tumblety was clearly innocent of the serious charges, but may have asked for trouble by using aliases.

Twenty years later he fell into a real scrape in England when he was arrested for sexually assaulting young men. He jumped bail and fled back to America, but some Scotland Yard men at the time, holding the naive belief that one sex maniac was much like another and all homosexuals were sado-masochistic, suspected that he might be Jack the Ripper. He was forced to abandon his lodgings in New York and lie low until the press sensation died down.

CELEBRITY SPOT

EUGENE DEBS

Eugene Debs, the great American labour leader, was killed by the Lindlehr Naturopathic Sanitorium at Elmhurst, Illinois. Unwell after a prison sentence, Debs went there for a rest. After a visit to Carl Sandberg he collapsed, and became unconscious. Since he didn't ask for a drink while he was oblivious, the hospital gave him no water for two days. Since he was on a fasting cure recommended by Upton Sinclair, they didn't feed him. An orthodox doctor visiting at Debs' brother's request, found him comatose, dehydrated, suffering malnutrition, and with symptoms of brain damage which the hospital had not noticed.

When his heart began to falter, the naturopaths gave Debs a useless cactus extract. When this failed they tried electric treatment and burned his skin. Finally, too late, they tried to give him digitalis – which could have saved his life given in the proper way earlier.

Debs died a day later, killed by naturopathic treatment.

PATENT MEDICINES

By the early 20th century, patent medicines were notorious, and led to necessary government regulation. Back in the 1840s, Disraeli had described the village of Willenhall where independent artisan locksmiths commanded so successful a trade that they could drink away three days a week. And while the parents were drunk on beer and gin, the babies were drunk on Godfrey's Cordial – a lethal mixture of alcohol and opium.

It had many successors. Mrs Winston's Soothing Syrup, Morrell's Teething Syrup, Grandma's Secret and Mother's Treasure were similarly noxious opiate compounds. Kopp's Baby Friend was probably the worst of the lot. This morphine based soother killed at least 11 children between 1905 and 1906.

Adults, too, could buy "tonics" with all the tonic effect of a bottle of whisky. Peruna's Catarrh Cure was 28% alcohol, and some users happily went on "Peruna jags".

In 1860 Professor Jaegger of Vienna made an extraordinary discovery. The human soul, he revealed, was not a spirit. It was an odour emanating from the person, and especially from the hair. To improve the soul, the good professor manufactured pills. His discovery found favour neither with Christians who believed in the soul nor atheists who did not.

The great conductor Sir Thomas Beecham was able to play whatever music he personally liked and treat orchestras with an eccentricity which became famous, because he was never dependent on his career to earn his living. He was heir to the Beecham Patent Medicine Company, and thus remained a rich man in his own right. To a public that knew not Mozart, his surname was famous for Beechams Pills – "Worth a Guinea a box" – which claimed to cure constipation, backache, cold chills, bad legs, "maladies of indiscretion", kidney and urinary disorders.

Analysed by British Medical Association chemists, they proved to contain aloes, powdered ginger and soap. Their actual worth was a farthing a box, and their impact on kidney trouble or syphilis could only be to persuade a patient to delay getting proper treatment, thus making his condition far worse.

Mayr's Wonderful Stomach Remedy

Mr Mayr developed to a fine pseudo-scientific level the old snake-oil salesman's trick of manufacturing fake gallstones for the body to expel without surgery. His "wonderful remedy" promised relief from indigestion, gases, dizziness, colic, torpid liver, constipation, gastritis, yellow jaundice, appendicitis and gallstones. His explanation claimed that: "The above ailments are mainly caused by a catarrhal condition of the gall bladder and duct, liver, stomach and intestinal tract, backing up poisonous fluids into the stomach and otherwise deranging the digestive system." Mr Mayr's marvellous remedy promised to remove them painlessly without physical operation and render the entire intestinal tract antiseptic.

The remedy was a bottle of oil and two powders. The patient was ordered to take one powder at 3.00 p.m., drink the entire contents of the bottle at bedtime, and take the other powder the following morning. Then. "When the bowels operate use a vessel and note the poisonous secretions removed by this remedy. In some cases dark green or yellow lumps varying in size from a fine bead to an olive – in severe cases even larger. In other cases quantities of thick tenacious slime or mucus. These accumulations are weakening and poisonous."

In fact, the first powder was Rochelle salts and the bottle was pure olive oil. Together these formed sodium soap in the intestine. The second powder was licorice root used as a laxative. The "gallstones" were merely lumps of soap formed by the action of alkali on the large amount of oil consumed.

Dr Tucker's Atomiser

Dr Nathan Tucker of Mount Gilead, Ohio, was the worst of the "addic-tionist" patent medicine manufacturers, marketing a drug he knew was addictive without being curative. Though in fairness one might note that he varied his prescription without warning from time to time, and some-times exchanged the addictive drug for sheer poison.

Still, in reported cases it was more often his preferred addictive drug that was actually responsible for killing his patients.

Dr Tucker sold an atomizer with his nostrum, and offered relief to the respiratory system from asthma, hay fever and catarrh. When the prescrip-tion was analyzed in 1903 it was found to contain:

COCAINE HYDROCHLORIDE 1%

POTASSIUM NITRATE 5%

GLYCERINE 35%

BITTER ALMOND WATER 35%

WATER 25%

VEGETABLE EXTRACT 4%

Two years later Tucker was selling

ATROPIN SULPHATE 1%

SODIUM NITRATE 4%

VEGETABLE EXTRACT 52%

But cocaine was reintroduced in 1906, making up 7% of the whole.

In 1908 The Lancet reported that a 36-year-old woman plagued by asthma had died of cocaine poisoning after using tucker's atomizer for two years. Later that year the cocaine poisoning of a five-year-old child in Shiloh, Ohio, was reported after it had been treated.

So when should you mistrust a patent medicine sold over the counter? Whenever it promises to cure too large a list of ailments.

Mrs Miller's Mild Home Treatment

Mild, indeed, was this remedy "especially prepared for the speedy and permanent cure of leucorrhea or ulcerations, displacement or falling of the womb, profuse, scanty or painful periods, uterine or ovarian tumours or growths, also pains in the head, back or bowels, bearing-down feelings, nervousness, creeping feeling up the spine, melancholy, desire to cry, hot flashes, weariness, and piles from any cause or no matter of how long standing." It consisted of boric acid, tannin, cocoa butter, and a trace of carbolic acid.

The advertising claimed that Mrs Cora B. Miller of Kokomo, Indiana, was "spending a fortune in giving medical treatment absolutely free to suffering women." The wheeze was to send the first treatment free and urge continuing it on a regular basis for $1.00 a time. It cost 6¢ to make, and Frank Miller who was actually trading in his wife's name, made more than $100,000 a year from this racket.

....

SPECIALIST CURES
....

The most feared diseases of any age offer fertile soil for the quack remedy. Patients terrified of receiving a "death sentence" may defer visiting their doctors and so allow the disease to take a firmer hold. Or they may grasp at the offer of a "certain cure" if they see it falsely advertised.

John St John Long, a handsome young Irish artist, started offering cures for TB in 1826. By the 19th century, incurable "consumption" had become the most dreaded disease. Long earned over £10,000 a year for rubbing a secret salve into his patients' skins. He was especially successful with women, but didn't save them. He was twice prosecuted for manslaughter. Once he was acquitted; the second time he was fined £250. Happily for medicine, he died when he was only 36.

Beating the Booze

Dr Lesley E. Keeley successfully transformed the sleepy little railway town of Dwight, Illinois into a great midwestern health centre. keeley attacked the medical side of the great social problem obsessing many 19th century Americans – the liquor trade. As a young railway surgeon working alone in his laboratory at nights, he satisfied himself that he had created a cure for drunkenness. Injections of bichloride of gold, he believed, would wean drunks off alcohol.

He tried it out on the town drunk in 1857 – and behold, the man was cured. By 1890 the town had six hotels, and drunks by the hundred were pouring in from all over the mid-west to attend the Keeley Institute. Keeley's attendants caught them as they fell out of their trains, gave them an immediate injection in the left arm, and hurried them off to the Institute. There they had to make instant financial settlement for a minimum stay of three weeks, during which they would be expected to take Keeley's internal remedy every two hours with four injections a day. The internal remedy was made to a specific prescription for each individual patient, and any swapping was forbidden.

Keeley barred cigarette smoking, gambling and swearing, and insisted that patients must bath twice a week. No form of tobacco was allowed for fifteen minutes before and after each injection, and strict silence was enforced on the queues in the injection room. Woe betide any patient heard using its nickname "the shot tower"!

Keeley allowed restricted use of alcohol to wean patients off their dependency without giving the "DTs". His attendants carried 4 oz flasks of excellent whisky at all times, and severe cases might be allowed up to 12 oz a day at the outset of their treatment.

He claimed a 90% success rate, and enrolled graduates in the "Bichloride of Gold Club". He undoubtedly believed sincerely in his treatment, and opened nearly 50 more branches across America. He died a millionaire, but it immediately became apparent that without his charismatic presence, bichloride of gold simply did not cure alcoholism..

Shedding a Few Pounds

Tex Guinan was better known for purveying alcohol. As hostess of a well-known New York speakeasy during prohibition she became famous for her nightly greeting of the customers, "Hello, suckers!" She also lent her name enthusiastically to promoting the obesity cure peddled by a man called Cunningham. According to the publicity material, the ample Tex declared: "In tights I was a sight at 204 lbs!" After trying the cure she lost 17Œ lbs in 10 days, whereupon, "Joy returned – I was found dancing before the mirror, singing as a full-throated lark sings at dawn."

Perhaps more to the point, her agent revealed that Cunningham was offering a contract that "made her eyes stick out."

The American Medical Association knew that Cunningham had formed various bogus patent medical companies. So one of their clerks wrote requesting the information advertised over Tex's name. The reply was gushingly personalized. "I am sincerely glad to get personally acquainted with you," Tex warbled, declaring, "I am a woman and am in this thing heart and soul out of the great joy it has brought me to be slender and see all others slender." A cure would cost $20.

The AMA clerk did nothing. Soon a follow-up letter offered to reduce the price to $10, assuring him that the "Tex Guinan Positive Fat Reducer... would render your chin, throat, arms, abdomen, hips, thighs and lower limbs... enchanting."

The AMA clerk, who was already cadaverous, smiled and did nothing. A third letter said, "Pardon me, dear, you may think me awfully conceited but I am proud of what great critics have said about my newly made form." A fourth letter lamented that the skinny clerk was still amongst the "piteous prisoners of fat, fat girdled, fat manacled, fat menaced," and offered the cure for $5.00 Still the AMA refused the bait.

Finally a fifth letter asked for the names and addresses of ten fat men or women, and offered the cure for $3.00. The AMA pounced and sent the money.

In return they received a quart of muddy liquid. 1 lb of alum mixed with 10 oz of alcohol was made up to two pints by the addition of water. A Los Angeles court issued a fraud order against Tex Guinan Inc., and the product quickly vanished from the market.

Practising as a pharmacist in Milford, Kansas, John Brinkley experimented by grafting a goat's testicle into a man who had been impotent for 16 years. When the man's grateful wife bore a son the following year, they named him "Billy"!

"Doc" John Brinkley

Brinkley's rejuvenating glandular implants became the biggest industry in Milford, and Brinkley, with his own radio station, became so well known that he almost became state governor on a write-in vote.

His licence to practice was withdrawn in 1929 when his "medical" qualifications were found to be bogus. Even so, earning over $1 million a year, he was able to lend one of his three yachts to the Duke and Duchess of Windsor.

CANCER CURES

Profiteering with Fake Cancer Cures

Koch's glyoxilade: an antitoxin discovered by Dr William F. Koch of Detroit was bought by 3,000 doctors at $25 per ampoule. For injecting it into patients in the forlorn hope that it would cure cancer, they were able to charge up to $300 a shot.

Krebiozen: brought from Argentina by the Durovic brothers, this whitish powder purported to be extracted from the blood of horses injected with the micro-organism responsible for "lumpy jaw" in cattle.

Thousands of ampoules of the drug were marketed at $9 each until 1963 when the FDA acquired the only sample ever laboratory tested. They found the "wonder drug" was the common amino acid creatin monohydrate.

Some doctors who made their own analyses reported that some of the ampoules contained nothing but mineral oil.

We have all heard anecdotal stories of cancer patients, given up by the doctors, who made miraculous cures after following diets of orange juice or grapes or beetroot juice. Since some cancers appear susceptible to patients' mental attitudes, this may be true for a few patients who mistrust science and believe in "nature". But such cures should never be attempted until after the doctors have given up. Cancers yield to surgery, if caught early enough. Delay may allow them to metastasize and become incurable. This is why cancer quacks are dangerous.

Dennis Dupuis, passing himself off as "Rupert Wells M.D., Professor of Radiology at the Postgraduate College of Electro-Therapeutics of St Louis" was a persistent quack who pretended to cure cancer at the turn of the century. The College was his own invention: he was self-appointed to the imaginary Chair of Radiology.

Like "Professor" Munyon he concentrated his advertising in religious journals across the USA, and claimed, "I can cure cancer at home without pain plaster or operation." The secret was "my marvellous radiotized fluid," marketed as "Radol". It was, of course, absolutely free of radiation and had nothing whatsoever to do with radio. Despite his claim that it was "a new and seemingly unfailing remedy for the deadly cancer... no matter what your condition may be," it was quite useless.

Dupuis sent out an average of 25 "cures" daily. In 1908 he sent out 7,800 treatments and reaped $70,000. Soon after that he was successfully prosecuted for fraud, and laws were passed to prevent the use of the US mail for such swindles.

Philip Schuch Jr.'s "Radio-Sulpho Cancer Cure" used a similar pseudo-scientific sounding name for an unscientific nostrum. But Schuch had an odd naturopathic end to his treatment. After washing an external caner with "Radio-Sulpho Brew" the patient was to apply a poultice of smelly limburger cheese!

Naturopath Harry M. Hoxsey started treating cancers in 1922 with an internal medicine of potassium iodide, red clover, licorice, burdock root, cascara and other roots; and an external application of corrosives like arsenic sulphide. He learned these "folk" remedies from his father while the old man was dying of cancer!

he was kicked out of Illinois in the late 1920s and went to Iowa. They kicked him out in 1930. In 1936 he settled in Texas and stayed there making a fortune until the FDA closed him down in 1960. Whereupon he skipped over the border to Mexico, where his head nurse still offers his "treatment".

Arthur Cox, claiming to be ҉ Osage Indian, sold an old "Indian herb doctor's" cancer cure. The patient would receive two bottles of liquid, two tubs of paste and a turkey feather. One bottle of liquid was horse urine. This was to be mixed with the clay from one of the tubs, using the turkey feather, and forming a thin salve to plaster over the cancer. The other tub contained petroleum jelly to cover the plaster and slow down its evaporation. The second bottle contained castor oil to keep the bowels open.

Cox was ordered to desist in 1947, and given a suspended one-year sentence. In 1952 he went to jail for persistently peddling his rubbish.

An eight-year-old girl from Los Angeles was about to have her left eye removed in surgery on her face cancer when her parents learned of a chiropractor who might be able to cure her without surgery. Over the telephone the chiropractor assured them that this would be the case. He charged $739 and set about "chemically balancing" her body with food supplements, laxatives and painful daily manipulation. The cancer soon grew to the size of a tennis ball and pushed the girl's eye out of its socket. She died within a few months and the chiropractor was charged with second-degree murder and given a prison sentence.

Charles "Chuckie" Peters was also eight years old when chemotherapy in a University of Chicago Hospital treating his leukemia proved so painful that his mother withdrew him and sent him to a "metabolic therapist". This quack gave Chuckie huge doses of vitamin A, which very nearly killed him. He lost weight dramatically; lost the power to walk; screamed if he was touched. Back in hospital he had two weeks sedation to recover from vitamin A poisoning. Happily the renewed chemotherapy was successful and he recovered from the leukemia, too. The metabolic therapy clinic settled out of court with Mr and Mrs Peters.

Max Gerson (1881-1959) devised a diet "cure" for cancer which is still sold in Mexico by his daughter. It involves much fruit and vegetables and frequent enemas, and bans salt, spices, sodium bicarbonate, alcohol and tobacco. Charlotte Gerson claims a high rate of successful cures, but has produced no follow-up figures. A sympathetic naturopath who checked up on 21 of Gerson's cures was startled to find that 20 had died within 5 years.

Zoologist Dr Laurence Burton invented "immuno-augmentation therapy" to cure cancer by strengthening the immune system with injected protein extracts. CBS Television's prestigious documentary programme "60 Minutes" gave the treatment a favourable report in 1979, with a distinguished physician reporting that one of his own patients had been "miraculously" cured by Burton.

What the public was not told, however, was that the patient relapsed and died two weeks later. Although Dr Burton died in 1993 his treatment is still sold.

Stanislaw Burzynski MD extracts what he calls "anti-neoplastons" from urine and claims to have helped many cancer patients get well. Sally Jessy Raphael's talk show featured four of them in 1988, all allegedly "cancer free". By 1992 three had died. The survivor had taken conventional treatment.

Dentist William Donald Kelly said cancers were simply "foreign proteins" caused by "a pancreatic enzyme deficiency", treatable by diet alone.

His licence was suspended for five years in 1976, but he set up a front "Institute", and then moved his operation to Mexico.

Actor Steve McQueen went there with lung cancer, and broadcast to say how much better he was getting – two weeks before he died.

LAETRILE

In 1963 a book by Glenn Kittler told the American public that "the day is near when no one need die from cancer. Laetrile, the revolutionary new anti-cancer drug... will be to cancer what insulin is to diabetes." The American public was bewildered to find that they could not obtain this drug. It was banned in the USA, and they had to go to Canada or Mexico to acquire it.

Laetrile was derived from the kernels of apricot stones. The laetrile molecule, it was alleged, penetrated to the site of the cancer where it was hydrolyzed by an enzyme, beta-glycosides, releasing hydrogen cyanide which killed the cancer. It sounded good – certainly apricot stones, like several other fruit seeds, can produce cyanide. So why couldn't Americans buy it?

To begin with, a commission to study Laetrile had been set up in 1953. Tests with controls on 44 cancer patients and innumerable mice had starkly shown that Laetrile had no effect whatever on cancer. In the second place, the authorities knew about the promotors of Laetrile.

Dr Ernest Krebs, who had a genuine degree, had been peddling patent medicines since the influenza epidemic of 1918, when he invented Syrup Leptinol, containing a rare parsley which he called an old Indian remedy. With rhubarb added it became Syrup Bal-sa-Me-A, a "miraculous cure". An enzyme called Chymotrypsin had subsequently been touted as a cancer cure. In 1926 Krebs extracted a drug called Sarcanicase from apricot kernels as an additive to make gutrot bootleg liquor less toxic. It was pretty poisonous itself and killed rats injected with it. Another apricot kernel drug followed called Allergenase, and claimed to be a "systemic detoxicant" curing arthritis, asthma and shingles.

In 1948, his son took up the apricot process and modified it to Laetrile.

Dr Krebs Jr. had never completed his doctoral studies, though he pretended that he had. His scientific inadequacy was only matched by his commercial amorality.

"The field of cancer chemotherapy is a law to itself. This jungle offers the greatest opportunity anywhere in commerce at this time...."

_____

"Push hard... and establish [Laetrile] as something precious that not even hospitals get for nothing."

_____

"One can usually buy even the top medical investigators as one does sirloin steak – and at about the same price."

DR ERNEST T. KREBS JR.

Happily, Dr Krebs Jr. was wrong about the venality of America's drug examining bodies and, until the 1980s, well after his father's death, Laetrile was prohibited and had to be smuggled in for those who wanted it.

Under the presidency of Ronald Reagan, "free enterprise libertarians" were able to insist that the position be reconsidered. Under political pressure and at great expense, four top research establishments tested Laetrile exhaustively.

The result? Laetrile was still proved to be totally worthless.

Killed by Laetrile

In 1972, when Laetrile was being shuffled into the USA under a backdoor disguise as "Vitamin B-17", three-year-old Chad Green, who suffered from acute lymphocytic anaemia, was being given "metabolic therapy" based on Laetrile in Massachusetts.

The Department of Welfare took his parents to court after hearing that the Laetrile was dangerously increasing cyanide in his blood, and heavy Vitamin A doses were affecting his liver. The court ordered Chad to be given orthodox chemotherapy, and Chad's parents fled to Mexico where they put Chad into Dr Contreras's Tijuana Laetrile Clinic. It killed Chad within a few months.

Profiting from a Global Tragedy: Bogus AIDS Treatments

By the end of 1985, Business Week estimated AIDS cure fraud as a multi-billion dollar business in the USA. Every cancer scam was adapted to AIDS: Laetrile, garlic pills, Burton's ammino-augmentative therapy, electric coils to pass voltage through beds, and a range of vegetarian-based diets. The instant extension of the same treatments to such a different disease spoke volumes about the sincerity of the purported "healers".

Mexican clinics varied the use of their old cancer scams with the marketing of new drugs that were hopeful, but as yet untested and so potentially dangerous.

And Not to Mention Pond Scum...

Dr John H. Renner of the Consumer Health Information Center sent students to ask health food stores in Kansas City whether they had products to protect against AIDS. Fifteen out of sixteen said they did, their useless nostrums including processed pond scum, hydrogen peroxide, and offers to freeze and store bone marrow for replacement if the donor should contract AIDS subsequently.

Prevention is Easier than Cure

A similar test in Houston checked 41 health food stores, asking for both a cure and a prophylactic. Every one of them offered a prophylactic. Thirty of them offered a "cure". Not one made mention of condoms or abstinence as guaranteeing safety.

Weirdest AIDS Preventatives

Lavatory seat covers and telephone covers have both been marketed as a guard against AIDS, though the condition cannot be acquired from either source. Weirder still was the offer of an AIDS-preventative toaster visor!

Two Great Cons

After the public learned about heavy water being used in radiation processes, two con-artists dreamed up Z-water, which gave off Z-rays, ("unknown to science", as they openly advertised). The Zerrett Applicator was a "plastic dumb-bell." (The prototype was a converted baby's rattle.) It cost $50 with your first bottle of Z-water. Put the water in the applicator, and it gave off Z-rays to expand the atoms in your body and promote health. ("Don't cross your legs. You might get a short circuit.")

Promotors William Ferguson and Mary Stanakis went to prison when Z-water proved to be indistinguishable from Chicago tap water.

Chester Nairn was imprisoned in 1961 for selling an ordinary kitchen blender as a wonder "extractor" which could get the vital elements out of raw fruits and grains. A list of cures ascribed to "Dr H. E. Kirshner" included: liquidized carrot, celery, spinach, cabbage and apple to cure cancer; carrot, celery and spinach for angina pectoris.

WHEN IS AN IMPOSTER NOT AN IMPOSTER?

In early Australia, it seems, William Kelly was visiting Melbourne in 1858 when, to his amazement, he saw a notice on a chemist's shop wall reading:

> *"To be disposed of on moderate terms – the 1st class Dublin Diploma of the late Dr T. Apply to his disconsolate widow at the old surgery in the tent next to the European National Restaurant, Clarendon Street."*

It was common at the time for men to "borrow" the names and diplomas of real doctors and set up practice in the outback.

When a law was passed to prevent this abuse by prohibiting the claim to any medical degree that had not been rightfully earned, an imposter passing himself off as a "specialist physician renowned throughout the colonies" was arrested and brought before the magistrates.

"Why have you put the letters MRCP after your name?" the bench asked him severely. "On your own admission you have had no medical training. Do not these letters state that you are a member of the Royal College of Physicians?"

"Oh no, sir," replied the quick-witted con-man. "They stand for Malvern, Royal Park, Carlton and Preston where I have previously been in practice."

The MDU's First Conviction

In 1912 the Medical Defence Union turned its attention to the case of Dr Richard Henry barber. Dr Barber had been practising in the north of England since 1907, when he wrote to the General Medical Council asking for his address in the register to be changed. He had left Gardiner, Oregon, where he had been practising since 1890, and returned to England to settle in Liverpool.

From 1907 to 1912, Dr Gardiner acted as locum to a number of doctors in the north of England, culminating in a year during which he took on the practice of a Sheffield GP who was ill. When the principal recovered, Gardiner set up his own practice in Rotherham.

However, many of his Sheffield patients complained about his treatment once their own doctor was back on his feet again, which determined the GP to make some enquiries. He wrote to America, and learned that Dr R. H. Barber had died in Oregon in 1904. He promptly placed the matter in the hands of the Medical Defence Union, and the General Secretary jumped into the role of Sherlock Holmes.

He traced the widow of the genuine Dr R. H. Barber in America, who agreed to come to England and give evidence about her late husband. He also began to make enquiries about the man practising under his name in Rotherham, and found that he had now added to Dr Barber's three degrees from Edinburgh another two to which neither he nor Dr Barber was entitled.

It came to the ears of the imposter that the MDU was making enquiries about him, and without further ado he absconded. The police joined the hunt, and by great good luck caught him boarding a liner at Liverpool on which he had taken passage as ship's surgeon, using the name and credentials of yet another doctor on the Medical Register. He was confronted with Mrs Barber who confirmed that he was not her husband, and was taken under police custody to London.

The real Dr Barber, it transpired, had enjoyed a very successful career in America, serving with distinction as an army surgeon in the Spanish American war. Back in private practice in Oregon, he died when he was called out to attend a patient in an accident some twenty miles away on a dark night. He set off on horseback, but mistook a mile-wide reach of the Siuslaw River for its fordable point, and died of exposure after making the crossing. The American authorities were properly informed of his death, but no one thought to advise the British General Medical Council to remove his name from the register.

Although one mystery had been sorted out, it still didn't explain the identity of the imposter. He refused to say. He tried to escape from the police on the way to London, and he shammed lunacy when he arrived there. Detective-Inspector Foster investigated his background, and established that he was a man called Harry Virtue who had already been convicted and fined for practising as a vet without a licence.

England has no such law as Australia's specifically prohibiting the use of unearned medical degrees. But Virtue pleaded guilty to fraud and perjury, and was sentenced to nine months imprisonment.

Stanley Clifford Weyman

One of the great con artists of all time, Stanley Weyman twice passed himself off successfully as a doctor. His most famous con was his insinuation of himself into the White House in 1921 by first telephoning Princess Fatima of Afghanistan when she was visiting America and telling her he was a White House protocol officer who would be arranging for her to visit President Warren Harding (and was entitled to a handsome monetary gift from her for his services); then telephoning the White House and saying that he wanted to arrange the visit on the princess's behalf.

That triumph (from which he had to flee quickly with the money) followed an even more successful impersonation. He had spent the previous year attached to a construction company in Peru, employed as its medical officer. It is not surprising that he was remembered better for the lavish parties he threw in the company villa than for any extraordinary medical achievements.

Weyman's next venture into medicine came in 1926. After the death of the Latin lover Rudolph Valentino, he turned up in Hollywood and announced himself as Valentino's one-time personal physician and friend. He was accepted at face value, and became involved in the arrangement of the star's funeral. Actress Pola Negri, who had played opposite Valentino, was impressed with his competence, and employed him as her personal physician for some years.

Weyman later drifted through a phoney legal practice and into journalism, until his sad death at the hands of an armed robber. By this time he was working honestly as a hotel manager.

FRED DEMARA
"THE GREAT IMPOSTER"

It started as a tale of heroism in the Korean war. The Royal Canadian Navy destroyer Cayuga returned from a tour of duty, and its press officer hastened to release the story of its young Lieutenant-Surgeon's devotion beyond the call of duty. Dr Joseph Cyr had performed difficult operations under the most unlikely circumstances. Using the Captain's cabin as his operating theatre he had removed a bullet from close to the heart of a Korean soldier. In an emergency field station he had performed a successful lung resection.

And his humanity had shown in the effective protests he made to improve the disgraceful conditions provided for convalescing Korean soldiers.

The coincidence that the Canadian war hero should have the same name as himself struck Dr Joseph Cyr of Alfred, Maine. Then he saw a photograph of the squat, crew-cut "Canadian", and gasped. That was no Dr Cyr! That was "Brother John" of the Christian Brothers' School in Alfred, whom Cyr had known a few years earlier when the brother was teaching biology. His name outside religion? The Christian Brothers believed it to be Cecil B. Harmann who had come to them after teaching biology in college.

Actually he was neither. He was Ferdinand Waldo Demara who had joined the Cistercians under his own name as a novice at 16; leaving them soon after to teach for the Christian Brothers in Rhode Island before enlisting in the army when he was 20.

He didn't like the army, and so began his peregrinating impostures. He deserted after a week and joined the US Navy, bringing forged credentials from Iowa State College, despite which he was not selected for officer training. He served at a naval hospital school in Norfolk, Virginia and picked up simple medical skills.

After deserting the navy he joined the Trappists in Kentucky as "Robert French", a psychology Ph.D. From the Trappists, "French" moved to De Paul University under the aegis of a teaching order, and studied scholastic philosophy. He went on moving from religious orders to colleges and back, with a spell as a hospital orderly, until the FBI caught up with him as a deserter. As a result of his capture he served an 18-month prison sentence and was finally given a dishonourable discharge from the army.

Freed, he started a new life as Cecil B. Hannan. On the Cayuga his first patient had been the captain, who had toothache. Demara sat up all night reading books on dentistry before extracting the tooth. Once the ship reached Korea there was a flood of wounded patients to treat: "I couldn't have been nervous, even if I felt like it. Practically everybody on the bloody ship was watching me."

Dismissed from the RCN and debarred from practising medicine in the USA, he made one more attempt to pass as a college teacher. But his face was well-known after articles in Life magazine and he was soon exposed.

318

Demara vanished from sight in 1952, only surfacing briefly in 1964 on a minor auto-theft charge in Los Angeles.

> *"I had to keep one basic principle in mind. The less cutting you do, the less patching up you have to do afterwards."*

FERDINAND WALDO DEMARA

The Fantasy World of Roy Grimshaw

The Pri-Med UK Private Medical Care and Screening Services Clinic ran for just 8 months in Lytham St Anne's. It offered vasectomies, abortions, dilation and curettage, smear tests and such services. Then in October 1982 its consultant surgeon, Roy Grimshaw, was stopped for a driving offence in his Jaguar, and told Bolton magistrates he was a busy doctor working any hour of the 24, and having to drive nurses home. They took pity on him, and spared his licence.

So one of the beaks was very surprised to see "Dr Grimshaw" again in a couple of weeks, teaching biology at Bolton North Sixth Form College. Grimshaw "the surgeon" was simply living out a fantasy life, and he was running himself into debt to support it.

Nor was he a safe operator. A woman who was satisfied when told her womb "needed flicking over" and returned when she was suffering renewed pain after three operations, was again trusting when told that her womb was now out of position and needed a plastic device to correct it. This was hopelessly wrong diagnosis: she had an ectopic pregnancy, and Grimshaw might have killed her had he proceeded.

He offered to "burn away" a gynaecological problem he pretended to find on a hairdresser he gave a smear test. She collapsed after he used valium as an anaesthetic. Grimshaw went to prison for six years, convicted of wounding, deception, supplying and obtaining controlled drugs, and perjury.

Moonlighting Cop

A Los Angeles traffic cop, suspended from duty for blackmailing a young woman to party in the bath with him when he should have given her a driving ticket, used his free time to work at Santa Ines Medical Enterprises, where his father-in-law was company secretary. Officer Kelly Klatt's wife Samantha also worked for the company, administering Wilmington Clinic.

Someone split to LAPD that Klatt was moonlighting for the clinic while suspended on full pay, and as a result of the investigation, the Klatts and Samantha's father found themselves arrested, along with a chiropractor and three Hispanics, all charged with operating bogus clinics.

The scam had run from 1983 to the arrests in 1989. The unqualified Hispanics posed as doctors, deceiving some poor Hispanics to come to them as patients, and employing other illegals at underpayment for over-long hours.

....

CREOSOTE EUGH!

....

A pharmacist in the north of England could not believe the prescription which ordered tincture of creosote to be taken by mouth twice daily. The noxious and potentially dangerous medicine, once a favourite of quacks, was virtually never used in modern times.

Her questions exposed the astonishing fact that the "Doctor" had been running a practice with 3,000 patients in the north of England for 30 years. With no qualifications!